A HEALING PLACE

Indigenous Visions for Personal Empowerment and Community Recovery

A HEALING PLACE

Indigenous Visions for Personal
Empowerment and Community Recovery

Kayleen M. Hazlehurst

Central Queensland
UNIVERSITY
PRESS

© Kayleen M. Hazlehurst 1994

First published 1994 by
Central Queensland University Press
Central Queensland University
Rockhampton, Queensland 4700

National Library of Australia
Cataloguing-in-Publication entry
Hazlehurst, Kayleen M., 1949-
A healing place: indigenous visions for personal
empowerment and community recovery.

Bibliography.
ISBN 0 908140 87 8.

1. Community development - Australian 2. Aborigines, Australian.
3. Social action - Australia. 4. Crime prevention - Australia
5. Indians of North America - Canada I. Title.

307.140994

Produced and distributed by
Australian Scholarly Publishing
4 Madden Grove, Kew, Victoria 3101

Printed and bound by Aristoc Offset,
3 Aristoc Road, Glen Waverley, Victoria 3150

*For all those
who have
gifted their lives
to the liberation
of the indigenous
heart, mind, and spirit*

Blessed and happy is he that arises

to promote the best interest of the peoples

and kindreds of the earth

(Baha'u'llah)

CONTENTS

ACKNOWLEDGEMENTS

I wish to express my gratitude to the following indigenous people for their inspirational leadership in the fields of alcohol and drug education and community regeneration, and for their generous assistance to the author over many years: Dr Maggie Hodgson, Nechi Institute and Eric Shirt, Poundmaker's Lodge; Dr Chester Cunningham, Native Counselling Services of Alberta; Andy and Phyllis Chelsea, Alkali Lake Band; Jean Jans, Weipa; Lana and Douglas Abbott and Douglas Walker, Central Australian Aboriginal Alcohol Planning Unit, Alice Springs; Bobby and Darren McLeod, Doonooch Self Healing Centre, Nowra; Basil Sumner, South Australian Aboriginal Sobriety Group; and the staff and regional representatives of the Aboriginal Co-ordinating Council, Cairns.

My thanks also to 'Bindi', Linda Waugh, for the beautiful original artwork she created for this book.

My special thanks to my three Aboriginal graduate students: Judy Atkinson, Coralie Ober, and Colin Jones for reading and commenting upon the manuscript and for taking these and other ideas into the field of action. Albert Einstein said that 'Imagination is more important than knowledge'. I wish for them, always, open and inspirational minds.

For supporting this research and writing during the course of my employment, I am indebted to the Australian Institute of Criminology, Canberra and the Queensland University of Technology, Brisbane. I wish also to thank the Queensland Drug Offensive Strategy, Queensland Department of Health, for its generous support for the publication of this book.

PREFACE

The heart-breaking and complex problems of addiction, family violence, and community breakdown are destroying the spirit and lives of too many indigenous people. Libraries are filled with chronicles of suffering and despair in Aboriginal history and contemporary communities. Stories of tragedy are not hard to find. But this is a book about hope. It tells of optimistic people and of places where a better future is being created. It attempts to bridge the gap between theories of prevention and practical needs for personal repair and community regeneration.

The techniques for personal and community healing described here take their lead from indigenous visions for community recovery expressed to me during my work over the last twenty years in Canada and Australia. The ideas are based upon discussions and workshops which I have either participated in, or conducted myself, with community groups, organisations and justice and welfare agencies, while I was with the Australian Institute of Criminology between 1984 and 1992, and at the Queensland University of Technology since March 1992; and upon research and communications I have had as a working anthropologist with caring practitioners and community action people in Australia, Canada, New Zealand, and the United Kingdom since 1972.

The book attempts to draw together and distil the ideas and experiences of social and institutional reform which have been shared with me, and which I have subsequently shared with others. It seeks to provide a coherent outline of the urgent issues which need skilled, 'hands-on' directions and solutions.

In comparing innovative indigenous programs and policies used in Canada and Australia, it gives examples of the 'well tried and true'. But, in this difficult and long fraught area, it also undertakes to shape a needed vision for change; to signpost this with arguments for the untried and the experimental; and to structure a framework for new directions which can be followed with confidence.

The book draws upon both conventional and action-oriented fieldwork, done during the course of my research, and upon consultancies and work with government and Aboriginal agencies in South Australia, Queensland, Northern Territory, Victoria, and New South Wales. I have incorporated the important findings of other scholars, professionals, and community workers and the pioneer contributions of various indigenous organisations and individuals in developing our understanding of present realities and future prospects. My personal experiment with the development of crime prevention strategies for Aboriginal communities (Hazlehurst 1989a; 1990) was an early response to develop practical means by which communities might play an active role in designing justice alternatives and preventative action. Reform of the criminal justice and corrections systems is now upon government agendas. But experience of introducing justice alternatives reminds us of how much more needs to be done in areas of prevention.

Racial tension and mutual disenchantment between black and white remain widespread throughout Australian society. These hostilities continue to traumatise communities and severely undermine efforts to create positive environments for change. Until the structure and balance of power relations demonstrate a heartfelt confidence in the abilities and talents of Aboriginal and Torres Strait Islander people, until there is active expenditure of energy and resources to understand and circumvent the factors of community decline, such sentiments will continue to be the cause of misery, pain, and social unrest for all concerned.

To the extent to which they remain in a state of welfare and bureaucratic dependence, Aboriginal and Islander people are differently seen as both 'victims' and as 'offenders'. Dependency and demoralisation are evidenced in excessive drinking, family neglect, unemployment, and criminality. For this, indigenous Australians are roundly criticised, despised, and devalued as citizens.

Yet do we anticipate a phase of social reconstruction? Will we stand behind Aboriginal people when they wish to command a degree of respect and autonomy in the areas of community development and social control? Any way forward must address the fundamental issue of Aboriginal community re-empowerment. For power and responsibility to be reinstated, it must also be relinquished by its former gatekeepers and guardians.

The first step for those who control resources is to begin to trust the people. Where there are signs of readiness or enthusiasm to take responsibility, national and state programs should be flexible enough to respond to them promptly. Program guidelines must be drawn up in ways which facilitate innovation rather than forcing communities to fashion plans to fit neatly into departmental boxes. If administrative or agency boundaries do not accommodate worthwhile ideas, then these structures and rules should be changed.

What Australian indigenous peoples and communities can do for themselves, as informed and skilled collectives, has scarcely been *envisioned*, least of all acted upon. The greatest gesture of reconciliation towards Aboriginal people by Australian governments on behalf of this nation would be for them to recognise the potential for community renewal and self-regeneration. Without the political will to create supportive institutional environments, or the imaginations to direct funding towards innovative community-healing approaches which *transform*, rather than nurse the ills of Aboriginal communities, governments will continue to fail in a domain where they have a historic opportunity to lead.

To continue to despise indigenous people for not taking charge of their own lives, while the custodians of power refuse them the legitimate means to do so, is patently unfair, profoundly impractical, and tiresomely expensive. We are all satiated with news of the over-representation of indigenous people in prisons and the annual round of riots. Yet to bring about real change in the interactional and behavioural patterns which continue to support 'the problems', will require nothing short of a colossal leap of imagination about what is possible within community functions and government administrations.

Intellectually, spiritually, and socially, the kinds of practical and policy reforms which promote personal healing and community renewal represent one of the freshest, most exciting, and challenging of grounds upon which any social scientist, legal thinker, or political leader might advance. Those who lead the way at present often have no formal qualifications. They are not academics. Nor do they occupy positions of power and authority. Yet their discoveries and innovations are revolutionary in human and psycho-social terms. There is much we can learn from them. This book explains the background to their thinking and promotes the techniques they have developed.

PART 1

Chapter one

THE HISTORY

THE ROOTS OF CONFLICT

Fierce Aboriginal resistance to European settlement, followed by 150 years of tutelage and welfare governance, have left Australia with a legacy of racial tension, bitterness, and social maladaptation. Conflict and repression accompanied white settlement over two-thirds of the area of the continent.

Australia's colonial and paternalistic past has had a profound effect upon the character and relations of Australian society — and is closer to present day policy and practice than most of us care to admit. Only thirty years ago assumptions among white officials that their exercise of authority over the daily lives of Aboriginal people was both legitimate, and essential to their 'civilisation', were widespread (Bird 1987). Changing attitudes in this area has been slow, even among more liberal-minded governments.

Neglect of the roads, drinkable water, sanitation, housing and educational needs of Aboriginal communities by local, state, and federal authorities was highlighted in the federal Human Rights Commission's *Toomelah Report*, following an inquiry into incidents of racist attacks and public disorder in New South Wales and Queensland border towns. Justice Marcus Einfeld reported that:

> Their treatment by government at all levels has been insensitive and uncaring. Their human rights have been ignored. This situation has persisted for decades despite the fact that authoritative attention has often been drawn to it ... The consequence has been high rates of preventable diseases, neglect of treatable conditions, and retardation of the development of children (Einfeld 1988: 61).[1]

In a study of poverty based on the 1986 Census conducted by the Social Policy Research Centre, University of New South Wales, it was noted that poverty among Aboriginal couples had fallen significantly since 1973. Social security increases had helped counteract the effects of unemployment for many families. It was found, however, that 50% of Aboriginal children (compared to 18% of non-Aboriginal children) still lived below the poverty line in 1986, and that Aboriginal families with employed adults were still significantly disadvantaged (Ross 1990; *Sydney Morning Herald* 7 August 1990).

Social indicators during the 1980s and early 1990s showed that Aboriginal standards of health, housing and employment opportunities had not risen proportionally with those of affluent Australian society. Aboriginal people only received the right to vote and equal wages in the late 1960s. Since the 1967 national referendum brought Aboriginal people theoretical equality of citizenship, there has been little relative improvement. Only 4.1% of Aborigines gain post-secondary education or academic qualifications. Unemployment is between four and six times the national average. The median Aboriginal family income is 54.4% of the median family income of all Australians. Only 18.9% of Aborigines work in white-collar occupations compared to 44.4% of other Australians (Australian Bureau of Statistics, 1987; 1994; Department of Aboriginal Affairs, 1984; *Times on Sunday*, 3 May 1987).

A large proportion of Aboriginal families still live in sub-standard and overcrowded housing or temporary shelters. Their average life expectancy is twenty years less than that of other Australians. Infant mortality is three times higher. The incidence of hepatitis B, typhus, trachoma, venereal disease, and early death from chronic alcoholism, remains significantly higher than in the general population. Young men in their twenties are hospitalised with cirrhosis of the liver, and other preventable diseases.

A two-year National Aboriginal Health Strategy Working Party, conducted under the direction of the Aboriginal Medical Service director Naomi Myers, reported that the estimated life expectancy for Aboriginal men was 56.3 (22 years less than for non-Aboriginal men) and 65 for Aboriginal women (15 years less than for all women). Mortality rates were up to 2.8 times higher (National Aboriginal Health Strategy Working Party 1989; Darby 1989). The Australian Institute of Health noted that trauma injury continued to play an important role in Aboriginal morbidity and mortality. Self-inflicted and accidental injuries were common (Wilson 1988; Hunter 1988, 1989, 1990a, 1990b; Thomson 1984, 1985; Thomson and Smith 1985; Thomson and English 1990; Bolger 1991; Hunter, Hall and Spargo 1991b, Reid and Trompf 1991).

In every community there are tragic stories of self-mutilation, drownings, motor vehicle accidents, and attempted suicides. Believing they have no future, so many young men and women have turned their anger and frustration against themselves. In the largest proportion of cases, injuries or crime are alcohol related (Hazlehurst and Dunn 1988). In a report presented to the Royal Commission into Aboriginal Deaths in Custody, the Aboriginal Co-ordinating Council, Cairns, expressed 'grave concern' over high death and homicide rates in the fifteen regional communities under their jurisdiction.[2] Men between the ages of 25–44 years were the highest risk group (ACC 1990: 8).

In spite of efforts by federal and state governments since the 1970s to identify and remedy current ills of Aboriginal Australia, there have continued to be losses of life, dignity, and liberty. In addition to overt and statistically measurable disadvantages, the suffering continues in more subtle, though equally pernicious forms.

INTERNALISED RACISM AND OPPOSITION

The afflictions which beset indigenous people — poverty, alcoholism, poor health, unemployment, and despair — are ills of a dispirited and conquered people. For a collective to lose its spirit is the greatest of calamities. The struggle for survival becomes a habitual state of siege and opposition — black against white, black against black. Views of worthlessness become assimilated into the individual persona. Helplessness grips the soul of the people. Unless a people have a vision of their own future they will remain defeated. They will always be vulnerable to self-oppression and oppression by others.

Australian commissions of inquiry undertaken by Einfeld (1988) and Moss (1991), and a number of individual studies, have clearly documented racial tensions in country towns where Aborigines cluster, in sub-standard coexistence, at the fringes of the white society, or between more isolated communities in rural regions. Paradoxically, severe friction also frequently exists between the black residents of these communities. Sometimes this can be traced to historic clan rivalries and disputes, irritated by colonial experiences of dislocation and placement of different groups upon a single reserve. But in the contemporary situation we also see the manifestation of what we might call 'the small bone syndrome' — a state of affairs common to situations of poverty where people are set against each other in constant competition over limited resources, mostly provided by the welfare state. The 'small bone' of government funding is never quite enough. But in the process of maintaining one's share, watching over one's shoulder, and looking out for the next one, a state of internal friction and dependence is consolidated. While people are divided in this way, they are inhibited from utilising community resources of solidarity and group action towards goals of economic independence and social well-being.

For Aboriginal people over the past fifty years internalised racism and powerlessness have become their worst enemies. Community stress, boredom, frustration, and peer pressure draw new generations into lifestyles of alcoholic excess and violence against those nearest to them — their families, friends, and neighbours (Wilson 1988; Bolger 1991). In Queensland and the Northern Territory black-on-black assaults have reached such appalling proportions, that Aboriginal leaders are now declaring a 'law and order crisis' in remote communities. A Townsville Aboriginal community worker, Gracelyn Smallwood, reported that the situation has become so severe that 'many communities are now collapsing. The entire social and family structure is breaking down'.

Reporting a death of a teenage girl resulting from multiple fractures and injuries inflicted by her boyfriend on a settlement near Townsville, Greg Roberts of the *Sydney Morning Herald* wrote:

> It wasn't an isolated occurrence. Since 1986, violence has resulted in more female deaths at both Kowanyama and Palm Island than the State's total number of Aboriginal deaths in custody ... Sexual offences have soared in recent years since communities gained access to X-rated and other pornographic videos, community workers say. After watching a video, two teenagers raped a five-year-old boy living on a Cape York community... 'That kind of thing would normally not even be thinkable among our people', Ms Smallwood said. 'These videos are being sold by the same unscrupulous individuals who make a fortune out of peddling sly grog on communities. The people who watch them think, if it's in the movie, it must be alright to go out and do it' (Roberts, *Sydney Morning Herald*, 11 August 1990: 69).

Alcoholism, violence, and social disintegration loosens rends and the family and community fabric. Children and youth run riot through the towns — having no respect for authority, either black or white. In some communities children as young as eight years old are perilously addicted to petrol sniffing. Alcohol consumption also begins at a young age as adult conduct is imitated. Despite community policing activities, or efforts in diversionary sentencing for juveniles and minor offenders, vandalism and disruptive behaviours threaten the well-being and peace of most Aboriginal settlements and neighbourhoods.

THE GENOCIDE QUESTION

Aboriginal people are dying prematurely from ill-health, addiction, accident, and despair. For many years protesting groups have asserted that acts of oppression and neglect by authorities have continued in the face of legislation which should outlaw these acts. Evidence of this is now emerging from national and international inquiries. International opinion asks why, in such an apparently affluent society levels, of poverty and demoralisation likened to Third World conditions exist in Aboriginal Australia today.

Reports of cases presented to the Royal Commission into Aboriginal Deaths in Custody read as a catalogue of humiliation and degradation (Muirhead 1988, 1989; Johnston 1991). Many Aboriginal families were convinced that official misconduct led to some cell deaths. Still grieving families experienced midnight raids on their homes and police harassment even as the inquiry into their son's death progressed. Some were convinced that their sons were murdered by officials; that prison officers or police had assisted in the so-called 'suicides'; or that they had driven them to suicide by physical and psychological abuse. In all Commission cases Aboriginal people felt that officials somewhere should be held accountable. They were distrustful of a system which, they perceived, was bent on covering up any official misconduct or culpable negligence.

The question of whether persons in positions of authority can be held accountable for the death of a prisoner as a result of psychological abuse raises new questions in law and professional ethics. Are these authorities responsible for the psychological well-being of their charges, as well as their medical and physical well-being? Many police and prison authorities would say 'no'. Custodians merely 'inherit' the psychological state of their prisoners. They are not responsible for them.

But it could equally be argued that a decline in the mental state of a prisoner, as a result of abuse by officers, should become a point of accountability. Until it does, there exists a very dangerous area in which official tyranny and harassment may reign free, with apparent public and legal consent. Physical and verbal abuse, denial of basic physical or medical needs, cruel and degrading treatment of prisoners, are causes enough to result in suicide or premature death. Such mistreatment clearly offends against at least four United Nations conventions.[3]

Economic interests are an important factor in all known cases of genocide. In his two formidable works, *Genocide: Its Political Use in the Twentieth Century* (1982) and *The Prevention of Genocide* (1985), the American Professor of Sociology, Leo Kuper, discusses contemporary theories and motives of genocide. In this context, the activities which have been perpetrated against Aborigines are instantly recognisable. Kuper explains that, 'racial or ethnic boundaries are usually not coterminous with class divisions ... Their role is most marked in the genocides of colonisation, in the sacrifice of indigenous groups to economic development ...' (Kuper 1985: 197).

Mining and pastoral industries have traditionally offered most employment to the Aboriginal work force in rural areas. Yet, fellow workers in these industries have not taken the side of Aborigines in their struggles for land rights. Is it merely coincidence that Western Australia, the state which retaliated most violently against federal efforts for national Aboriginal land rights in 1983, was also the state with the highest rate of Aboriginal deaths in custody? (Muirhead 1988: 84). During the Royal Commission on Aboriginal Deaths in Custody, racial hostility in that state was raw and undisguised. The Western Australian Police Union and the Western Australian

Prison Officers' Union objected to their members having to give evidence at the Commission's inquiries. With the financial backing of the Western Australian government they held up inquiries for some weeks by their institution of a legal challenge to the validity of the Commission's proceedings. A Western Australian Supreme Court injunction brought a halt to the Inquiry in that state late in 1988 until their case was dismissed by a Full Bench of the Federal Court in February 1989.[4]

It is not surprising that Aboriginal people suspect a connection between official expressions of non-cooperation with the Royal Commission into Aboriginal Deaths in Custody in certain states and the higher rates of Aboriginal custodial deaths in those regions. It is also not without significance that those states have been tardy in resource sharing, in the promotion of Aboriginal economic independence, and in the introduction of criminal justice reforms for Aborigines.

Genocide is seen as one of the worst crimes under international law. Ethnocide and cultural genocide also constitute serious violations against humanity. All indigenous peoples have experienced painful histories of physical and cultural attack in the process of the occupation, colonisation, and expansion into their territories. Some have suffered unashamed campaigns of genocide and dispossession, even into the twentieth century.

Less obvious, however, are continuing practices which disadvantage indigenous people through poverty from birth until death; omnipresent policing or welfare officiousness, which bring fear and uncertainty into family life; limited educational opportunities which stunt the development of children and the emergence of responsible leadership; discriminatory experiences from such early years which result in low self-esteem — the crippling enemy of aspirations and dreams. For many indigenous communities the burdens of everyday existence become so great that mere survival is the pre-eminent achievement. Too many do not survive beyond infancy or youth.

Genocide and cultural genocide can take many forms. Where a society has been founded upon conquest or social injustice it should not be surprising to find strains of this disease lingering in other, more subtle forms. Injustices of policy and administration based upon notions of racial and intellectual superiority are no less dangerous. They may actually be more so. Unconfronted, they may remain in place to injure many generations.

No society benefits when one section languishes in poverty and subjugation. Unemployed, demoralised, and increasingly alienated populations threaten the peace and security of all. The savings to the tax payer in unemployment benefits, medical care, policing and incarceration costs alone would justify the increase of economic well-being and self-sufficiency of indigenous peoples.

We cannot hope to reconstruct human psyche overnight, nor perhaps for many decades. But stern human rights legislation and constitutional safeguards could begin that process. Such undertakings would protect Aboriginal people from immediate abuses. Secondly, by introducing greater security and opportunities for self-determination, Aboriginal people may regain some control over their own lives. Land rights and the political facilitation of self-determination are central to contemporary indigenous rights and future well-being (Williams 1985, 1987a, 1987b; Grabosky, Scandia, Hazlehurst and Wilson 1988).

The High Court's Mabo judgement, the subsequent development of federal and state legislative responses, and the reconciliation process set in motion by the federal government, have only begun the enormous task of clarifying and resolving the many issues of contention (Commonwealth of Australia 1993; McRaie, Nettheim and Beacroft 1991).

Although the worst violations of human rights are being resolved in law, the Australian national inquiries of 1987 and 1988 have indisputably revealed that there are issues of policy and practice which have for many years resulted in neglect and discrimination against Aboriginal people.

There is an underlying dissatisfaction with the quality of services provided by all levels of government to Aboriginal communities. In some cases local government bodies have charged Aboriginal communities *as if* services of an equal standard to neighbouring white communities are being provided, even though they are not (Einfeld 1988). Aboriginal insistence on participation in service delivery is a powerful indication that they wish an increasing and genuine degree of self management and community control.

THE CULTURE OF OPPOSITION

Over the years responses of resistance have become so much a part of the 'Aboriginal experience', that they are now given cultural expression in patterns of opposition towards all agents of the law or government. In its worst manifestation this culture of opposition takes shape in wanton irresponsibility, excessive use of alcohol, and other forms of belligerent self-destructiveness. Willing participation in the 'hand-out' economy has gone far beyond the role of the welfare recipient. 'Making the government pay' (for the sins of the past) is maintained as a matter of principle, as much as a matter of economic necessity.

In like manner, fully-employed Aborigines have vowed that they will not even pay parking fines because Aboriginal people, they feel, 'have paid enough'. Thus, they expose themselves to heavier fines, and the possibility of imprisonment for fine default. What we are witnessing here is not merely alienation, but passive resistance.

The end result, however, hurts Aboriginal people more than the systems they are trying to punish. Sadly, the worst forms of opposition entrap individuals and families in horrendous cycles of misery, and cause stagnation in community leadership. What once seemed the most promising form of political action, namely protest politics — while useful in raising public awareness during the sixties and seventies — is today unfruitful. Being both racially grounded and oppositional in stance, protest politics often fails to identify its non-Aboriginal friends in the wider community and government, or to rally them to its cause. One of the most important lessons of the 1993 negotiations over native title legislation is that a sustained and flexible commitment to participate in the legislative process can produce outcomes of great benefit to Aboriginal people. It indicates that a new form of Aboriginal leadership, displaying a broader sociopolitical consciousness, and adept in high level inter-racial diplomacy, is emerging in Australia.

AN UNHEALTHY HYBRID

While it may be readily acknowledged that, for a significant majority, flight from the realities of poverty, supervision, and despair occurs through the neck of a bottle, the phenomenon of Aboriginal alcoholism is significantly more complex. A century of conflict with European authorities over the possession and use of alcohol now forms a very solid part of contemporary Aboriginal 'self/other' ('us' against 'them') identity.

Introduced concepts of paternalism and male dominance severely undermined traditional socioeconomic and gender relations in the first instance. More recent liberal ideologies — particularly relating to concepts of equality, citizenship, and human rights — overlay earlier frameworks. In western society today paternalistic codes have been more readily displaced, or at least balanced, by liberal and feminist ideologies. With the relatively limited impact of feminism in remote Aboriginal communities, and seeming continuity of imposed governance through the delivery of police and government services, a rather different hybrid has emerged.

The dominance of the male factor, individualism, human rights activism, and efforts to resurrect 'traditional rights' have blended into a terrifying and oppressive new culture of drinking and violence. The sacred right of males to drink — and to excess — overpowers all reason or impulse for the common good. Communal and family values, and their traditional guardians, the women, have been violently oppressed. Unless some sanity and balance is restored, Aboriginal social and cultural life, and possibly whole generations, will be at risk.

COMPANIONSHIP AND OPPOSITION

In communities where both companionship and opposition are expressed through social and swill drinking, the loyalties of non-participants becomes suspect. Non-drinkers are accused of being 'whitemen'. Young people clamour for their share of 'social acceptance', the marks of adulthood, by joining in 'adult' activities — drinking, aggressive displays of 'who's the boss' in the home, destruction of property and imprisonment. One form of subjugation is replaced by an enslavement of a more lethal kind.

High levels of official intervention — now as much a matter of necessity — occurs in the guise of law enforcement. Black/white hostilities and oppositional life styles are enacted through accelerating cycles of 'drunk and disorderly' — arrest — despair; 'drunk and disorderly', — assault and battering — imprisonment and despair; and eventual early death.

There is no doubt that many Aboriginal people live in fear and apprehension of government authorities; that many live their lives in a constant state of siege and confrontation with the police. Yet, action to reverse the situation has been a case of 'too little, too late'. Lack of community support, general apathy, and the belligerent refusal to change, cripple efforts of the few brave souls who work for the majority. If exhaustion doesn't defeat them, community attitudes which blame the helper or blame the system ('we are being set up to fail') soon will. The expectation of failure permeates public, official, and Aboriginal thinking about Aboriginal operations.

Based upon historical and contemporary memory of injustice, charged with the righteousness and expediency of protest, and embellished with myths of separation and tradition, the culture of opposition takes hold. Most Aboriginal political bodies are structured and attuned to calling white society to account for all that ails, weakening themselves as autonomous and self-determining agents for change. Communities are not geared to examining their own consciences. In a large number of areas Aboriginal councils are responsible for, and derive considerable profit from, the import and sale of liquor to their own people. The corrosion is complete. 'We live with lies', wrote Judy Atkinson:

> We claim our young men are in jail because of fine default and drunk and disorderly. Yet 53% of these young men who died in prison cells over the last ten years were in prison for violent crime (Atkinson 1990a: 12).

THE CHALLENGE OF THE FUTURE

Although public awareness is important, reconciliation will not come about merely through disseminating the 'true' colonial experience by correcting the history books. Nor will the answers be solely monetary. Though desirable, neither the transfer of lands in compensation for past losses, nor the endless sinking of monies into the provision of welfare services will be the determining factor in the improvement of the quality of life.

Aboriginal people may now bask in the uncertain victories of acknowledged native title, monetary compensation, and European guilt. But ultimately, it is they and their children who suffer the loss of wasted lives. Revolt against colonialism continues through life-styles of alcoholic excess and crime. After a two hundred year history of conquest, paternalistic governance, and active opposition, the structure and impulse of Aboriginal social life have been almost destroyed.

Liberation of three kinds is required. *Decolonisation*, which inaugurates the release from dependency and tutelage, will occur through increasing decentralisation and distribution of the management of Aboriginal affairs to Aboriginal organisations and agencies. Secondly, *community reconstruction* — the revitalisation of community life, and the redrawing of the domains of community leadership — will bring about renewal of a most profound kind. The dual action of 'letting go the power' and 'assuming responsibility' which these two necessarily entail will only effectively be achieved by negotiated agreement, mutual respect, and collaboration between white and black.

True freedom, however, will also require a revolution of a third kind. It must first be won in the hearts and minds of the people. It requires release from internalised shackles of racism, self-hate, and nurtured hostility; and it must be won at home. It will be won when creative and perceptive leadership is directed towards the needs of the people for spiritual repair, for reinstated honour, and for the development of healthy and safe communities. This *spiritual liberation* of Aboriginal Australia will begin with a positive sense of destiny — the shaping of a 'vision' of their own future:

> We must understand the influences of our colonial past. We must acknowledge its negative impact upon us as individuals and as a people. *But then we must move on.* We must learn to forgive the whiteman if we are to let go of our bitterness and our self oppression. If we are to grow we will need to work together for change. This is our path now, this is the spiritual way (Indian alcohol counsellor, British Columbia, 1990).

◆ ◆ ◆

[1] The housing, health, welfare, economic and inter-racial situation described by Einfeld in the *Toomelah Report* is typical of the majority of country towns with significant Aboriginal populations.

[2] The Aboriginal Co-ordinating Council consists of a secretariat of representatives from four regions: *Southern*: Cherbourg and Woorabinda; *Northern*: Palm Island, Yarrabah, Hopevale and Wujal Wujal; *Gulf*: Doomadgee, Pormpuraaw and Kowanyama; and *Peninsula*: Injinoo, New Mapoon, Umagico, Weipa South, Lockhart River and Old Mappoon (ACC 1990:3).

[3] The *Universal Declaration of Human Rights* (adopted by General Assembly resolution 217 A (III), 10 December 1948); *Standard Minimum Rules for the Treatment of Prisoners* (adopted by the First United Nations Congress on the Prevention of Crime and the Treatment of Offenders, 1955; also approved by the Economic and Social Council by its resolutions 663 C (XXIV) 1957 and 2076 (LXII) 1977); *Declaration on the Protection of All Persons from Being Subjected to Torture and Other Cruel, Inhuman or Degrading Treatment or Punishment* (adopted by General Assembly resolution 3452 (XXX), 9 December 1975); *Code of Conduct for Law Enforcement Officials*, (adopted by General Assembly resolution 34/169, 17 December 1979).

[4] The *Age*, 24, 25 November 1988, and 22, 29 December 1988; *Sydney Morning Herald*, 24, 30 December 1988; *Canberra Times* 29 December 1988; Hazlehurst and Hazlehurst 1989: 44.

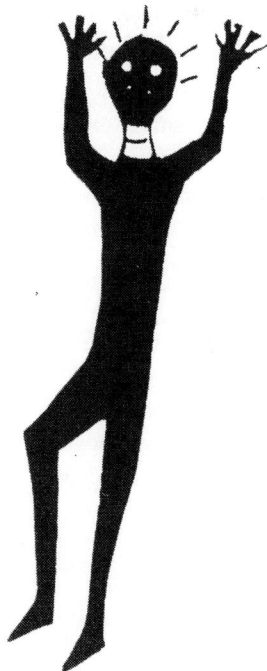

Chapter two

THE 'LIVING HELL' OF 'LOST' COMMUNITIES

Long ago grog and family fighting/killing didn't belong to our culture. Why let this destroy us now?

Its bad to fight one another. It's no good. Look out! We must look out for each other (*Family Fighting/Killing Wrong Way!* 1989).

THE ROOTS OF VIOLENCE

According to Judy Atkinson (1990a; 1990b), and Barbara Miller (ACC 1990) colonial conquest and settlement set in motion patterns of dominance and violent oppression which became entrenched into white/black relations in Australia; and which have become reflected in, and carried forward by, Aboriginal people in Aboriginal personal and community life.

As Miller writes, the 'pain and bitterness of these memories passed on from generation to generation still chills the blood of Aboriginal people ...' (ACC 1990: 24). Sunday afternoon man-hunts, malicious poisoning of water holes and flour, rape and ongoing sexual exploitation of black women by white men devalued the human worth of generations of men and women:

> The level of violence, and death by violence in Aboriginal communities which in turn contributes to the high rate of imprisonment of Aboriginal people and consequent deaths in custody can be understood against the backdrop of the structural violence white Australia has perpetrated on the original owners of the land (Atkinson 1990a: 4).

In the early 1980s Paul Wilson traced epidemic levels of alcoholism, self-mutilation, inter-personal conflict, and murder directly to the colonial and post-colonial experience in northern Queensland. People of different tribes, dispossessed and herded together into new areas for settlement, continued to live under stress and tension. 'White Australians have created historical and social conditions which are violence provoking', wrote Wilson (1988: 3). Other researchers have noted that the condition of conflict which Aborigines have felt themselves to be in with white authorities, or perceptions of such, has led to a state-of-siege mentality. Years of supervision and deprivation have, in turn, provoked resistance and opposition against wider society (Cunneen and Robb 1987: 190–197, 207; Beckett 1964: 40).

The issue of alcohol, and Aboriginal access to it, is embedded in the history of Australian race relations. The *Licensed Publican Act* (1838) forbade the supply of liquor to 'any aboriginal native of New South Wales or New Holland'; all Australian states and territories subsequently followed suit (McCorquodale 1985). After a long period of prohibition, drinking rights came to symbolise equality and full rights of citizenship.[1] Even women, many of whom bear the brunt of the violence and drinking, and who may want to see canteen outlets on communities closed down, can be adamant about the right of their men to drink (Brady 1990: 138; Hunter, Hall and Spargo 1991a; 1991b; Sansom 1980).

Historic grievances and loss, and the sense of powerlessness and frustration which they arouse, are turned inward. Many communities display the classic symptoms of internalised oppression — despair, shame and self-loathing, alienation, self-destructive behaviours and recurrent violence against close relatives. Excessive bouts of drinking, without apparent regard for personal welfare or the welfare of family and community, and excessive family and community disharmony, are supported by historical experience and muddled reasoning concerning human rights.

PSEUDO-CULTURE AND MYTHS

There is considerable evidence throughout communities in Queensland and the Northern Territory of myths, articulated and circulated by younger Aboriginal males, that violent assault upon women is in keeping with Aboriginal customary law and tradition. This has resulted in dispositions towards non-interference by both police and community leaders, and judicial leniency towards male offenders. Yet it is a view which is seldom upheld by middle-aged women or elders of either sex.

Nor is there any historical or anthropological evidence to support the view that systematic and condoned spousal assault was customary. In fact Aboriginal women traditionally had a high status within their communities, with a strong economic and ritual role of their own. They were co-owners of land, provided and distributed about 80 per cent of food staples, and had autonomy in the care of the land and the maintenance of sacred ceremonies. Women occupied a strong power base along with the men in political decision-making and social control.[2]

Audrey Bolger has marshalled significant evidence *against* the proposition that family violence was traditional:

> It is apparent that today true traditional violence accounts for only a minority of the incidents of abuse against women. By traditional violence is meant the punishments for transgressions which were part of the means of social control in Aboriginal society and were meted out to both male and female offenders (Bolger 1991: 49).

Family fights, or fights between partners, were easier to control in the open camp setting of traditional groupings. Relatives of disputants were always handy to intervene. Public displays of shaming were less likely to result in the severe and purposeless injuries of alcoholic assaults. Traditional punishments of sorcery, ritual spearing or blows to specific parts of the body, were conducted by authorised persons, under the sanction of the whole community (Brady 1990: 141; Bolger 1991: 55; The Law Reform Commission 1986; Sansom 1980; Bell and Ditton 1980).[3]

'Legitimate' violent punishments could also involve death, and were administered, one could argue, in an impersonal fashion similar to the way in which floggings, hangings, and the electric chair have been throughout western history (Bolger 1991: 49). But in the traditional setting, of course, such punishments were not carried out wantonly in alcoholic rage, but in accordance with certain codes and prescriptions understood by everyone.

Nor were uncontrolled and undeserving assaults upon a wife condoned. Under customary law, improper mating, marriage outside one's ascribed marriageable kin group, or violence against a member of another kin group (even one's wife) would more surely provoke retaliation from the victim's kin. With the breakdown of much of the fabric of traditional law and custom, many of these principles today are only vaguely recalled and acted upon.[4] Their misuse makes a mockery of traditional social values to a dangerous and increasingly frequent degree.

There is strong evidence, Bolger contends, that Aboriginal women have become victims of what one informant called 'bullshit traditional violence'. That is, assaults are being made upon women 'for illegitimate reasons, often by drunken men, which they then attempted to justify as a traditional right'. These assaults are supported by other men, many of whom are employed by councils and government agencies, who feel they should not interfere in domestic bashings. It is small wonder that women do not have a lot of faith in police or government authorities when this occurs. Older members of the communities know this is wrong:

> When asked if it was traditional for men to beat their wives, older women
> were unanimous that it was not and many men who were asked agreed.
> However, women said that men were working the law 'two ways'
> involving either traditional or white law to suit themselves and distorting
> traditional law in the process (Bolger 1991: 50).

Merv Gibson (1987: 3), in a paper presenting 'a contemporary Aboriginal viewpoint', cites 'sharing' as another example of Aboriginal traditional culture being distorted in the modern day setting. A man takes the family income and spends it on alcohol, leaving his family without proper provision for food and clothing:

He then shares the alcohol with his cousins and thus justifies the action: 'as a true expression of cultural identity and as a fulfilment of cultural and kinship obligations'. Wrong, says Gibson, rather the man is using 'Aboriginal tradition to justify what is in essence selfish exploitation based on an individual physical desire for alcohol'... (in Bolger 1991: 51).

Police, particularly in remote areas, have been hoodwinked by the 'traditional law' argument, resulting in widespread dereliction of duty in the protection of Aboriginal women during domestic disputes. Claims by young men that police should not interfere with their 'customary right' to 'discipline' their wives and children have been a convenient strategy to ward off arrest and prosecution. Due to high numbers of violent incidents in communities, it has also proved to be convenient for police to treat 'domestics' as 'nuisance crime', extending tolerance well beyond what is now acceptable in wider society.

While anthropologists, police, and other white authorities have contributed to the creation and perpetuation of these myths, Gibson maintains that they are not entirely to blame. Aboriginal men, including those in powerful positions, have much to gain from such distortions: '... for as Aboriginal women say, men have been eager to use both traditional and new laws to their advantage' (in Bolger 1991: 51).

In her research for the Royal Commission into Aboriginal Deaths in Custody, Marcia Langton found that the concentration of anthropological field workers upon the role of Aboriginal men in the past has obscured and distorted the role and status of Aboriginal women. In the Northern Territory the issue of violence against women was being trivialised by the legal system. Courts and police have been letting offenders off lightly because of assertions that rape and wife bashings were customary and of little consequence in Aboriginal society (Langton 1991; Langton and Ah Matt et al. 1991).

With uncompromising clarity, Langton maintained that brutality could not be justified by explanations of culture, poverty, or struggles for survival:

> There is no excuse that justifies this treatment of women and children. And the white people who do offer excuses out of some belief that they are being respectful of Aboriginal culture are being misled ... (Langton in Balendra 1990: 23).

Where these had, in the past, been 'arbitrarily' employed by Aboriginal men to 'inhibit and terrorise women, and to cast them as whipping posts for their frustrations, the role of feminism is to defend the rights of women As WOMEN'. If a stop was not put to these trends, Langton said, there would soon 'not be an Aboriginal culture left' to defend (ibid).

This position had been put forward several years earlier by the Law Reform Commission. In its inquiry into 'The Recognition of Aboriginal Customary Laws', the commission concluded that: 'minority values, cannot as such, justify the violation of basic human rights' (1986: 84). It is disturbing that these messages have not been reaching those responsible for justice administration in Aboriginal communities.

The real danger emerges when 'myth' and 'pseudo-culture' affect the impartial application of the criminal law. I have had police tell me that, 'even when these women have broken arms and smashed jaws, they will not lay charges against their husbands — so what can we do?' Victims, on the other hand, complained that instead of offering them the needed protection from violent partners, police officers tended to leave Aboriginal women to their fate. 'I watched with tears rolling down my face as they walked out the door and left me with him'.

DISHONOURED WOMEN

Researchers have asserted that racial violence victimises Aboriginal women on two accounts. They belong to neither the dominant culture, nor the dominant gender (NCVAW 1991: 7). Aboriginal women are continually exposed to the physical dangers, financial hardships, and domestic disruption of alcohol abuse. An eighteen month survey of 120 Aboriginal households, undertaken by the Secretariat of the National Aboriginal and Islander Child Care, found 61 cases of child sexual abuse and 59 cases of rape. About 85 per cent of the juvenile victims were female. Most incidents were carried out in their own home by a member of their nuclear or extended family, and went unreported (*Adelaide Advertiser*, 22 May 1991).

Judy Atkinson, a researcher of Aboriginal background, gives a horrific account of young women being subjected to individual and gang rape time and time again — young men raping older women, old men abusing young girls, and the neglect and sexual abuse of children and infants. 'Anal and vaginal gonorrhoea and syphilis are common, and in one case a seven year old's reproductive capacity was destroyed.' Every form of abuse is occurring:

Physical — bashings, kickings, burnings, knifings, assault with axes, pickets and other weapons.
Sexual — rape, incest, enforced sexual acts
Verbal — name calling and verbal put-downs
Mental — emotional stress, fear, guilt, shame
Social — public humiliation, denial of friends, family or social services;
Financial — denial of the means to feed and keep the family or pay the bills, financial

blackmail, threats and theft of welfare cheques, incomes and pensions. Money is being squandered by one member of the family on alcohol and gambling.

In response to the growing concern of Aboriginal women in remote communities, a series of interviews about alcohol-related violence, and its effects upon Aboriginal family and community life, was conducted on video throughout Australia by Atkinson in 1990. One interviewee described family violence as 'a cancerous disease that is destroying us, eating the very heart of our culture and our future as a people' (*Beyond Violence: Finding the Dream*, 1990). Sue Wright, coordinator of the federal government's Remote Areas Project on domestic violence, spelt out the problems:

> Women are being badly hurt and dying because of violence and in some places rape and sexual abuse of women has become common place. The sexual and physical abuse of children is also increasing. Our whole Aboriginal race is getting out of control. We are losing one another. We are losing our families, we are losing our self-identity ... A lot of women are taking a lot of bashings out there and it is amazing how the human body can stand up to the treatment they get week after week, sometimes day after day (in Balendra 1990: 23).

While not all the victims of violence are women, a much smaller minority of women commit violence. Some of the injuries which women sustain, however, are very serious (Bolger 1991: 18). In a Pitjantjatjara community visited by Maggie Brady, 25 per cent of all female injuries were to the head (compared to 7 per cent of male injuries):

> Lacerations are usually inflicted with bottles, iron bars and bricks, which are wielded as weapons during fights. In this community, alcohol related crimes are virtually all against the person rather than against property, although some property damage does occur (Brady 1990a: 138).

At the *National Forum on Domestic Violence Training* organised by the Office of Status of Women, Department of the Prime Minister and Cabinet, in Adelaide between 26–28 April 1990, it was reported by Aboriginal speakers that Aboriginal women were so badly and so regularly being beaten that they no longer had the capacity or will to care for their children. 'If we are being raped and bashed how can we look after our kids?', these women asked.

Even more so than the problems faced by abused non-Aboriginal women, the socioeconomic position which Aboriginal women have occupied in Australian society has made their plight doubly lamentable. As the least educated, most impoverished, least employed, and most powerless sector of Australian society their 'invisibility' has been until recently almost complete, wrote Jocelynne Scutt (1990). White women would be advantaged when black women become visible in Aboriginal culture, she said, and their cause given proper recognition by Anglo-Australia.

WRECKED MANHOODS

Various 'reasons' are given by men for violence at home. Common 'blaming the victim' kinds of comments recorded by Bolger were:

> 'It serves her right — she was drinking too.'

> 'It was her fault — she back-answered him when he was drunk.'
> 'She asked for it — she didn't have his tucker ready when he got home' ...[and]

> 'Sometimes women need a good hiding.' (Bolger 1991: 55).

The National Committee on Violence Against Women (NCVAW) asserts that domestic violence is not about sex or love, it is about power and control — or the lack of it:

> Violence against women is a product of the social construction of masculinity; the set of traditions, habits and beliefs, which permit some men to assume dominance and control over women and thus, to assume the right to use violence as a means of exercising that dominance and control (NCVAW 1991: 8).

There is a close relationship between the 'original aggression' argument — concerning the effect of colonialism upon Aboriginal culture — and the NCVAW line of thinking. The behaviour of Aboriginal men, particularly since the withdrawal of restrictive church and mission administrations, must be seen *par excellence* as the classic depiction of 'constructed masculinity'. It is a pattern of dominance, these authors would say, quite unlike traditional cultural experience.

Atkinson is clear in her assertion of this connection. 'Spousal assault', she says, is 'learned behaviour'. It was learned by Aboriginal people from the initial aggression of white occupation, and has since been transferred throughout the fabric of Aboriginal society over several generations of exposure to male-dominated colonial and paternalistic administrations. The violent and jealous behaviour of male partners, and their desperate need for dominance, has resulted in terrible mistreatment of

Aboriginal women and children. Many women, said Atkinson, live in 'spiritual and mental incarceration in their own homes':

> This abuse begins with the belief that a man has the right to dominate his wife and children. This is a fundamental structural problem, which began with the subjugation of one culture by another in 1788. It was an act of violence then, and it continues to be so (Judy Atkinson, notes from the *National Forum on Domestic Violence Training*, Adelaide, April 1990).

A range of historical and psychological reasons for this unhealthy change could be offered. With nomadic inter-dependence between men and women destroyed, with the mutual obligations to family and moiety removed, and with the strict codes of traditional law supplanted — 'just wanting to be boss!' may well have become a primary obsession. Robbed of the right to pursue traditional activities, and denied opportunities for positive achievement and self-worth within the Australian economy, adult men become preoccupied with overt displays of 'manhood' in their home. This 'loss of role' among 'male providers' is a common theme of discussion concerning social problems in Canadian Indian communities as well. Impoverished women, it would seem, deserve less of our concern because they at least still have the role and function of 'mother'. In reality they are left little choice.

While researchers, community workers, and Aboriginal women in particular, are sympathetic to explanations of the possible stresses and fears which impel men to violence, they are increasingly giving voice to the urgent need to confront and stop this dangerous trend. There is no acceptable reason for 'giving someone a hiding'. Even though this is a difficult area, and precisely *because* it is fraught with complications, community programs *must undermine every justification* until perpetrators take responsibility for their violent responses.

> Everyone, everywhere must become intolerant of violence against women and uphold the belief that no woman deserves violence and that the use of violence is a crime (NCAVW 1991: 2).

In addition to the obvious humanitarian ones, there are some good reasons why every means to defeat patterns of aggression should be used. The abuse of others shatters the credibility of people as care-givers and as leaders. A tyrant in the home is an unstable protector and mentor of the family. A bully on the council builds a base of support upon very shaky ground. 'Me first' forms of tyranny will always result in subjugation rather than respect.

It is an ironic and sad fact that aggression can ultimately destroy the aggressor — whether male or female. As well as making themselves miserable, aggressors will be disappointed by the lack of cooperation and loyalty they receive from those they wish to dominate. When aggressors do not win the love or regard they expect, family life becomes strained and eventually impossible. 'When people are injured and demoralised, children are not tended to, and the dinners do not get cooked,' pointed out one community worker.

Failure will be heaped upon an aggressor's unresolved rage — leading to dangerously high levels of frustration. Victims will be blamed for the little respect received, for loss of pride, and lack of personal fulfilment. Aggressive and self-destructive behaviours ruin social relations and erode human trust. Many do not wish to follow such people on their chosen paths of destruction, but will 'play along with them just to keep them quiet'.

Men who themselves become victims of the machismo myth, fail in every area of social life — as brothers, fathers, husbands, and leaders. As their insecurity increases, violent men are perceived by others as representing cowardice, weakness, impotence, and ineptitude. The television hype and 'roaring bull' machismo of young male culture soon betrays them. Violence does not symbolise strength or power, vitality or intelligence, and fails to win the desired homage. But it surely results in wrecked manhoods. To Aboriginal men who believe otherwise, Atkinson issues this piercing challenge:

> We need to stop oppressing ourselves. We need to stop functioning like conquered blacks.[5]

BLIGHTED CHILDREN

> A turtle will give birth to a turtle ... Stress gives birth to stress. Violence gives birth to violence (Mam 1991: 9).

Aboriginal women are increasingly concerned about the plight of children who are exposed to lifestyles of alcoholism, binge drinking, and violence. Children who learn self-abusive and family-abusive behaviours from their parents' generation will apply it quite early in their own lives. It will soon be manifested in juvenile behaviour towards other children, community property, and eventually family members. Infants and young children become increasingly in danger of assault from older and adolescent boys, grandmothers become fearful of grandsons, mothers of sons and sons-in-law.

Children who are exposed to spousal assault are more likely to become batterers in their own personal relationships, or to accept the role of victims. By the time young people have reached early adolescence lifestyles of violence have already taken root — ensuring their recurrence through the generations.

On one community a local health worker pointed out that many teenage
boys bash-up their girlfriends in much the same way as their fathers bash
their mothers ... Many children grow up thinking that violence is a
'normal reaction to problems and anger' (Queensland Domestic Violence
Task Force 1989: 261).

It is not just male children who are psychologically affected by repeated experiences of
violence and distorted perceptions of 'tradition'. For victims, particularly female
children, the myths are likely to become 'a self fulfilling prophesy' (Atkinson 1989: 9):

The sad thing is that many young women now believe that it is
traditional for men to beat their wives, since this is the everyday reality of
their lives. Older women may reject this as a distortion and a myth, but
they worry about the implications of acceptance of this and other
'bullshit' tradition for the next generation (Bolger 1991: 51).

The Aboriginal Co-ordinating Council (ACC) in Cairns has for some years employed
male and female family violence counsellors on its staff to work with Aboriginal
communities. The ACC consists of 15 Aboriginal councils responsible for
approximately 12,000 people living in trust communities in this northern Queensland
region. Every means possible, I was told, should be employed to stop family violence
in Aboriginal communities. Next to excessive use of alcohol, it is the most likely cause
of Aboriginal injury and homicide today. It should be stopped, not only for the sake of
those who fall victim to it, but because early experiences of family violence induce
patterns of violence and criminality in Aboriginal youth and children (discussions
with ACC June 1990):

No-one is suggesting that all Aboriginal people are violent or that all
women are being assaulted and harassed. ... However, it appears to be a
widespread phenomenon and women want it to stop, not only for their
own sakes but for the sake of their children and families (Bolger 1991: 38).

VIDEO-PORN AND AIDS:
NEW SCOURGE OF VIOLENCE?

Over a 15–20 year period community workers have observed changing patterns of
physical behaviour and sexual offending among Aboriginal men and boys which, they
are convinced, have been induced by exposure to violent images in the media. This
'new scourge of violence' in remote communities has been attributed by local people

to the introduction of a diet of macho and violent television programs and, more recently, of violent and pornographic videos available through local distributors and inter-state mail order outlets.

Women complain that they have been asked to participate in these viewings and to imitate sexual acts which are offensive or distressing to them. Assaults on young children, infants, and animals by young males, sometimes roving in gangs, escalates after shipments of pornographic videos.

This draws our attention to another frightening dimension of social dysfunction. To add to the existing problems of alcoholism, ill health, abuse and neglect — there is the increasing danger of AIDS. Promiscuity is not the only transmitter of the HIV virus, the rising incidence of sexual assault can also provide a medium. 'Safe sex' is seldom a primary concern of the rapist, especially a young uninformed one. What chance do children have in guarding themselves against this disease? In one group of town camps Bolger was told that 'there was no girl over the age of ten years who had not been raped ...' (1991: 32). I have heard similar estimates, sometimes with even lower age thresholds, in several communities I have visited. By the time they have reached sexual maturity many of these children will have been subjected to numerous sexual violations. What good is AIDS education to them?

These problems must surely trouble the consciences of even the most liberal-minded opponents of censorship. With the presence of AIDS in some Aboriginal communities we simply do not have another decade to ignore issues of social decline. Yet governments continue to make decisions concerning pornography with little evident regard for its effect upon indigenous people:

> ... while the people who sit in the Legislative Assembly in Canberra consider pornography does no harm, they have not considered the circumstances of young males living in isolated and depressed circumstances in remote Australia. Sometimes such videos, brought in by white men as forms of entertainment, are the only understanding our young men have of mainstream culture. While the rest of Australia has received the message from law-makers and others in authority that such videos are 'ok', there are voices of concern coming from Aboriginal women who say violence and sexual abuse has increased since pornography entered communities (Atkinson 1990b: 7–8).

While the mail-order traffic in X-rated and R-rated videos is subject to federal and state government legislation, the running of illicit and illegal videos is difficult to police. Where the impact is felt most, there are few local government or community controls over the nature, volume, or viewing of such material. Profits to be made by delivering these videos, it would seem, have attracted the same kinds of people who have conducted sly grog operations over the years.

To unscrupulous interests, Aboriginal society is 'a sitting duck'. In one northern Queensland community I visited it was the non-Aboriginal owner of the community garage who ordered in this material from Canberra, and rehired these to the Aboriginal men at a considerable profit. It was the Aboriginal women who were asked to perform the acts that were seen on these videos, or the young children who were assaulted by highly excited teenagers after a viewing. Without proper authority to set up their own controls these communities are a vulnerable and ready-made market for the worst of what western society has to offer.

The story gets worse. A four year old boy was severely traumatised when he watched an imported South American 'snuff' movie with his uncle. The details are too gruesome for print. But there is no reason to believe that Aboriginal people could not become the target of 'video nasty' distributors.

Neither police, health and welfare, nor criminological studies have seriously investigated the effect pornographic and violent audio-visuals may be having upon Aboriginal communities. Community workers say they see a connection between households with video machines and the failure of infants in those households to thrive. The relationship between video violence, assaults against the person, and other social indicators needs to be explored. These are important studies waiting to be undertaken.

During the 1980s Aboriginal imprisonment rates and deaths in custody captured public and academic interest. But it would be small consolation if video-porn, and its relationship to community violence and the spread of AIDS, becomes a fashionable new domain of research and government concern a decade too late. Aboriginal women continue to have their lives and bodies shattered from alcohol-related violence. Community workers continue to express their distress about escalating sex crimes among boys, teenagers, and men in communities where X-rated and R-rated videos are readily available. Even if alcoholism and community violence do become the focus of attention, within a few years they could be overtaken by a crisis of even greater proportions as a result of the spread of AIDS and other sexually transmitted diseases. Why has the response to these appeals for action been so slow ?

Unless Aboriginal people are empowered to introduce by-laws and other controls to ban the importation of harmful materials and products, with these controls being given the full enforcement of the law, the rates of violence and the spread of disease in their communities will continue to soar.

A word for those who are indifferent or complacent. If we assume that, so long as the assaults are 'black-on-black' we need not be concerned about Aboriginal violence, we ignore the fact that inter-racial violence plagues nearly every continent of the world. If we assume that fatal diseases will stay within the confines of remote communities, then we have forgotten the evidence that such diseases respect neither gender, class, colour, creed — *nor physical boundaries.*

It is only a matter of time before the non-Aboriginal community will feel the extreme effects of Aboriginal violence, alcoholism, and ill health. To wait until then is not simply inhumane — it is insanity. Men and women need to stand together against this problem. Governments should do whatever they can to support and promote their stand.

LOST COMMUNITIES

In its submission to the Queensland Domestic Violence Task Force, the Aboriginal Co-ordinating Council expressed deep concern about the levels of violence on its Deed of Grant in Trust communities. This was confirmed by the findings of the Queensland Task Force during its inquiries in 1988, and earlier in a New South Wales Task Force on Domestic Violence in 1981. In the 1988 report of the Queensland Domestic Violence Task Force, *Beyond These Walls*, Aboriginal trust areas and communities were said to provide glaring examples of a community life which promotes family violence. Social ills of all forms — overcrowding, unemployment, poor health, alcoholism, and interpersonal conflict were rife in these communities, with few preventative or helping services available.

In a study on Palm Island, Queensland, it was noted that over 70% of assaults on women were committed by drunk boyfriends or husbands (Barber, Punt and Albers 1988). In the Northern Territory Aboriginal women represent about 11.5% of the population. In 1988, 17% of the 1811 violent offences recorded that year were against Aboriginal women (Bolger 1991: 11). In his study of the changing patterns of Aboriginal mortality in the Kimberley, Western Australia, Hunter observed:

> Kimberley Aboriginal males were more likely to die from motor vehicle accidents, accidents or suicide than Aboriginal females. However Aboriginal females were more likely to be victims of homicide (1989: 11).

Aboriginal women are dying far too frequently from violent assault at the hands of their husbands and boyfriends.[6] The lives of Aboriginal men are twisted and wasted in prisons of addiction as well as gaols of concrete and steel. The minds and futures of children, as young as infancy, are being deformed by exposure to the misery of criminal acts which can not be justified by arguments of 'culture' — neither under traditional or criminal law, nor under any international human rights conventions.

What Bolger described as one of her most 'significant findings' was the 'similarity of the violence suffered by Aboriginal women' to those stories collected by Scutt (1983) among their 'non-Aboriginal sisters'. The types of abuse by men, either drunk or sober; the excuses and reasons — either real or imagined; and the unwillingness of women to talk about them. There were differences, usually relating to cultural factors or living conditions and levels of abuse. Aboriginal men were more likely to use weapons — 'sticks, stones, star pickets'. 'But the overwhelming impression is one of comparable experiences', Bolger concluded (1991: 37–8).

'What is clear from all this evidence', wrote Atkinson, 'is that violence is a way of life and that few Aboriginal women and children have access to the protective services required':

> The law, in fact, has not addressed this problem of serious sexual assault preferring to deal with the more minor social disorder problems like drunkenness and disorderly conduct ... Whatever the cause, both Government and Community has to take the first and most essential step and admit there is a problem. The problem is of such immensity and complexity that there are no quick and easy solutions. Nonetheless the problem must be addressed now (Atkinson 1989: 13–14).

The question of the adequacy of the law on Aboriginal and Islander communities, pointed out the Queensland Task Force into Domestic Violence, is something which 'deserves concerted attention' and urgent consideration by decision makers (1989: 266). What is clear is that community support for the legal protection, counselling, and support of victims, or the rehabilitation of perpetrators, is either insufficient or totally absent from those violent pockets of Australian society which need them most.

The number of sobering-up centres can be counted on one hand and are run with varying degree of success. Some are little more than shacks which act as flop houses. There are no whole-community detoxification programs and few shelters for women and children who suffer from violent assault. The child welfare, health, medical, and police resources on Aboriginal communities are desperately over-stretched by alcohol related violence. 'It is often the wives, mothers and grandmothers', wrote Sharon Payne, 'who are left to deal with the violent mental and physical problems associated with alcohol abuse' (Payne 1990: 10). Nothing short of comprehensive preventative and treatment programming will reverse this trend.

TAKING RESPONSIBILITY

Violence will stop only when men stop being violent and when the community stops condoning it (NCVAW 1991: 9).

In the mid 1980s d'Abbs noted that opposition to alcohol abuse in communities came mainly from older men and married women with children. Women, particularly, criticised the setting up of clubs and canteens and called for their closure. But at public meetings, where alcohol restrictions were discussed, it was usually women's views which were most likely to be suppressed or ignored by community leaders; and visiting officials seldom set up separate meetings with the women (d'Abbs 1987; Barber, Punt and Albers 1988; Brady 1990).

As levels of alcohol-related illness, injury, and personal assault reached a critical stage during the late eighties (Reid and Trompf 1991) there was a groundswell of opinion in northern Queensland that the issue of family violence should be squarely addressed. At the forefront of this activity was the Cairns-based Aboriginal Co-ordinating Council. ACC researchers and workers took both the Queensland government and Aboriginal community leaders to task over these issues.

In the Northern Territory, Aboriginal women began to hold separate women's meetings and actively to speak out against the injuries and deaths being caused. On 5 May 1990, about 200 Aboriginal women from surrounding towns and isolated settlements journeyed to Alice Springs to stage a protest. Once too ashamed to discuss domestic strife openly, these women conducted a march through the streets of Alice Springs, appealing to government officials for assistance in seeking the means to prevent alcoholism and violence in their communities (Balendra 1990: 23).

Educational resource materials and video packages produced in the Northern Territory, Queensland, Western Australia, and Canberra between 1989 and 1991, made available to community workers, community support groups, and women's groups, new ideas and materials for discussion. Some videos were run on Aboriginal television programs.[7]

A series of community healing, family violence, and customary law conferences organised in Alice Springs, Adelaide, Brisbane, Cairns, and the remote north of Queensland started to draw together Aboriginal people for sharing and mutual support.[8] Through these exchanges, women's groups, and special committees against family violence and child abuse gained a little more direction and confidence. Some government programs have been funded but there is still much to be done in programming for detoxification and preventative action.

In *Through Black Eyes: A Handbook of Family Violence in Aboriginal and Torres Strait Islander Communities*, developed by the National Aboriginal and Islander Child Care, the message of community responsibility and community control was strongly emphasised:

> Family violence is our big shame. It affects everyone, women, children, men — the whole community. It can happen to anyone, black and white, rich or poor. It is happening in our Communities; the remote areas, bush and town camps, trust areas, reserves, country towns and big cities ... Family violence is everyone's business; we need to look to our Communities to take up responsibility for this problem (*Through Black Eyes* 1991: 3-4).

The way out of the maze of problems concerning the old law and the new, and the way forward for the future, was perhaps best expressed in the words of an elder from Kowanyama, northern Queensland:

> We can't go back. The old law was for the old problems. Now we got this new law — this whiteman's way. And we got these new problems. This law doesn't fix them either. It's no good. What we got to do is put them both together — the old and the new. Mix them up. And they'll be hard and strong like cement (Harry Daphney, Kowanyama, *Beyond Violence*, 1990: 8).

'We are all hurting — the Elders, our men, our women and our kids', wrote the Secretariat of the National Aboriginal and Islander Child Care, 'especially our kids':

> They look to us for love and support and guidance. We need to tell them that family violence is not our way! We need to give back to them the old cultural values of respect for themselves and others, of peace, of caring, of looking out for one another and the safety and protection of their families (*Through Black Eyes*, 1991: 4).

More than this, said the SNAICC, our children are the key to our future. 'They are the means by which we will be woken from this nightmare!' (ibid).

COMMUNITY RE-EMPOWERMENT

> We have the answers here in our community. Sometimes we don't realise how strong we are, what we can do (Weipa South, Qld, resident, *Beyond Violence*, 1990: 8).

Aboriginal community workers and researchers in Queensland are now urging women to talk about family violence among themselves, and to set up regional conferences for this purpose. This has been a great breakthrough, as only a few years ago it was a taboo subject which induced great shame among the women.

There has also been a growing interest in Queensland in establishing a network of Aboriginal women's support groups. The intention is not to exclude men, but initially to help women understand that nobody deserves to be battered and beaten, and to help them consider their alternatives. These groups help victims to become united in their opposition to family violence, to become stronger in their capacity to reverse this trend, and later to involve men and youth in the needed programs against violence.

Why not holistic?

Awareness is the first step in this direction. The *Through Black Eyes* handbook urged concerned men and women to 'BREAK THE SILENCE' on abuse at both the individual and community level. We can do this, it said:

Individually
- by speaking out about rape or child sexual abuse
- by believing the victims when they tell you about it. By re-affirming that the abuse was not their fault
- by helping and supporting them in any way possible.

As a community
- by acknowledging rape or child sexual abuse as a Community problem and responsibility
- by condemning rape and child sexual abuse as practices and setting harsh punishment for the abusers
- by taking it seriously, and making it top priority
- by initiating community awareness programs, preventative action groups, and setting up crisis lines and centres with specialised counselling for both victims and abusers
- by standing up for our women and children and giving them the support and protection of their Communities (*Through Black Eyes*, 1991: 25).

In recent years indigenous people in Canada, the United States, New Zealand, and Australia have begun to seek ways to re-empower their communities. The philosophy of 'self-determination', which is supported by international law conventions for all indigenous populations, represents a turning away from the repugnant colonial relationship, and a growing indigenous role in areas of social, economic, and political development.

Since the 1970s Aboriginal people have sought increased involvement in the running of local affairs, business enterprises, and service delivery. With the exception of legal services, which have had a significant degree of success in making legal counsel accessible to Aboriginal people throughout the country, Aboriginal professional and paraprofessional involvement in the criminal justice system has been limited. Nevertheless, community policing, elder advice to magistrates, and community court options have improved justice delivery to community groups (Hazlehurst 1991).

Indigenous leaders have increasingly recognised that community ownership of community problems, and community ownership of community solutions, are fundamental to the process of re-empowerment. Freedom from violence is an essential element of this process of liberation:

We are building something new. Something that belongs to us. We are working together. And it's good. We can see the results (Broome, WA, resident, *Beyond Violence*, 1990: 8).

◆ ◆ ◆

[1] The 1967 national referendum sought to remove from the Australian Constitution discriminatory provisions against Aborigines, and to grant Aboriginal people equality of citizenship, including the right to drink (Fletcher 1992: 1-2; Gumbert 1984: 20-25).

[2] Bolger pointed out that Aboriginal women have always known that domestic violence was wrong, and not upheld by traditional law. But it took anthropologists some time to recognise this, mainly because the discipline was for some time dominated by males who spoke primarily to Aboriginal men in their studies of Aboriginal society. 'This bias has now been largely corrected', wrote Bolger, 'mainly by women researchers who have been in a position to hear women's side of the story' (Bolger 1991: 50; see also Goodale 1971; Berndt 1979; Hamilton 1981; Bell 1983).

[3] Anthropological literature has documented spearing in the thigh of men, and blows to the arms of women as customary sanctions.

[4] As in some cases the inebriated 'were able to place their blows to specific parts of the body, suggests that strong cultural factors were at work' (Brady 1990: 141).

[5] Notes from the *National Forum on Domestic Violence Training*, Office of Status of Women, Department of the Prime Minister and Cabinet, Adelaide, 26-28 April 1990.

[6] It has been pointed out that, in one Queensland community, more women died as a result of violent assault than all the Black deaths in custody in that state for the same period (Atkinson 1990b: 6; Balendra 1990; Hammond 1990, Brady 1990; Devaneson 1986; Hunter 1989; Reid and Trompf 1991).

[7] See section on Reference Materials, at the end of this chapter.

[8]*National Forum on Domestic Violence Training*, conference organised by Office of Status of Women, Department of the Prime Minister and Cabinet, Adelaide 26–28 April 1990; *Aboriginal Family Violence Seminar*, Cairns, 15–17 May 1990, organised

by the Aboriginal Co-ordinating Council with Office of the Status of Women and Queensland government support; *Two Laws Conference*, organised by the Foundation for Aboriginal and Islander Research Action (FAIRA) and the University of Queensland, Brisbane, 5–8 December 1990; *'Healing Our People' Conference*, organised by the Australian Institute of Criminology, Alice Springs, 2–5 April 1991; *Remote Areas Aboriginal Women's Conference*, Laura, Cape York Peninsula, 1-4 July 1991.

Chapter three

VISIONARY PROGRAMS

Women are clearly saying they are tired of the violence and want it to stop. The first stage in working out how to stop it is bringing it out in the open, talking about it (Bolger 1991:38).

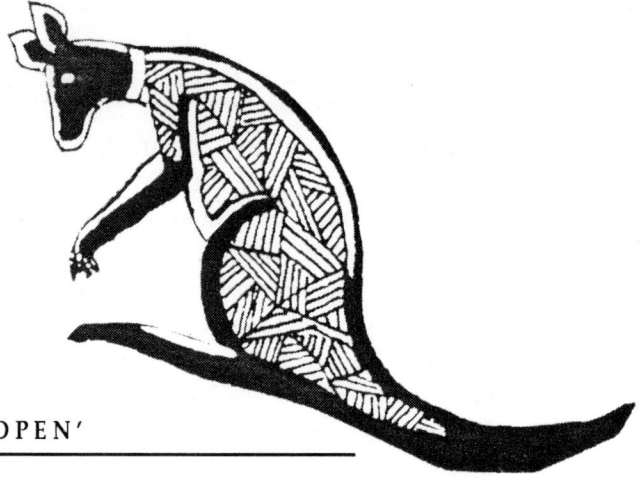

'BRINGING IT OUT IN THE OPEN'

It has taken a long time for Aboriginal and Islander women to speak out against family violence. Of the many stories collected in her Northern Territory study, Bolger said that it would be doubtful if Aboriginal women would have related such stories for publication five years earlier. In addition to Aboriginal women tiring of community violence, the activities of several agencies since 1989 have helped to raise Aboriginal and Islander awareness. The message that 'people don't have to put up with this violence' has gone out to the town camps, towns, outstations, and trust areas of Queensland, Northern Territory, New South Wales, South Australia, and Western Australia.

Issues of family violence were brought into focus through the efforts of the National Domestic Violence Task Force, as part of a broader campaign implemented by the federal Office of the Status of Women, Department of Prime Minister and Cabinet. Between November 1989 and May 1990 Judy Atkinson, who was employed as a consultant to the National Domestic Violence Education Program, travelled to all states to speak with Aboriginal and Islander women and men about family violence and to find out about community projects being used to overcome it.

The *Beyond Violence — Finding the Dream* (1990) handbook and video package was compiled as part of the Aboriginal and Torres Strait Islander sub-program of the National Domestic Violence Education Program, and was jointly sponsored by the Office of the Status of Women, and the Office of Aboriginal Women, within the Aboriginal and Torres Strait Islander Commission (ATSIC).

In 1989 the Northern Territory Department of Aboriginal Affairs funded the setting up of a Remote Areas Domestic Violence Project employing Sue Wright and Gamiritj Gurruwiwi to visit communities regularly to discuss their problems. These women now run *'Family Fighting/Killing Wrong Way!'* workshops for communities using the manual, handbook, posters, and video kit of the same name produced by the Aboriginal Resource and Development Services, United Aboriginal and Islander Christian Congress, and the Department of Northern Territory Aboriginal Affairs, Darwin.

WOMEN TALKING TOGETHER

Aboriginal women are frequently the ones who shield their men from the police, even when it is they who are the victims. They do this for reasons well-known to domestic violence workers everywhere — the aggressor is also a loved one (father, husband, boyfriend or son); the victim may convince herself that she 'deserved it'; she does not want to break up the family; has no money and nowhere else to go; or does not want to leave the children behind.

Aboriginal women cannot or seldom wish to flee their communities. There are both financial and emotional reasons for this. Relatives, friends, and familiar surroundings offer comfort and security. Women's refuges, in the few places where they exist, provide only temporary shelter.

But another theme has been constant in talks between Aboriginal women on this subject. They have a justified concern for the safety of their menfolk when they are exposed to the criminal justice system. Put quite simply, they are afraid the abuser will be subject to depression or mistreatment in police cells or prisons. They may die in custody or may come home even more outraged than when they were taken away. The extensive publicity given to the Royal Commission into Aboriginal Deaths in Custody has increased rather than dispelled these fears.

MEN'S PROGRAMS

Through conferences and forums women from many walks of life and cultural backgrounds have found similarities of experience and thought. 'Our men are victims of the attitude that domestic violence is OK', said Josepha Kanawi, from the Law Reform Commission, Papua New Guinea:

> Instead of taking our men to task, and telling them 'you are bad', women
> need to stand together and say 'you need to change your attitude'. Its a
> family issue *and* a national issue.

> We need to say to them: 'You are not the enemy! The enemy is the
> violence!' (Josepha Kanawi, notes from the *National Forum on Domestic
> Violence Training*, Adelaide, April 1990).

Many Aboriginal women share this view. 'No one will ever convince me that the answer to violence is to pick the man up and put him in prison', declared Atkinson at this same forum. 'Prison is one place where men have learnt violent behaviours'. If given the opportunity, 'our men will feel pride in their role as guardians of law and family':

Community needs to stand up and say 'Stop the Violence'. When men and women stand together it's far stronger than just women standing up on their own. Sometimes we don't know how strong we are. We have the answers ourselves in our community. By taking control of our problems we are taking control of our future (Judy Atkinson, notes from the *National Forum on Domestic Violence Training*, Adelaide, April 1990).

Atkinson went on to raise some direct questions about aspects of women's behaviour and attitudes which may be contributing to patterns of violence. Perhaps mothers could be stronger in censuring aggression in boys. Women could play a part in setting standards. Hitting and swearing should not be acceptable:

As wives and as mothers we need to ask ourselves, 'do we pamper our boys?'. 'Do we let him hit his sisters?'. 'Are we, as mothers, partly responsible for the males the way they are and for the domestic violence towards women?' We see boys putting down and humiliating their sisters. More often mothers try to protect their sons. We expect girls to be strong.

Women get killed, men go to prison and our kids carry it on into the next generation. We love the men, we don't want to leave them. We just want them to stop the violence. *When women get continually bashed their spirit is hurt*. It affects *all* the family of all ages (Judy Atkinson, notes from the *National Forum on Domestic Violence Training*, Adelaide, April 1990.

Many Aboriginal women do not share the sentiments of western feminists that tougher legislation and prison sentences should be used on their violent men. They want safe homes and safe communities. They say, quite adamantly, that *they want the violence to stop*. They want their husbands and partners to receive help so they will learn how to stop. They want their sons to learn how to break the cycle of offending.

Aboriginal women tend to avoid prosecuting their men for physical assault, rape or incest, said Atkinson. However, this does not mean that police should leave them at the mercy of a drunk and violent husband — 'ignoring their screams for help'. Police can intervene. 'If the aggressor cannot be calmed down it is safer for everyone that he be placed in police cells overnight, until he has sobered up'. Most violent drunks say they do not remember what happened the next morning, and their women frequently concede — 'he didn't know what he was doing' (ibid). Awareness that there is an official responsibility — Police, Community Councils, Health Services — to work with Aboriginal communities to prevent domestic violence is one area which needs to be highlighted.

In seeking solutions it is necessary to begin to *'name our villains'*. That is, to give an identity to those things which are hurting us as individuals, families, and communities — rather than to let them continue in the nameless grey light of uncertainty and confusion. When people are not clear in their minds about the kinds of activities or behaviours which are harmful they will find themselves trapped in fearful relationships, which are supported by cycles of anger, mutual blaming, and denial. Solutions will be impossible.

Aboriginal women have identified *violence* as one of those most immediate obstacles to peaceful family life. They are now seeking longer-term solutions. *Denial of self-responsibility* in individuals who drink and become violent continues to be a major source of disempowerment to men, women and children. Like the villain of *alcoholism*, they want alternatives which address the root causes of these social ills. They want to eradicate them in the lives of the next generation. The catch-phrase at women's meetings today is *'Stop the Abuse'*. They see an urgent need for men's programs which will provide a place for men to talk about problems of personal and community violence, and for the habitually violent to receive help.

Aboriginal women do not want their men imprisoned. Neither do they want the violence to continue. They want community healing.

'STOP THE ABUSE' PROGRAMS

The National Aboriginal and Torres Strait Islander Family Support Program, introduced by the federal government in 1990, made funding available for programs for family support and family violence projects and the production and distribution of resource materials. This program increased opportunities for community-based activities, particularly those arising from the state and regional initiatives of the Office of Aboriginal Women within the Aboriginal and Torres Strait Islander Commission (ATSIC). Under this program communities were able to apply for funding for projects to the Women's Issues Officer at their nearest ATSIC Regional Office.

In 1988 Western Australian Aboriginal women's groups became involved in a 'Stop the Abuse' campaign with the support of the Department of Aboriginal Affairs (now ATSIC). Colourful posters and brochures, including one designed by the Aboriginal artist, Sally Morgan, have been very popular and have received wide distribution.[1] Three hundred people attended a series of five day 'speakout' forums held at different centres around Perth.

Information sharing groups and gatherings have been run in South Australia, Victoria, and New South Wales. The highlight of a large conference organised in May 1989 by the Cawarra Women's Shelter, Mt Druitt, Sydney was a play about family violence written by a group of Aboriginal women. The major funding for this conference came from the NSW Department of Family and Community Services. In Queensland, kits on family violence and child abuse have been produced by the Aboriginal and Torres Strait Islander Corporation for Women, Brisbane, and the Aboriginal and Islander Child Care Agency Ltd with ATSIC funding.

In northern Queensland the Aboriginal Co-ordinating Council (ACC), Cairns, wanted to take an holistic approach. Since the late 1980s a team of ACC workers has been responding to community requests for help with setting up workshops, support groups, and preventative programs. Team members include an alcohol abuse worker, an AIDS awareness worker, community development and child-care workers, a recreation liaison officer, and a domestic violence worker. The elected councillors who make up ACC were encouraging the team to visit each of their communities.

'BEATING THE GROG'

The message of the Central Australian Aboriginal Alcohol Planning Unit (CAAAPU) is 'Let's Beat the Grog Together'. Aimed at the 'bush mob' and 'town mob' of the Central Australian region, this Aboriginal organisation recommends 'sharing and caring' as the key to success.

The CAAAPU was established in March 1991 with funding from the federal Department of Health and Community Services. Its initial team of four was based in Alice Springs, and worked with 45 Aboriginal communities and organisations, involving community workers, consultants, and interpreters. CAAAPU members travel widely from bush to town organising meetings and talking to people. In addition to sending out a regular newsletter they make good use of the local Aboriginal radio station, Imparja television, and the ABC.

As alcohol abuse is the biggest problem facing the Aboriginal people in Central Australia, CAAAPU tackles the 'grog' issue directly. In 1991 Doug Walker, the coordinator of CAAAPU, himself a recovered alcoholic, spent four weeks at the Native alcohol treatment centre, Poundmaker's Lodge, in Alberta. He was also joined by Doug Abbott, along with his wife Lana. The Abbotts were very experienced in this field. Doug Abbott was the co-founder of Northern Territory based, Aboriginal Alcoholics Awareness (AAA), and Lana Abbott was the Senior Health Worker with the Central Australian Aboriginal Congress for ten years. As well as attending the Poundmaker's Lodge treatment programs they visited a number of successful outreach and after-care programs in Alberta.

'We've gained a lot from the Indian mob. Actually seeing what has been done has given us confidence that we can do it here too', Doug Walker explained in an article published in the *Aboriginal Law Bulletin*:

Our goal is to get a comprehensive action plan that brings together all the elements needed to really make big changes in all our communities. The key factors include first class, culturally centred treatment and training. And to be effective these programs must be developed, controlled and staffed by Aboriginal people (Doug Walker in Wynter 1991: 7–8).

In evaluating one sobering-up shelter in Alice Springs, a researcher found that in the four and a half years of its operation police made 3700 apprehensions for public drunkenness; 121 people were apprehended for a third of these; and one man was apprehended 409 times.

CAAAPU was convinced that prevention and treatment are far cheaper and more effective alternatives to constant policing and gaol. It was abundantly clear to CAAAPU'S experienced membership that effective and high quality treatment for detoxification was needed in Central Australia to break the cycle of alcohol and substance abuse. It was simply not enough to sober people up and send them out again to the same environment and expectation of drunkenness.

CAAAPU began targeting communities to help them develop their own local and regional plans for 'getting off the grog'. At the same time they lobbied the Northern Territory government and the private sector to orient their support for treatment, training facilities and community education (Wynter 1991: 7-8).

CAAAPU took action in making their vision of a treatment and training centre for Central Australia come true. In November 1991 they invited Eric Shirt from Poundmaker's Lodge, and two experienced helpers to assist the local people to run their first alcohol counsellor training program followed by a 28-day treatment program.

On 1 September 1993 CAAAPU began a full-time Aboriginal alcohol treatment program with funding secured from the NT Department of Health and Community Services, 'Living with Alcohol' Program. In the first six weeks over 50 people had volunteered themselves for treatment, coming from Alice Springs and the country regions, Tennant Creek, Adelaide and even as far away as Sydney. Meeting a need, and reaching the goal of setting up of *their own* treatment program created a great sense of achievement and pride in CAAAPU workers. 'But we couldn't have done it without training', said Lana Abbott. 'Training was the key' (personal communications 14 October 1993).

COMMUNITY AWARENESS CONFERENCES
AND WORKSHOPS

As part of its national campaign against domestic violence, the Office of the Status of Women (OSW) mounted an Aboriginal awareness program in far north Queensland with keen Aboriginal support in that area. About two and a half weeks after they had held the *National Forum on Domestic Violence Training* in Adelaide, some of the same organisers assisted in the running of the first Aboriginal family violence seminar in northern Queensland. Between 15–17 May 1990 a 'Holistic Domestic Violence Initiatives and Awareness Workshop' was organised in Cairns, by the Aboriginal Co-ordinating Council with OSW support and funding from the Queensland government. While this was largely a gathering of about 150 Aboriginal women, it also had a small attendance of Aboriginal men, with a smattering of government, community policing, health, and welfare representation. At this gathering Judy Atkinson launched her *Beyond Violence* package.

A number of resolutions arose from the ACC 'Holistic Domestic Violence Initiatives and Awareness Workshop'. Participants stressed that Aboriginal and Islander people should be allowed to develop programs which include the needs of the whole family — men, women, and children. Aboriginal communities should be allowed to deal with their own offenders and the extended family unit should be involved in decision-making processes when dealing with juvenile offenders. Family support worker training and community-needs awareness skills should be developed. There was strong support for training in mediation, peace-making, and crisis intervention techniques. ACC communities needed the power to make their own by-laws regarding matters such as alcohol use and the control of violent videos. More government funding was needed for the development of educational resources, workshops, and recreational programs for communities.

A year later an even more important gathering was organised. In the first four days of July 1991 over 500 women attended a *Remote Area Aboriginal Women's Conference* held in Laura, Cape York Peninsula. The perception of the need for a major 'women's sitdown' had first arisen from an *Aboriginal Women's Futures Conference* held the year before in Townsville. The Laura gathering which was set up in a remote camp setting, away from the luxuries and limitations of hotel venues, allowed Aboriginal and Islander women to deal with business which was of major concern to them, the well-being of their families and communities.

The 'sitdown' provided an opportunity for the women to talk, in an informal way, on matters of alcohol, petrol sniffing, and related health problems; on violence and the lack of support for victims; on the pressures and mental stress experienced by young people; on police reluctance to assist Aboriginal women and children; on the need for more Aboriginal Support Centres and Shelters where women can escape the violence; and on the need for abused women to develop their self-esteem in order to make changes in their lives.

At one workshop it was proposed that: 'Parents need to understand their behaviour acts as a role model'. House-bound mothers needed special attention and support. There was a need to challenge a number of misconceptions and myths in the community and to stop blaming the victims. 'Solutions cannot begin until we start talking about the problem', it was concluded at another workshop. 'We need to empower communities and families to attend to their own responsibilities'. Alcohol-free recreation, concerts, and festivals, such as the recent *Caring for Country, Caring for Countrymen* cultural festival provided a good example of a community response. It was felt that more of these could be planned.

Workshop participants pointed out high unemployment and low self-esteem among Aboriginal men. There was an urgent need for men's programs. There should be greater involvement of police in the control of perpetrators of violence, and more Aboriginal police aide training on the subject of family violence. A need was also seen for more Aboriginal policewomen, and female police aides, in every community. Mental problems and violence were widespread, but the women did not see prison as the solution. Issues concerning womens' health, Aboriginal legal services, land rights, mining, the environment, education, government funding, ATSIC and other government services were also discussed.

Educational programs and new skills training were seen by the participants to be of central importance to future solutions:

> We must use education for developing awareness, healing skills, developing our own Murri recovery groups, setting up Alcohol prevention programs, after-care and follow up. When we succeed we should celebrate. We need to look at traditional medicine and spiritual healing strategies (Working Group for Follow-up of the *Remote Areas Aboriginal Women's Conference*, Laura, Cape York Peninsula, July 1991).

VISIONS FOR THE FUTURE

In the two decades of experience in the use of preventative approaches by Native people in Canada the concepts of 'healing' and 'community re-empowerment' have become intrinsic to the process of achieving self-determination. These concepts are also pertinent to the present situation of Aboriginal and Torres Strait Islander people. In my search for fresh approaches I was strongly influenced by the indigenisation of problem solving and action-planning occurring in Canada — particular regarding the severe social maladies of alcohol and drug addiction and community violence. I made two trips to Canada, first in 1989 and again in 1990 to look specifically at Native crime preventative and action-oriented approaches.

In 1989 I was graciously received by the visionary Metis chairman, Chester Cunningham, and his outstanding staff, of the Native Counselling Services of Alberta (NCSA). This private Native-run organisation, which was founded some eighteen years earlier, had made ground-breaking progress in the areas of Native court services, youth treatment, and prisoner rehabilitation. Two areas of their work particularly interested me. Their Family Life Improvement Program (FLIP), was run by skilled Native workers. These workers used a refreshing combination of small hands-on workshops, whiteboard instruction, peer group support, and light-hearted games to tackle chronic problems of addiction, domestic violence, parenting, child neglect, and family breakdown. Participants were also taught skills in personal development, and in dealing with welfare and other government agencies. The FLIP program, being very popular, was run on an ongoing basis from the NCSA offices and was also taken into prisons as a part of this organisation's prisoner support activities.

The second area which captured my attention was the work of the NCSA research section, who were at the time creating a new community-based crime prevention program. We exchanged literature, ideas, and videos and it was this work which eventually became the basis of my *Crime Prevention for Aboriginal Communities* manual published by the Australian Institute of Criminology, Canberra, towards the end of 1990.

The central themes and techniques of this preventative approach were of particular interest to Judy Atkinson, during her consultancy on the National Domestic Violence Education Program, and later to Coralie Ober who worked for the Queensland Corrective Services Commission. Drawing on the *Crime Prevention for Aboriginal Communities* manual, both Atkinson and Ober recast the presentation of these ideas for Aboriginal communities in the production of two workbooks of their own.[2]

Techniques for shaping a vision for the future, forming action groups and support groups, identifying problems, and seeking holistic solutions were seen to be the most useful:

- The community, itself, can be the most powerful source for personal growth.
- We need a real vision of our future. We need to know where we are going, and what our hopes are for our children and for our children's children.
- Our survival depends on the repair and strengthening of our identity and cultural foundations.
- We want to live with dignity and confidence in the world we live in today.
- To deal with these new pressures and change, we need to gain new skills and to select new tools which will carry us forward as a united people (Hazlehurst 1990).[3]

'Finding Our Dream' — a vision for the future — became Atkinson's primary preoccupation. During her six month trip around Australia she talked with Aboriginal and Islander people about the theme of a violence-free society. She asked them: 'What would our community be like without crimes of violence?'. From this trip it became apparent that there was an acute awareness of the issues and problems. Atkinson collected a smorgasbord of Aboriginal ideas for change, and a good reference indicator of helping-organisations for Aboriginal people, which she published in her *Beyond Violence: Finding the Dream* manual and video:

> When we take responsibility for acts of violence such as domestic violence and sexual abuse we acknowledge that others are hurt physically, emotionally, mentally, and spiritually. We can see the long term damage we are doing to ourselves, our families and our communities (Atkinson 1990:6).

The responses Atkinson drew from her interviewees on the subject of violence were powerful and clear sighted:

> If we don't speak out nobody will know what is happening. Women are so battered I don't know how their bodies get up in the morning and tend to children ... or not attend to them (Darwin, Northern Territory).

> Our children are the ones who are hurt the most. And they are the least empowered (Perth, Western Australia).

> A lot of young fellows don't understand their traditional customs and abuse them ... I don't agree with customary law when it's not being practised properly (Palm Island, Queensland).

> The problem must stop being trivialised by the legal system and by others as somehow based on customary law (Alice Springs, Northern Territory).

> People get hurt physically — you can see the bruises and black eyes. A person gets hurt emotionally — you can see the tears and the distressed face — but then you've been hurt spiritually like that — it's real deep hurt and nobody, unless you're a victim yourself, could even understand because you've been hurt by somebody that you hold in trust (Hobart, Tasmania) (Atkinson 1990: 6–7).

'The community can stand together to STOP THE VIOLENCE — STOP THE ABUSE', Atkinson's manual asserts. And her interviewees confirmed this feeling:

> We're killing ourselves. If we don't do something NOW there won't be a future for us. It's not a women's problem. It isn't a man's problem either. It's a community problem and the whole community has to be involved, to be told what's happening. We all have to change our attitudes, take responsibility for finding solutions (Melbourne, Victoria).

> Sometimes, when we look at the problems, they seem like a large mountain. But we can move that mountain, one rock at a time. All of us working together (Weipa South, Queensland).

> We have the answers here in our community. Sometimes we don't recognise how strong we are, what we can do (Weipa South, Queensland).

> We are building something new. Something that belongs to us. We are working together. And it's good. We can see the results (Broome, Western Australia).

> Our vision of who we are is lost. We have to find it again (Atkinson 1990: 5–24).

THE 'HEALING OUR PEOPLE' CONFERENCE

Between August and early September 1990 I visited the Alkali Lake Indian community in British Columbia to discuss with them our common concerns, how they began their community detoxification project, and what similar strategies might be adopted in Australia. In Edmonton I visited the impressive 'Poundmaker's Lodge' Canadian Native detoxification program, and its associated training centre for alcohol workers, the Nechi Institute on Alcohol and Drug Education (Crossingham 1987).

I was also able to attend an exciting *Healing Our Youth* conference, held in Edmonton between 18–21 September 1990. Largely organised by the Poundmaker's and Nechi Centre, this conference drew together some of the brightest teachers of innovative programming for the treatment of at-risk families and youth throughout Canada and the United States. Observing the workings of these programs, and rubbing shoulders with their many dedicated workers, was both humbling and inspiring. 'Humbling', because I realised how timid and unimaginative our approaches still were in Australia. In all areas of justice reform, community policing, correctional policy and community programming we continued to congratulate ourselves for achieving so very little, in relation to what we *might* be achieving. 'Inspiring', because it opened to me a new world of potential and possibilities.

No less inspiring was the powerful presence of positive thinking, *even joyful thinking*, among these workers. The companionship in seeking new directions produced a wonderful experience of discovery and self-discovery. There was a fraternity of sharing and mutual support, a sense of *brotherhood and sisterhood* born of sorrow, and nurtured through hope. This sharing of ideas and activities for social reconstruction induced an elation and confidence in these 'survivors' and 'workers' — many of whom were the same people who had turned their lives to helping others like themselves. In dealing with some of the most terrible social problems known to humankind, *these* people actually seemed to be having fun! My observations on this second Canadian trip fortified me, and gave me courage to urge more assertive approaches in the tackling of alcoholism and community violence in Australia. Between 2–5 April 1991, the Australian Institute of Criminology, in collaboration with an Aboriginal working committee and community leaders, organised a four-day *Healing Our People: Aboriginal Community Justice and Crime Prevention Forum*, in Alice Springs. As an employee of the Institute at that time I asked if the conference could radically depart from the Institute's more formalised academic conventions. To its credit, the Institute was receptive to this. It allowed me to plan a forum structured largely upon hands-on experiential workshops, emphasising themes of inter-personal and spiritual healing and community re-empowerment. I hoped to involve workshop leaders who would examine customary ways, along with new skills, for the handling of contemporary social problems.

The Alice Springs conference focused upon community-based solutions to addiction, family violence, crime and juvenile problems in Aboriginal communities. Forty innovative Aboriginal and Islander community leaders, elders, and health and alcohol workers were asked to speak or run workshops. In addition, three Canadian Indians noted in this field were brought over especially for the conference: Eric Shirt who, as a founding member of Poundmaker's Lodge, Edmonton, had advised on the establishment of similar programs throughout Alberta; and Chief Andy Chelsea and his wife Phyllis Chelsea who in 1970 were the first members of their reserve community to sober up, and to begin the highly successful community detoxification program at Alkali Lake, British Columbia. Both programs have continued to inspire, and to actively help, many other Native peoples in Canada and the United States toward community detoxification.

At the beginning of 1991 the idea that Aboriginal people might become 'responsible', or indeed sufficiently empowered to take 'control over their own problems' was radical for Australia. After three decades of Aboriginal protest politics

— a philosophy which denounced colonial and paternalistic governments as being 'responsible for all Aboriginal ills' — it was perhaps even a little dangerous. In a climate where condemnation was the more popular activity, shifting responsibility was not the politically fashionable thing to do at this time.

Initially the concept of 'community healing' met with a mixed reception during my personal exchanges with Aboriginal friends and colleagues. I explained that this was a different kind of 'responsibility'. It was the first step in getting 'out from under' the welfare relationship. As long as people were sick with alcoholism and oppressed by community violence this would never be possible. Taking responsibility for community problems was a means of taking back control of community life. We talked it over in this fashion. I left my friends to think about it for a while and several days later they came back to me, confirming that they wished to have a conference where new skills for empowerment were explored.

In fact, the *Healing Our People* forum excited a great deal more interest in the Aboriginal community than the AIC organisers could ever have anticipated. Once a working committee was formed, flyers sent out, and the news released that three Canadian Indians had been invited as keynote speakers to the conference, the applications to attend began to pour in. In the last week the Institute's fax machine ran hot with conference registrations — 5, 10, 15 and even 20 bookings at a time. We soon surpassed our 180 participant limit, stretched this to 280 (about 90% of whom were Aboriginal or Torres Strait Islanders). In the last few days we had to turn away well over 100 more applicants — much to everyone's distress. Next time, we agreed, such a conference will be held at a larger venue.[4]

As the convenor I spoke very briefly at the opening session to explain what we hoped to set in motion through the *Healing Our People* forum. The indigenous message which seemed to be growing loudest in recent years within Australia and overseas was that renewal will involve liberation from dependency of all kinds — not just from colonialism, and alcoholism, but also from self-oppression. And in the community by innovative programs and by setting up networks of personal support (Hazlehurst, *Healing Our People* forum, Alice Springs, 2 April 1991).

Indian speakers who attended the '*Healing Our People*' gathering shared their experiences of individual recovery and whole-community detoxification. Workshops explored old ways and new skills for strengthening individuals and communities. Topics addressed during the conference included:

- Treating alcohol and drug addiction
- Healing family violence
- Supporting victims of violence
- Treating alcohol and drug abuse
- Action Planning for Crime Prevention

- Helping our youth
- Developing a community approach
- Conflict Resolution and community peacekeeping
- Innovative programs for offenders
- Aboriginal post-release schemes
- A holistic approach to community health

There were videos, some emotional moments, and a lot of laughter and warmth. Many participants said they felt renewed, inspired, and gained a fresh confidence in their abilities.

Judy Atkinson also attended and ran one of the workshops at the *Healing Our People* conference and we discussed future areas of need for these kinds of events. She was still having problems with some of the women who did not want her to openly discuss family violence, incest, and rape. Long, gruelling, 'women's business' meetings ended in tears and despair. I kept encouraging her to go on with her work and not to give up.

In the evenings our Indian friends also assured us that this stage of denial was a part of the process. Their people had also to go through this. There had been a lot of resistance in Indian communities at first. But as people became free of addiction, other hurts came to the surface. When hard issues, such as sexual abuse and incest, were tackled through educational workshops, the process began to have a cleansing effect upon everyone concerned. Writing about this phase Maggie Hodgson said:

> Dealing with issues which arose as soon as they surfaced in the
> community was possible because the community trusted ... it became
> very apparent the community was experiencing another layer of healing,
> a deeper level of healing. People were trusting enough to say they had
> been abused and were willing to talk about it (Hodgson 1987a:8).

With a swiftness which I was now beginning to associate with a quiet revolution, Atkinson and her women organisers went on to organise the significant *Remote Area Aboriginal Women's Conference* held in Laura three months later.

Over a period of about three years the decision to run 'new skills' and 'solution-oriented' preventative conferences in Australia was strongly influenced by a cross-fertilisation of ideas between Canadian and Australian indigenous peoples. From what I have observed in the unfolding events, the most significant fact is this: that the philosophy has preceded the action. In the Canadian experience it has been the aspirations for empowerment which have led people to find the strength and the means of transforming individuals and community life. Taking responsibility for community healing begins the process of taking back control. There is power in powerful ideas. This is the key. From this, all else flows.

◆ ◆ ◆

[1] Morgan's poster read: 'Aboriginal Women are Watching you. Strong Aboriginal Women say STOP THE ABUSE. Stop raping our children' ('Stop the Abuse' Campaign sponsored by the Western Australian Aboriginal and Islander Women's Congress and the Department of Aboriginal Affairs).

[2] The manuals referred to here were *Beyond Violence: Finding the Dream* compiled by Judy Atkinson 1990; and *A Community Work Book*, compiled by Coralie Ober in 1991.

[3] As it was intended to be used as a community work book the *Crime Prevention for Aboriginal Communities* manual (Hazlehurst 1990) was written in the first person.

[4] Between 22–25 June 1992 the Australian Institute of Criminology organised an *Aboriginal Justice Issues* conference in Cairns. With the assistance of three hotels, this attracted a gathering of over 500, mostly Aboriginal, participants — an indication of the growing interest in this area.

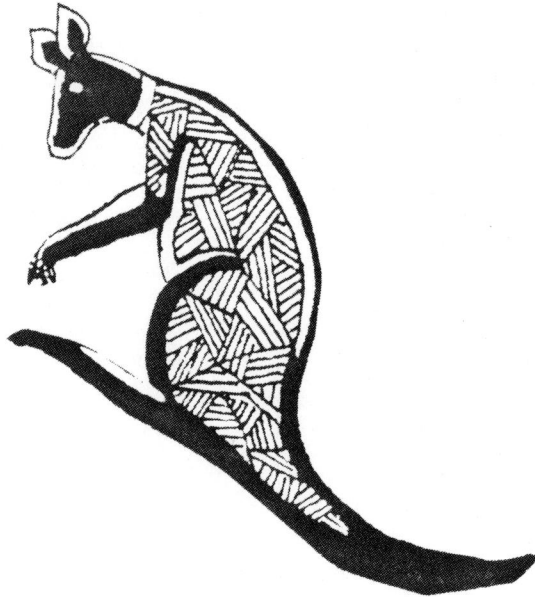

PART 2

Chapter four

INTERVENTION AND HEALING

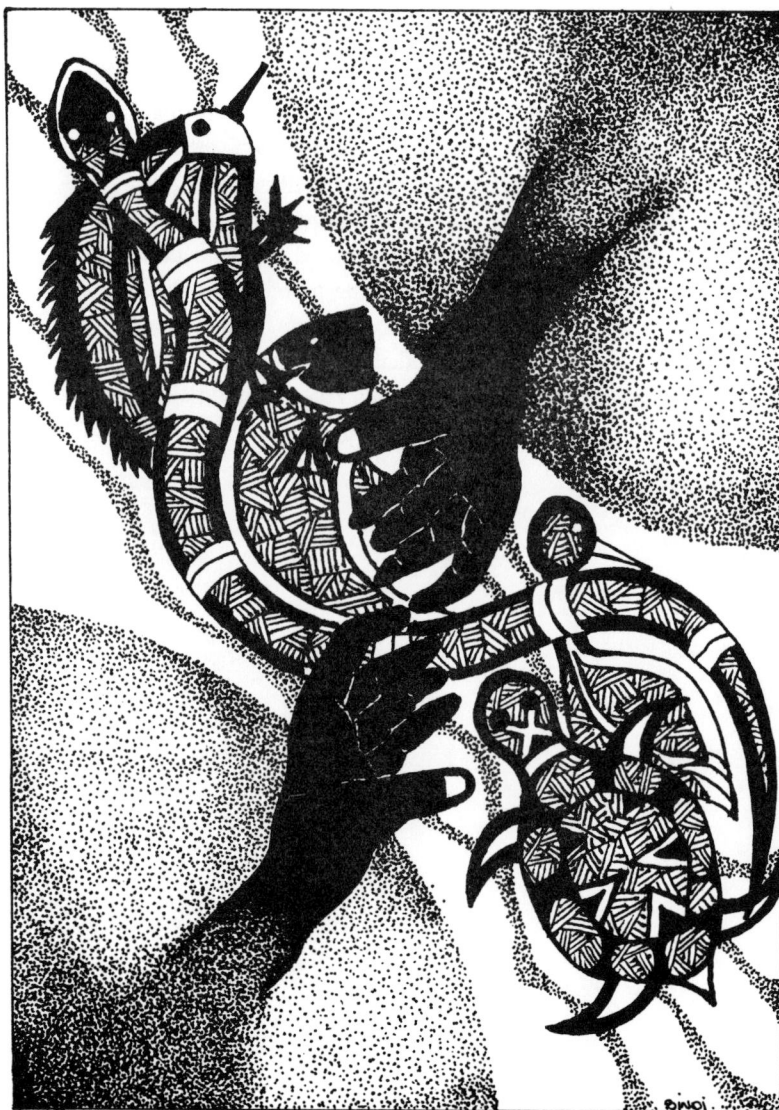

Booze has snapped more wedding rings, sold more homes, bankrupted more people, blighted more children, defiled more innocents, twisted more limbs, smashed more vehicles, wrecked more manhoods, dishonoured more womanhood, filled more jails, broken more hearts, caused more suicides, armed more fools, drained more blood, blinded more brains, blasted more lives, dug more graves, made more insanity, and created more living hell for more good people than any other single scourge that ever took root within the human race ('Poundmaker's Lodge, Alcohol and Drug Abuse Treatment Centre', leaflet ca. 1988).

INTERVENTION AND HEALING

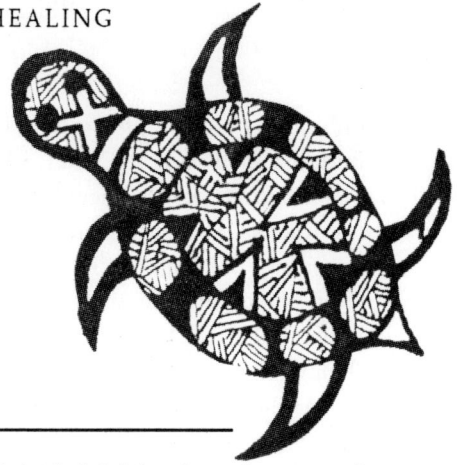

WHAT IS ALCOHOLISM?

The historical and intercultural contexts of Aboriginal drinking have been much studied but little understood. The National Aboriginal Health Strategy Working Party presented an Aboriginal perspective of causation in the following statement:

> ... there is consensus in the Aboriginal community that understands the 'alcohol problem' from a community perspective, as a symptom (ultimately a symptom of dispossession) of alienation, and discrimination which leads to loss of self esteem (1989: 194).

Since the nineteenth century, alcoholism, and its physical and social consequences, have been the centre of various theoretical and moral debates. Medical scientists have recorded patterns of biochemical and epidemiological evidence. They have also raised questions of genetic transmission and susceptibility. Social scientists have contributed historical, sociocultural, and cross-cultural explanations. Psychologists have examined the psychosocial factors contributing to alcohol use. Anthropologists have developed an ethnographic analysis of the function of drinking relations in contemporary cultures. Each have contributed, to a degree, to our pool of knowledge on why people drink (Hunter, Hall and Spargo 1991b: 5-13).

There are fundamental differences in opinion among medical and social science researchers on the use of alcohol in indigenous cultures. Medical researchers tend to examine the kinds of problems — particularly those related to physical and mental ill-health, the distribution of consumption, and the prevalence of alcohol-related disease — which are common to all cultures. These problems, they feel, should be directly and immediately addressed.

Social scientists have drawn attention to the negative impact of a range of social, economic, and environmental pressures upon Aboriginal culture over the past 200 years (Kamien 1975; Beckett 1964, Haebich 1988, Tatz 1980). Psychologists have identified psychosocial factors of stress in drinking behaviour (Mail 1989; Albrecht 1974).

Anthropologists have focused on belief and behaviour which they attribute to 'normative' or 'deviant' patterns of drinking. This research has attempted to understand alcohol abuse on its own terms, as a cultural experience and practice (Berndt and Berndt 1985: 521, 94; Hazlehurst 1986: 211-213; Heath 1987: 41; Sackett 1988: 73; Brady and Palmer 1984: 72; Brady 1985, 1989; Marshall 1983).

Room (1984) questioned whether anthropological research, in its objective of presenting the 'native view', was condoning substance abuse, or at the very least down-playing its negative effects. It was criticised for having an ethnographic, if not vested, interest in keeping things as they were (Brady 1991: 57, Duquemin, d'Abbs and Chalmers 1991: 13).

Anthropologists have also raised the question of 'who owns the alcohol research' concerning indigenous people, and are considerably preoccupied with raising funds to expand Aboriginal alcohol-related research, and to make it more relevant to policy and programs.[1]

Despite widely different approaches in addiction research, there is a general consensus about the personal damage and social pathology of alcoholism. Whatever the role of substance abuse today in Aboriginal social exchange or in helping people to cope, it exposes people — individually and communally — to great risk.

THE CONSEQUENCES OF ADDICTION

Understanding the physical, mental, and social consequences of addiction is the first step to recovery. The prevalence of health problems associated with the excessive consumption of alcohol (including kava) and drug abuse (especially psychoactive drugs, and petrol inhalation), are undeniable. The health effects can range from minor discomforts to critical illnesses and death.

Trauma resulting from violence induced by alcohol or drug abuse is immediately apparent. Broken limbs, smashed faces, bruised bodies are common place. Extreme cases of assault, rape, and murder are far too frequent. Less obvious hazards, with lethal consequences, are the effects of damage to livers (in the case of alcohol) and lungs (drug abuse, or petrol sniffing). Severe brain damage and loss of mental and motor powers can be attributed to all three forms of substance abuse. Illnesses commonly induced by alcohol and addictive substances include:

- liver cirrhosis
- high blood pressure
- heart disease
- obesity, gastritis
- pancreatitis
- viral hepatitis
- a large number of cancers
- chemical or drug dependence

- risk to central nervous system
- lowered immune system
- newborn drug toxicity
- fetal alcohol syndrome
- low birth weight and birth defects
- tremors, sweats, reduced sleep
- strokes and seizures
- loss of memory, blackouts
- brain damage, death.

Another effect is the injury or death which results from accidents, mishaps or violence:

- injuries from falls, burns, or fights
- drownings, aspiration, or poisonings
- injuries from machinery, tools, or weapons
- motor vehicle accidents
- destructive behaviour
- physical and verbal assaults
- abuse of partners and children
- arson, rape, murder, suicide.

Alcohol use has also been identified as a major contributor to domestic assault, child neglect, poor family nutrition, poor school performance, and a general failure to thrive in infants and children. (For detailed breakdowns on alcohol and drug-related causes of ill health and death see Thomson and English 1990: 70-75; Holman et al 1988; Watson 1988; Hunter, Hall and Spargo 1991b; Reid and Trompf 1991.)

PSYCHOLOGICAL PROBLEMS

In a Kimberley study (Hunter, Hall, and Spargo 1991b) revealed widespread concern among Aboriginal drinkers and non-drinkers alike (both male and female) about the personal and social problems which arise from drinking. Psychological reactions included feelings of anxiety, depression, panic, and paranoia — sufficiently intense to seek help from family and friends. Seven percent of the sample experienced frightening visual hallucinations, 10% heard voices, 10% reported an impulse to harm themselves (e.g. by self-mutilation), and 11% experienced an urge to commit suicide.

Psychological reactions varied by age and gender. The four symptoms of panic, paranoia, and auditory and visual hallucinations occurred with the highest frequency among Aboriginal men between the ages of 31 to 40 years, with a similar but less pronounced pattern occurring among Aboriginal women (Hunter, Hall and Spargo 1991b: 52-53).

Psychological reactions include:

- anxiety
- stress
- paranoia
- panic
- auditory hallucinations
- visual hallucinations
- inability to cope
- loss of control
- depression
- suicidal feelings
- disorientation
- insanity.

SOCIAL AND CULTURAL CONSEQUENCES

In a paper delivered at the *Healing Our People* forum at Alice Springs in April 1991, Torres Strait Islander leader, Steve Mam, expressed concern about the loss of the 'personal and collective propriety' which had traditionally provided the checks and balances in human relations in Torres Strait Islander communities. The disciplinary role played by elders in the cultural setting serves to teach 'respect of others', and to remind people of their 'obligations to the community'. Shaming played a large part in this process.

With the decline of the cultural system, and the increasing dominance of the 'British system of law', the influence of personal, family and collective morality declined. When the ethical codes and leadership of traditional law are removed, said Mam, the 'stresses of cross cultural living', particularly those experienced by a 'cultural person living in the British values system', become themselves a source of aggression and misunderstanding. Alcohol and drugs are used to escape from these stresses. But the outcome is disastrous. The effects of drugs and alcohol make 'that person think more and more about himself or herself, and less and less about his or her family and society and the obligations that go with it'.

The most obvious downstream effect of alcohol and/or drugs is the gradual breakdown of culture. With that breakdown comes the loss of respect with the loss of personal and collective propriety. The end result can only be violence ... because the known boundaries which keep culture alive are being removed (Mam 1991: 8–9).

Domestic violence, child abuse, assault and injury, the destruction of property, delinquency and incarceration are problems which Aboriginal people must face on a recurring and sometimes daily basis. These problems are emotionally and physically stressful to individuals. They stress family and inter-family relations. They stress council resources which might otherwise be put to better use in the arenas of economic and community development. They undermine, and in some areas totally halt, the transmission of traditional life. They make the ordinary business of community management and the achievement of community goals extremely difficult for leaders. In some cases they corrupt local leadership.

Not infrequently they result in the resignation of service personnel. Being required to swing from crisis to crisis, police, hospital staff, service agency workers, teachers and community workers are kept in a constant state of apprehension or fatigue. A treadmill of 'reaction and rescue' is set in place which exhausts the creative imaginations, energies, and skills of even the most willing human beings over time.

Involvement with the criminal justice system seems another inevitable consequence of alcoholism. In the Kimberley study, 55% of an Aboriginal interviewee sample had been in a police lock-up on one or more occasion. 'Of these, 92% had been in a police lock-up during the past year ...'. For both men and women the highest rates occurred between the ages of 25 and 40 years, with a steady decline after this. But incarceration rates were considerably higher among Aboriginal male drinkers than among female drinkers. Abstainers were the least likely of all to be incarcerated (Hunter, Hall and Spargo 1991b: 54–8; Brady 1990a).

There was a strong correlation between imprisonment and drinking patterns. Imprisonment rates were extremely high among young men who drank:

> The frequency with which a person was incarcerated in a police lock-up, was strongly related to the frequency with which that person drank, and the quantity that they consumed when they drank (Hunter, Hall and Spargo 1991b: 62).

THE INDIGENOUS EXPERIENCE

But what is the Aboriginal and Torres Strait Islander experience, and what are leaders saying about alcoholism today? In most cases their commentaries on the effects of alcoholism on their people are graphic and blunt; their appeals for the autonomy to overcome these problems, urgent and uncompromising.

In his opening address at the *Healing Our People* forum Geoff Shaw, General Manager of the Tangentyere Council, Alice Springs, said that Aboriginal people would welcome the opportunity to develop a positive approach:

> These issues are complex and pervasive, their effects are destructive and brutalising, and their underlying causes often seem unsolvable. In this environment it is not surprising that people dealing with these issues on a day-to-day basis, often become demoralised and develop negative attitudes. This is further exacerbated by the constant need to raise the level of awareness in the wider community.

> All too often we have to present graphic illustrations of the problems, to make people aware of the issues, and to tackle apathy, ignorance and racism ...

> And so it is particularly pleasing to participate in a conference which will help our people learn from one another's achievements, and to help build our confidence and morale through demonstrating how we, as a community, can tackle our problems ...

> First, I will present what I believe are some fundamental principles for achieving community-based solutions to the problems of substance abuse, crime and violence. In particular the need for self-determination and self-governance ...

> Redressing the situation hinges on the establishment of a formal recognition of the inalienable right to maintain our social and cultural values ...

> Self-governance at a local level provides the means for relating and responding to the needs of the immediate community, and offers the chance of regaining self-esteem and hope.

> It allows the communities to draw on their social and cultural values to address local problems; to tackle problems in culturally relevant ways where past attempts by western institutions, or using western methods, have failed (Shaw 1991).

In giving recommendations for the prevention of alcohol-related violence, Torres Strait Islander leader Steve Mam pointed out that:

... it will be difficult to effectively treat violence in the environment that has a visible lack of morals, ethics, and a sense of responsibility ... Something needs to be done about restoring people's values and learning self respect with consideration for others (1991: 18–19).

Where the 'institutionalised' efforts of police and corrections had failed to teach respect, Mam concluded, the form of treatment similar to that used by Alcoholics Anonymous was more likely to succeed.

Formally organised sports programs, board games, card playing, bingo, and other recreational community activities, offered a safe avenue for the expression and management of stress. Verbal communication was also critical, as there is a tendency for a cultural person to keep his pride in his pocket. 'It takes a lot of courage to say "I have a problem and I need help"'. Most people needed someone they can turn to and trust — if not an elder, then someone else. Support groups like Alcoholics Anonymous are 'a very good method of combating and treating violence for Torres Strait Islanders' (Mam 1991: 17–20).

Geoff Shaw was particularly supportive of the Canadian Indian models which have been adapted to community and cultural needs:

The message of Phyllis and Andy Chelsea, and Eric Shirt, bring to this conference a striking example of the success of this approach. Through local-governance, the process which has allowed them to take control over their own lives, the Cree Indians of Alberta, Canada, have made outstanding progress in managing alcohol abuse and related social problems (Shaw 1991).

Shaw went on to outline projects which the Tangentyere and Central Australian Aboriginal Congress had been developing to combat alcohol abuse and related problems in Central Australia. There was a long-term strategic plan to formulate educational, training, counselling, codependency and rehabilitation programs for research, monitoring and treatment of addiction. Community-based action groups can adapt and indigenise treatment programs to suit local needs and cultural realities. In the Northern Territory the Aboriginal Alcoholics Awareness group (AAA) is an active community-based initiative which has grown out of this objective.

Aboriginal staffed night patrols also focus on trouble spots in town camps and urban areas. They counsel Aboriginal people in the prevention of problems, mediate disputes and sort out problems with children, transport people to hospitals and the women's shelters, and liaise with the police.

The Tangentyere Council had also successfully implemented the Community Development Employment Program (CDEP)[2] in seven town camps and hoped to expand this to all eighteen camps which would involve a work force of some 350 people. The Council saw this as a constructive means of bringing back self-esteem and purpose to people's lives as well as helping the community. There were also issues of law and legislation, Shaw pointed out:

> Aboriginal people have long recognised that while alcohol is not the only source of problems of violence, it is nevertheless a major contributing factor. Because of alcohol's devastating effects, we have campaigned vigorously for fundamental changes in the laws and policies which control the distribution of alcohol.

The Tangentyere Council, he said, is urging the Northern Territory government to recognise the need for 'Special Measures' by:

- the restriction of the numbers and trading hours of liquor outlets;
- directing that a proportion of revenue collected from alcohol sales go to alcohol education, treatment and/or rehabilitation;
- requiring that the issuing and monitoring of liquor licences take account of public health issues and the effects on Aboriginal communities;
- taking a more rigorous approach to prosecutions for the sale of alcohol to intoxicated persons or minors;
- making licensees legally liable for injuries and damage caused by intoxicated patrons.
- banning advertising of alcohol.

These objectives, he pointed out towards the end of his speech, were in keeping with National Human Rights and International Civil Rights Conventions which recognised the right of indigenous peoples to respond in a spirit of self-determination toward their own cultural and social needs (Shaw 1991; also Lyon 1990).

SOBERING-UP CENTRES ARE NOT ENOUGH

For some time Aboriginal leaders have been asking the government and the police not to arrest intoxicated Aborigines, but to allow them to be dealt with by sobering-up centres. Some centres, in those few places where they have been established, have their own pick-up services to keep drunks away from trouble and to give them safe accommodation overnight. Where they do not exist police feel they have little alternative but to put drunks in police cells overnight 'for their own protection and for the protection of others' — even where drunkenness has been decriminalised.

But overnight accommodation in police cells or sobering up centres is simply not enough. A dry bed might prevent a death that night, but it will not prevent the dying. Only holistic treatment of the disease of alcoholism will bring about cure. For want of genuine treatment and rehabilitation, the endless cycle of picking up drunks, who 'go back on the grog' once they are returned to the community, becomes an exhausting and fruitless task.

There is the further problem of educating public opinion. The need for this was perhaps best illustrated in a newspaper article, written by Matthew Warren for the *Australian* (14 February 1989), where a decision by the South Australian Health Commission to build a $185, 000, 12-bed sobering-up centre in the hospital grounds at Port Augusta created a 'hysterical' public response. Because local residents feared the possibility of disturbances by 'intoxicated Aborigines' the local government council demanded that the centre be built outside of town or in the prison grounds. If there is to be any genuine public support, governments and the wider community will need to be made aware that *prevention and cure* are the primary goals of treatment.

COMMUNITY ACTION AND INTERVENTION

> Sobriety gives a feeling of conquering something inside, and that has to
> be experienced rather than explained (Milera 1980: 36).

Increasing numbers of communities have been seeking to set up women's refuges, children's shelters, and women's resource centres. In addition to providing immediate protection and shelter to those suffering from abuse, refuges seek to offer outreach support for women to re-establish themselves after marriage breakdown. Women's resource centres provide a location for fellowship, information distribution, and training. They can become a hub of communication and activities — women's meetings, arts and crafts, health, birthing and child care, sewing, domestic skills, and care for the old and sick in the community. They become a place of mutual support and personal fulfilment.

Sobriety societies may also act as resource centres for men, women, and youth — conducting regular counselling and workshops on alcohol-related problems. The Mura Kosker Sorority, for instance, runs programs for Thursday Island women on domestic violence and child abuse. In New South Wales the first live-in Aboriginal alcohol rehabilitation program, Benelong's Haven, opened in 1974. In its first seven years of operation Benelong treated 1,200 men and women, and claimed a 25% sobriety success rate. Residents 'step into a cohesive community that will be demanding, giving and forgiving'. The success of the New South Wales rehabilitative programs such as Benelong's Haven, Namatjira House, Oolong House, and similar programs run in other states, has been attributed to the blending of Alcoholics Anonymous principles of caring and sharing, with Aboriginal spirituality and values of extended family (Miller 1982; Milera 1980; Hazlehurst 1986).

Since it was set up in the inner city of Adelaide in 1973, the South Australian Aboriginal Sobriety Group for Drug and Alcohol Rehabilitation has provided a range of services including alcohol counselling, emergency accommodation, referrals to other agencies, youth recreation, transport and a Mobile Assistance Patrol. The group also runs a Dry Hostel and a Wet Hostel — but feels this is simply not enough. After almost a decade of experience in alcohol and drug rehabilitation the director of the SA Aboriginal Sobriety Group, Basil Sumner, concluded that there is no such thing as drinking in moderation for Aboriginal people and rejects the 'Drink wise, drink safe' approach as dangerous and misleading. 'It's all or nothing', he stressed. 'We have *got* to get off the alcohol.'

The Adelaide centre struggles under very limiting and difficult conditions. It is inadequately funded and seriously understaffed. 'Aboriginal workers are expected to be on hand seven days a week, 52 weeks a year. There is no time for holidays', reported Sumner to *'The Window of Opportunity'*, intersectoral drug conference (Adelaide, 4 December 1991). In his view the most important factor for future detoxification of Aboriginal people would be the introduction of more far-reaching programming:

> We need our own rehabilitation centre. We have got to get together for some strategic, long term planning. We need a good prevention program (Basil Sumner, interview 4 December 1991).

The view that sobriety is the 'only cure' was expressed by Milera, another Aboriginal ex-alcoholic, over a decade earlier. On the importance of rehabilitation Milera was unequivocal:

> I have seen rehabilitation centres in Adelaide, Sydney, Kempsey, Broken Hill, Moree and Alice Springs. I have read of rehabilitation centres all over Australia dealing with the problem of alcoholism among our people. *I do not think that there is, or ever will be, an unsuccessful rehabilitation centre* (Milera 1980: 36).

Upholding and strengthening the family, and undertaking activities which lead to the rebuilding of Aboriginal society and Aboriginal culture, are critical in turning the tide of ill health and addiction. Aboriginal communities have a legitimate claim on state resources for the development of rehabilitative and healthy life-style activities.

CRISIS INTERVENTION

In any community, undercurrents of tension are likely to stress and fracture relations between individuals and families. Inter-family fighting may be a regular occurrence. In addition to street offences, answering calls to assist in domestic situations is the most frequent task of police. Police need better ways of determining which are 'private matters' (that is, matters which can be handled by the families themselves), and which require police action.

In the event of a disturbance the primary objective of officers is that no harm should come to any party. They will be making decisions as to whether injury to persons or property will result; whether weapons are available or may be used; or whether other residents are affected by the noise or disruption. Action will need to be taken if a serious offence has already been committed, and to ensure that injured individuals receive proper medical treatment and are protected from further harm. In many incidents peace can be restored simply by sitting down and talking with the persons concerned, perhaps with the assistance of an Aboriginal officer or a reliable family member or friend.

Police need to know the location of available shelters, safehouses, and social welfare services — particularly when negotiations between disputants break down, and individuals are clearly in need of assistance or protection. Specialists can also be brought in to assist the police — an Aboriginal elder or JP, a mediator, a district nurse or child welfare agent, a women's shelter worker, a doctor or psychologist. If there is a community action group, a support group which can give assistance to victims, or individuals who have the authority or skills to play a crisis intervention role, the community should make sure the police know this, as it provides officers with viable options to arrest.

Strategies and skills which are an asset in crisis intervention include:

- separating and calming disputants;
- listening;
- avoiding controversy or taking sides;
- negotiation and mediation;
- managing conflict and peace-keeping;
- helping adults and youth in crisis;
- personal counselling;
- social agency referral;
- victim support, and
- offender support.

It is preferable that some form of intervention is used *before* a situation becomes dangerous and requires law enforcement. A local action group can help in this regard if some of its members have crisis intervention skills and if the group has thought through possible crisis strategies. Police have quite a wide discretion in the way they handle cases. When setting up intervention training local police and police aides should be invited to train alongside the Aboriginal workers. This way they will become committed to the same preventative agenda.

These skills assist people in dealing with family violence, mental illness, emotional or alcoholic rage, sudden death, distressed victims and bereaved families. Such training and experience also throw light on the psychological and social factors involved and will help an action team make more informed decisions.

DISPUTE RESOLUTION AND MEDIATION

Many Aboriginal people are alienated from the criminal justice system and feel they have good reason to distrust the courts because of their past experiences with them. They have a very real fear of state police authorities in the settlement of family or community conflicts. Cumbersome and highly technical judicial processes, coupled with cultural and linguistic difficulties, present formidable barriers to the uninitiated. For the courts, the provision of interpreters continues to be a problem. The use of words, voice tone, body language and the ventilation of emotions differ between Aboriginal and non-Aboriginal cultures and have in the past led to fateful cases of misinterpretation and miscarriage of justice.

Conflicts have a great deal to do with socioeconomic conditions and the social values of the persons involved. There can be serious conflicts *within* a cultural group. There can be disharmony between men and women, younger and older generations, and factional tensions between families and clans which may have lasted for many years. Some feuds are handed down over several generations. Where there is ongoing scarcity of welfare resources, where one sector of the community carries social responsibilities different from those carried by others, or where differences of exposure to outside influences through education and the media exist, all these provide fertile ground for intra-community conflict.

Minor disputes can escalate into assault, injury, or even death. Unresolved conflicts between individuals, neighbours, and family groups have enormous human costs, let alone the costs in time and resources of police and courts. Early intervention and settlement of disputes is by far the best solution. Understanding other people's situations and perceptions is central to successful dispute resolution.

Mediation services specialise in the provision of socially and culturally relevant intervention by training mediators from a range of social and ethnic backgrounds.

Approximately half of the mediators working for the NSW Community Justice Centres, for instance, have non-English speaking credentials. Wherever possible centres try to 'match' the mediators to the disputants on the basis of gender, age, and ethnicity (NSW Community Justice Centres 1988; Hazlehurst 1989b).

Professional mediators act to defuse disputes through a process of discussion, reasoned exchange, and negotiation. People are helped to talk through their problems and to come to a satisfactory settlement. Mediators seek to conduct mediation sessions in such a manner that disputants are able to explore all their options and arrive at a mutually acceptable solution and settlement of the dispute.

In a paper published in 1988 I suggested that a broad range of social problems and minor offences might be more effectively handled by mediation processes within Aboriginal communities: for instance in cases of juvenile vandalism, public disturbances and domestic disputes; issues concerning customary law and kinship rights and obligations; discrimination and racial tension; conflicts with police, landlords, and local government authorities; conflicts over property and resource rights, or in negotiations with state and federal government agencies or mining and pastoral interests (Hazlehurst 1988).

Alternative Dispute Resolution programs could also be introduced into Aboriginal communities as part of existing Aboriginal Community Council or community justice arrangements or, in more traditional communities, by giving more support to elder tribunal arrangements already in existence (Williams 1987: 40–95; Hazlehurst 1988b; 1991).

Community Justice Panels have been set up in Victoria as an attempt to play a peacekeeping role and to bring Aboriginal values to bear upon Aboriginal offenders. Community panels seek solutions to social problems through a mediation approach without resorting to the legal system. They may also target the specific needs of children and youth. Panels consist of Aboriginal volunteers with the support of professional agencies, police, prisons and the courts. They also help in providing advice, supervision, and post-custodial assistance.

There has been growing interest in the introduction of conflict resolution skills and mediation programs for the management of community and family disputes throughout Australia generally. Several states now have set up alternative dispute resolution services modelled on the successful NSW Community Justice Centres (CJC) program. It has been estimated that services provided to Aboriginal participants by well established agencies have been at a rate roughly representative of their population in centre localities (that is, just over 1% through CJC Centres in NSW).

Where conflict resolution initiatives have been introduced police have found the referral of difficult and intractable cases to mediation services an increasingly useful option. The success rate for the settlement of family and neighbourhood disputes is notably high (over 80% is claimed by most agencies). These services greatly increase community control over the settlement of local problems and disputes, and have had the effect of significantly lowering offending and imprisonment rates.

A Community Justice Program (CJP) was established in Brisbane, under the jurisdiction of the Queensland Attorney-General's Department in July 1990. By the end of that year trained community mediators were providing services to the south-east Queensland area, including metropolitan Brisbane, Logan, and the Darling Downs region, and were extending them to Toowoomba, Townsville, Mt Isa, and the Gold Coast during 1991 and 1992. In addition to having ready access to Aboriginal/Islander and non-Aboriginal mediators, Aboriginal communities in this region have been able to approach the program for workshops, community mediations, and mediator training.

Since 1989 the Aboriginal Co-ordinating Council (ACC) wanted to set up a Northern Queensland Aboriginal Mediation Service. The first step in this direction occurred when CJP and ACC collaborated in the running of mediation training for a group of Aboriginal/Islander community representatives and professionals in June and September 1992. With the engagement of eleven new recruits (including eight Aboriginal/Islander mediators), dispute resolution services have now become available to communities in the Cairns region.

WHOLE-COMMUNITY MEDIATION

The introduction of whole-community mediation in Queensland has led to collaboration between the Brisbane Community Justice Program and Aboriginal community workers with promising results. When 'grog running' and drinking reached a crisis point at Doomadgee in February 1991 there were serious levels of conflict between two sections of the community. The issue received national coverage through the press and on a '60 Minutes' television program.

When in March that year a request for intervention was received from members of the Doomadgee community, three mediators with appropriate skills and background were selected — Joan Welsh and George Belfrage (mediators from the Brisbane office) and Coralie Ober (an Aboriginal and Islander Liaison Officer with the Corrective Services Commission).

Prior to the first visit to Doomadgee the team of three met in Cairns for a two-day discussion with the executive of the Aboriginal Co-ordinating Council to outline the role of the Community Justice Program's intended plan for Doomadgee.[3] Two of the mediators also attended the April *Healing Our People* forum in Alice Springs as part of their preparation for the forthcoming community mediation. A three day, 'pre-mediation', visit to Doomadgee was arranged in order to conduct a series of talks with the primary parties involved in the dispute, to explore their concerns, develop trust in the mediators, secure commitments from parties to participate in the mediation, and to establish a mediation agenda. Although things were difficult, it was found that 'people were keen to find ways to solve the problems' and were prepared to be involved in the process.

Amidst what was later described as 'the changing dynamics of the community', arrangements for a large public meeting were made in order to mediate between the 'major stakeholders' in the dispute. A week later the three mediators returned to Doomadgee for a further three days. Approximately 100 people attended the meeting. The issues were complex, but it was found that, 'Adherence to the [mediation] process resulted in positive outcomes':

> The setting of the agenda for the mediation was part of the process of empowering the parties and of making them equally responsible for the resolution of their dispute, and equally able to negotiate.

> The agenda setting and exploration of issues continued until lunchtime, with most parties communicating their view of the issue to the other parties. Neutral observers noted that members of the community were acknowledging other perceptions of the issues, and their own part in the dispute for the first time at a community meeting.

> Although alcohol was central to the conflict, it was by no means seen as the only issue.

> Representatives began to accept responsibility for resolving the conflict, by discussing possible actions and other ways of behaving, and negotiations on issues continued until late afternoon ('Doomadgee Dispute', internal paper of the Community Justice Program, 1991a: 2–3).

While formal agreements cannot be published,[4] the program acknowledged that the settlement of the Doomadgee conflict — the first whole-community mediation to be conducted in Australia with Aboriginal people — was very promising. The agreement related to the management of alcohol and included the establishment of new structures for managing community concerns in the future.

The contrast of mediation to the adversarial legal and criminal justice system, and its disempowering effects, was most striking. Parties were allowed to 'own their own conflict', rather than having to endure intervention from police or governmental agencies. 'The process supported the existing cultural structure in the community, rather than imposing an invasive power structure'. The community was left feeling responsible for their own concerns (Community Justice Program, 1991a). As one

Aboriginal participant said: 'Mediation is something we have always done. It comes naturally to us'.

Because of the number and depth of internal conflicts which such a forum inevitably drew out, not all the agenda items were discussed and settled at this community meeting. However, the Community Justice Program later reported that exposure to the process had been a very positive one for the people. The immediate crisis was resolved by the community itself, and the door-to-door delivery of alcohol was stopped. The mediation process improved communication between different groups, where formerly there had been little or poor communication. The parties involved experienced effective ways of behaving, which might govern future relationships; and an awareness of new skills for alternative dispute resolution was imparted.

A letter of thanks from the Doomadgee Aboriginal Community Council to the Community Justice Program provides a strong testimonial to the effect of one community mediation upon Doomadgee:

> In general there has been a marked improvement in attitudes and in the level of tolerance and acceptability of each other and other people's problems. To me, it now appears that people will try to help each other out, or accept that each person is different ...

> The results have been great. There has been an increased interest in sporting and recreational activities, there appears to be less violence, more outstation work and in my opinion more Community pride ...

> Whilst [at the Doomadgee Rodeo] there was no alcohol on sale (it was present) there was a greater tolerance to those who consumed alcohol. Those consuming liquor did not drink in the open and certainly did not create any undue disturbance ...

> These sporting and recreational events, the movements to the outstations and general tolerance increase have been a direct result of the mediation. I state this with authority having been the organiser of these events ...

> I personally commend the Community Justice Program and look forward to the input of mediators in the areas of land rights, mining and community negotiations (correspondence Doomadgee Aboriginal Community Council to the Community Justice Program 9 August 1991).[5]

Since this time other whole-community mediations, meetings and liaison efforts have been facilitated by the Community Justice Program (O'Donnell 1992).[6] The Queensland Community Justice Program wishes to increase the presence of Aboriginal and Islander persons on their mediator panels and to explore ways of enhancing the delivery of mediation services to Aboriginal and Islander communities. In 1992 a 30-minute video on mediation for Aboriginal and Torres Strait Islander communities was commissioned by the Community Justice Program. The video, 'Talk About It', which was produced by Marcia Langton and Lew Griffiths, included a re-enactment by members of the Doomadgee community of the settlement process which had occurred in their community a year earlier. This video is now available from the Community Justice Program, Queensland Department of the Attorney-General.

Without a doubt, dispute resolution illuminates a new road for action. It provides alternatives to the anxiety and suffering of conflict. But it must be kept in mind that the numerous, and complicated nature of, Aboriginal community issues makes a holistic approach vital. The inter-generational influences of alcoholism, the rape of the minds and the spirits of the next generation, and the lack of meaningful community activities, underpin the loss of community pride and dishonour the lives of women and men. Dispute resolution cannot be expected to eliminate the complex and tragic causes of these problems. Nor can they be easily 'negotiated'.

Other helping and healing projects will need to occur simultaneously with, and as a support to, the provision of mediation services. Mediation will help the healing process, but it cannot provide all of the solutions. This was the conclusion of Queensland mediators as a result of the whole-community experiences of the Community Justice Program (Joan Welsh, mediator, Community Justice Program, discussions with the author, 6 January 1992).

'BITING THE BULLET' OVER ALCOHOLISM

In too many Aboriginal communities today, alcoholism is the most common cause of ill-health, psychosis, and early death. It is the most common cause of infants and children failing to thrive. It is the most common cause of illiteracy, of lost opportunities and wasted human potential. It is the single most influential cause of violence, incarceration, and domestic misery.

We might debate 'the problem' of addiction. We might conduct research upon its social dimensions and physical manifestations. We might offer up compassionate analyses of why people drink, sniff petrol, or take drugs — which cannot be faulted for their historical accuracy or cultural relevance. We might even experiment with half-way measures ('dry areas', 'restricted areas', 'drunk buses', 'sobering-up' centres, and 'drink safe drink wise' programs) but these serve only to displace the problem or to divide the strong in the community from the weak. In all of this apparent 'activity', we are doing nothing more than marking time. (O'Connor 1990; d'Abbs 1987, 1990; Brady 1990b).[7]

Canadian Native alcohol workers, healers, and program administrators are quite emphatic in their approach towards addiction. They treat it as a disease, for which there is a cure:

> Alcoholism is an illness. You can do nothing successfully when you are sick. We need to get the people well. We need to treat the disease of alcoholism, before we can achieve the full potential of the people.

> When it comes down to it, we cannot avoid the simple fact that alcoholism destroys. It steals lives, ravages families, and enfeebles communities. Alcoholism is the villain, not each other. It is our common enemy. By working together — with love, understanding and mutual support — we can remove the suffering. We can save lives. If this is seen to be 'taking a hard line', then it is the hard line which we have no option but to take (Eric Shirt, Poundmaker's Lodge, conversations with the author, 2–5 April 1991).

It would seem that much of our thinking in Australia in the past has reflected an unwillingness, or a lack of know-how, on how to bite the bullet over alcoholism. But before we proceed we must first come to a fundamental understanding of the nature and effect of alcoholism. Our analysis of the situation can be simple. Our conclusion need be no more profound than this: — that every day we wait to take action to free people from addiction will be another life lost, the spirit and vitality of another young person extinguished. There is only *one solution*, and that is *cure*.

◆ ◆ ◆

[1] Sparked by Room's criticisms, and deeply concerned that their research should be more effective in impacting upon 'policies, programs and the quality of Aboriginal life', a group of researchers involved in Aboriginal alcohol problems met in May and later in December 1990 to explore this issue (Duquemin, d'Abbs and Chalmers 1991: 13).

[2] CDEP was established in 1977 as an income support and community development program for remote Aboriginal communities. This is seen as a 'work for the dole' program, as participants forego individual access to social security entitlements in favour of CDEP paid employment. Equivalent funds are paid as

block grants to communities which then utilise this wage pool for part-time employment for community members on a range of useful and needed community projects (Altman and Daly 1992).

[3] It was regarded a matter of protocol and courtesy to obtain the consent and support in principle of ACC to work in one of their member communities.

[4] The content and settlements of all mediations are confidential.

[5] A second community mediation was conducted by the CJP in Doomadgee in April 1993, further indicating the satisfaction of this community in the results of mediation.

[6] On 14 October 1991 a community mediation was held on Palm Island on the issues of alcohol, community violence, and child abuse. Between 19–21 August 1991, at the invitation of the Division of Aboriginal and Islander Affairs, the Community Justice Program facilitated a meeting of Aboriginal and Islander community representatives and relevant government departments to develop a Strategy on Caring for Returned Human Remains and Burial Artefacts. In a report entitled, 'Towards Self-Government' the Legislation Review Committee acknowledged (1991: 17) the potential contribution of alternative dispute resolution to the maintenance of 'peace, order and good government' in Aboriginal and Islander communities (Community Justice Program 1991b).

[7] In his South Australian study, O'Connor (1990) found that most approved or pending 'Dry Area' applications responded to public drinking and anti-social behaviour around public areas, such as pools, beaches, and town squares. Aboriginal youth were an obvious target of these applications. More importantly, he pointed out that most community members, police, agency workers, and town council representatives agreed that 'Dry Area' declarations only served to move drinkers into less publicly visible areas. When drinking parties relocated to road sides, river flats, or other more isolated areas the danger of drinkers dying of injury, illness or exposure increased significantly.

Chapter five

'GETTING OFF THE GROG'

Be Truth at all times. Know those things that lead to your well-being and those that lead to your destruction (Elders, Alkali Lake, British Columbia).

LET'S LOOK AT THE ALCOHOLIC

Irrespective of the theories regarding alcoholism, its causes, and consequences — a controversy which might involve us in endless contention — let's look at alcoholism as it affects the alcoholic.

Medical and psychiatric opinion agrees that alcoholism is a chronic and progressive disability with physical and psychological aspects, which is characterised by the victim's abnormal drinking behaviour and eventual loss of control. The Heartview Foundation, Dakarta a private non-profit alcohol and drug treatment centre, has provided treatment for dependent persons and their families since 1964 and now provides services throughout the United States and Canada.

In recommending intervention, the Heartview Foundation, pointed out:

> Neither the explicit causes of the illness, nor the changes it brings about in the body are completely understood. Nor can the disease be 'cured', in the sense that the alcoholic can ever expect to return to a pattern of 'normal controlled' drinking (Heartview Foundation, booklet, [nd]: 2).

The Heartview Foundation listed some of the characteristics of the encroaching disease:

1 Constructing an alibi-system
The growing psychological obsession with drinking, even when 'dry', requires the development of denial through rationalisation. A rationalised self-image enables alcoholics to lay blame for all their troubles to causes other than drinking or themselves. Projecting the blame on to other things and other people evolves into an elaborate self-preserving alibi-system. 'There is no money for food because his wife has spent it all' or 'the government doesn't give enough'.

The physical compulsion to drink, and unpleasant withdrawal symptoms, increase as addiction takes hold. In practical terms, alcoholics are people whose drinking interferes with, and continually causes problems in, the emotional, moral, health, and financial aspects of their lives. It directly interferes with their family relationships and affects their ability to get along with people. 'It is the alcoholic's inability to cut down on his/her drinking, in spite of the trouble it causes that distinguishes them from other drinkers' (Heartview Foundation, booklet, [nd]: 3).

This process of rationalisation grows as the illness progresses. It may start when a drinker thinks of a drink as a relief from stress, and continue until the early stages of memory loss and eventual blackouts. The more dependent alcoholics become on the effects of alcohol, the more they will need to rationalise, conceal, or justify their behaviour. As questions and criticisms from family and friends increase, excuses and explanations multiply and become more elaborate. Violence may be resorted to when no other means will do. This, in Alcoholics Anonymous (AA) terminology, is called 'Stinking Thinking'.

2 'Hitting bottom'

Alcoholics have great difficulty distinguishing abnormal drinking behaviour from normal drinking behaviour. This is particularly true when they surround themselves with drinkers like themselves. Throwing up and passing out become a 'normal' part of drinking:

> The middle stage is characterised by loss of control when the alcoholic can no longer predict the outcome of drinking with any reliability. The late stage alcoholic demonstrates total loss of control, prolonged binges, and physical and moral deterioration. Finally, the facts of what drinking has become are impossible to explain away, the alibi structure collapses and the alcoholic either accepts help or dies from the illness (Heartview Foundation, booklet, [nd]: 4).

This stage is what in AA language is called 'hitting bottom'.

3 Seeking help

Countless alcoholics have died from accident, suicide or physical complications. Clinical experience has shown that 'hitting bottom', that moment of defeat when alcoholics might ask for help, can be induced at a much earlier stage — before their lives and bodies are horribly mangled by the disease. The earlier the treatment begins the greater likelihood of recovery.

Intervention in the illness of alcoholism requires two things:

- opportunity for treatment and
- motivation for treatment.

Through treatment the early stage alcoholic, and the potential alcoholic can be surrounded with the evidence of the illness. By a continuous barrage of information: the facts, the truth, and the seriousness of the disease have a therapeutic value. It is a situation of 'creating a crisis' in the life of the alcoholic through awareness. *It is a case of 'raising the bottom' to break the fall, as soon as possible in the cycle of the disease.*

4 *Providing motivation*

Getting the alcoholic or similarly addicted person into treatment is the first and most crucial step of recovery. He or she must be a willing participant. Providing the motivation is an essential part of treatment. The Heartview Foundation explained this stage of the process in this way:

> Motivation is partly a process of collapsing the alibi structure in order to get the alcoholic to accept the need for treatment. Logically, it is a task to be undertaken by those closest to the alcoholic — family, close friends and co-workers — for whose benefit the alibi structure was largely erected in the first place.
>
> But their success in this effort will depend entirely on how well they understand the illness. Motivation, therefore, is something to be done by those closest to the alcoholic, with explicit and continuing advice from someone who understands not only the illness of alcoholism but the process of recovery as well (Heartview Foundation, booklet, [nd]: 5–6).

Motivation occurs when:
- alcoholics admit they are sick
- alcoholics are no longer able to 'escape' from the truth of their condition
- alcoholics are surrounded by the facts of their illness, its symptoms, and seriousness
- they learn to know their disease and what will happen without recovery — ill health, hunger, broken families, disturbed children, accidents, death
- family and friends support and participate in the program of healing; and when
- communities provide back-up and support when patients return home.

The Heartview Foundation stressed that we should not underestimate the power of the 'grim realities' of alcoholism in procuring a motive for treatment and sobriety. *Surround alcoholics with reality, not criticism. Help them to understand the true nature of their illness.*

'FINDING OUR SOBRIETY'

If there is to be any recovery at all the alcoholic must stop drinking. Heartview Foundation states that 'Recovery is a process not a condition' ([nd]: 8). Alcoholics must first recognise that they suffer from a chronic, but *treatable* illness. The AA experience, with tens of thousands of alcoholics throughout the world, has shown that confirmed alcoholics can never return to a lifestyle of moderate drinking. They can only control the disease if they stay off alcohol for the rest of their lives. Simple abstinence, however, does not guarantee recovery on its own. The alcoholic will also need to heal the long-term effects of the addiction through self-understanding and improved life-styles.

Alcoholism is a fourfold disease: physical, sociocultural, mental, and spiritual. Each area of the problem must be properly treated. Where one or other aspect of the disease is ignored, or where problems or issues are unresolved, the person may easily slip back into old patterns of drinking. Those who have been involved for many years in healing the complex illness of alcoholism have discovered that the most effective treatment requires a multifaceted and holistic approach.

Native addiction treatment and healing programs follow a philosophy of personal, social, and spiritual reconstruction of the individual through the support of the collective. They are about showing people that they have choices, and about helping people discover choices they did not know they had.

These programs have found that the creation of an inner life will sustain the alcoholic through these difficult phases, and will pave new ways of thinking and behaving which will encourage personal growth.

Treatment and healing are for all those who wish to improve the quality of their lives, and the lives of their relations, friends, and communities. Positive action inspires in people a new sense of purpose. What begins as a process of self-help, very often evolves into a personal mission, or even a profession, of helping others. Helplessness is replaced by a new vision for the future.

THE POUNDMAKER'S LODGE MODEL

Through his many years of experience with the Poundmaker's Lodge, and similar Native alcohol treatment programs throughout Alberta, Eric Shirt found that: 'healing required three things: the *Right Place, the Right Time, and the Right People*' (Eric Shirt, notes from the *Healing Our People* forum, Alice Springs, April 1991).

In addition to their common histories of colonialism, there are many other experiences which Aboriginal people share with the Native peoples in Canada and the United States. With the self-determination movement of the mid-1960s Native people came to realise that alcohol and drug abuse were major barriers to the fulfilment of Native potential and aspirations. For two decades they have grappled with chemical dependency and have laid a firm foundation for culturally relevant prevention and healing of addiction for Native people.

Today, there are many excellent examples of treatment programs for Native peoples in North America. One of the oldest and must successful Canadian models is the Poundmaker's Lodge, located on the rural outskirts of Edmonton, in Alberta. The Poundmaker's Lodge, and its associated training centre, the Nechi Institute, is now housed in a modern $6.9 million facility built with funds from the Alberta Alcohol and Drug Abuse Commission and the Alberta provincial government. Since its beginnings in 1973, this Alberta program has treated and trained thousands of Native people in substance abuse prevention.

The interior architecture of the Poundmaker's Lodge reflects the ambience of the outdoors — the strong bond between the people and nature is seen in the generous use of wood and stone, open spaces, Native paintings, and artefacts. The facility comprises a 54-bed treatment wing, and a 34-bed counsellor training section, offices, conference rooms, a kitchen and dining area, recreation and vocational areas, a beautiful stone sweat lodge for traditional and spiritual activities and a large cultural centre where joyful alcohol-free dances and Pow Wows are frequently held.

TRAINING AND PROGRAM DEVELOPMENT

Poundmaker and Nechi Programs are founded upon the principle that Native people will be most effectively counselled and rehabilitated by other Native people. Support and funding had to be raised for both treatment and training programs. In the early years this challenge was overwhelming. 'Not only were there no suitable facilities in Alberta, there were few Native people who possessed the knowledge, skills and attitudes required of an effective alcohol and drug counsellor' (Poundmaker's/Nechi Centre, leaflet, [ca. 1988]).

Fundamental to the centre's program, therefore, has been the development of relevant treatment, and the specialised training of Native counsellors. Program development and counsellor training fit together, hand in glove. While operating separately, Poundmaker's Lodge and the Nechi Institute are located on the same premises and work cooperatively, each drawing upon the other. Each bases its programs upon a common understanding of the historical relationships and social aspects of the Native experience.

The historical cycles of colonialism, welfare dependency, poverty, and conflict with non-Native society; and the social issues of ill health, poor housing, unemployment, and violence are all seen to be part of the complex cause and effect of alcoholism. These are discussed and explained to participants, and an understanding of them forms part of the treatment and training. Other common assumptions include:

- Alcohol and drug abuse are learned behaviours, derived from the interaction of the individual with the social environment.

- Maladaptive behaviours can be replaced by adaptive ones, in the context of a clearly defined community which provides a sober reference and which encourages learning and healthy change.

- For maximum effectiveness, training/treatment programs must incorporate the traditions and mores of the client's own culture and society. Where they are accepted, these will serve, further, as deterrents to addiction.

- Participants and counsellors who are Native, and who have themselves emerged from life situations marked by alcohol or drug abuse, can have a powerful impact in the service and management of rehabilitative systems. The fact that they can refer to their own experience inspires respect and trust in their clients.

Native ceremonial Sweat Lodge (Native Counselling Services of Alberta, 1993)

The 30-day Poundmaker's treatment program for adults combines the latest techniques in individual and group counselling, spiritual meditation, prayer and cultural studies, healthy lifestyle training, arts and crafts, and recreation and social activities. A resident elder and nurse are in regular attendance.

Ritual and cultural activities are used to create a familiar environment which reinforces positive Native images. The sweat lodge is a particularly important aspect of the personal purification and spiritual strengthening of participants.[1] Strict rules are imposed on participants and visitors concerning the prohibition of alcohol or drugs on the premises, the respectful treatment of property, keeping rooms tidy, and the taking of responsibility for small chores.

YOUTH AND AFTERCARE

The Poundmaker's Lodge program is linked to an aftercare program to ensure that every client receives maximum benefit from treatment and rehabilitation. It also provides an intensive 90- day addiction program for Native youth between the ages of 12 and 17 years who have had problems with alcohol, drugs, and solvent abuse.

In 1990 an Adolescent Centre was established at St Paul, Alberta, with designated Open Custody status. This allows the Solicitor General's Department to refer eligible young offenders and those on probation, or with open custody or temporary release status, to the care of the program. The Native youth program includes addiction treatment, school education, life skills development, family therapy, recreational activities, medical care, and counselling in Native culture, customs and spiritual values. It has its own follow-up and aftercare support.

NECHI INSTITUTE OPERATIONS

The Nechi Institute began operations one year after the Poundmaker's Lodge, in 1974. The purpose of the institute is to provide training and educational programs for individuals and service agencies. Trainees are taught to understand the background to, and illness of, addiction, to counsel the addicted and their families, and to work with communities. Training includes issues of family violence, addiction and suicide prevention, aftercare, research, and program management. Nechi has conducted training in most provinces and territories of Canada, and Nechi-trained staff are prominent in community activities, inmate treatment programs, pre-employment programs to assist recovered alcoholics and addicts returning to the work force, Human Services development, youth summer camps, media and newsletter communications, suicide prevention programs, and the development of curriculum materials for alcohol and drug prevention for schools.

A CATALYST FOR CHANGE

Treatment and training programs are designed to affirm for Native participants their:

- identity as a people;
- ability to control their own destiny;
- personal and community spirituality;
- ability to become responsible for, and to improve the general well-being of, their own people; and
- their potential to assume leadership in their communities.

Alberta has many different tribal and language groupings (Blackfoot, Cree, Blood, Beaver, Stoney, Chippeqyan, Sarcee, as well as Metis) who are dispersed widely between rural reserves and urban settings. For almost two decades, Poundmaker's programs have attempted to *find common ground* and to overcome apparent differences between Alberta's Native peoples. The program encourages participants to set aside old tribal and family conflicts. Native people are united against the *common enemy of alcoholism and drug addiction* (Poundmaker's/Nechi Centre, leaflet, [ca. 1988]).

Poundmaker's Lodge programs have acted as a catalyst for positive change in Native communities. Activities they have generated include the setting up of alcoholics support groups, community development, self-esteem building, cultural awareness, youth education programs, and alcohol-free recreation. The inter-tribal, and inter-provincial exchange of ideas, and the sharing of successes, have been encouraged through Native newspapers, national awareness conferences, training programs, and sober Pow Wows.

TESTING THE EFFECTS?

Since 1983 the Nechi Institute has developed a data base of information on Nechi trainees to assess the effect of Nechi Alcohol and Drug Education Programs upon their clients' lives, and that of their communities. In 1991 a survey study of this information was conducted. As such a study could not yet be done in Australia (as we have no similar extensive programs) its findings provide extremely interesting insights for other groups wishing to pursue a path of community detoxification.

In 1992 the report, *The Eagle Has Landed: Data Base Study of Nechi Participants*, was published. Of those interviewed, 52% described themselves as having been an 'Adult Child of An Alcoholic'; 48% as a 'Co-Dependent'; 24% as a 'Problem Drinker'; and 8% as a 'Drug Addict'. Respondents who had stopped drinking or using other substances were asked if there was a specific reason which led to their decision to abstain. 'The family' figured prominently in 115 of 409 responses, particularly the respondent's children:

> This included a large number of respondents who reported that they wanted to raise their children in a safe and sober family environment, that they were afraid their children would be removed [by Child Welfare] from the home [or would not be returned] because of their alcohol or drug abuse ... A smaller number of other respondents however, also indicated that they were about to start a family, or planned to do so in the near future (Nechi Institute 1992: 19).

A second powerful reason given was concern about the respondent's mental, emotional, spiritual, or physical health:

> This included the 78 respondents who reported that they were simply 'sick and tired of being sick and tired', persons who had experienced numerous blackouts and severe hangovers, individuals who reported a variety of physical conditions brought on or complicated by a history of alcoholism, as well as those persons who reported they had almost died or were afraid that they would die or be killed as a result of their abuse.

> In addition, eight other respondents reported that their mental health had deteriorated to such a point that it had prompted their decision to stop using alcohol or drugs (Nechi Institute 1992: 19).

For 37 other respondents, some personally traumatic incident or tragedy within the family unit or community at large had precipitated the decision — such as a serious accident, the death of a close family member through alcoholism, being out of control, getting in trouble with the police, spending too much time in prison, or feeling life was on a downward slide.

Some indicated that their decision to refrain from the use of alcohol or drugs was influenced by several factors, relevant to their particular situation. A mixture of negative and positive reasons were given. In the respondent's own words:

> 'Health reasons, plus there were now four sober people in my community and I thought if they can do it, I can do it.'

> 'To save the family that threatened to leave me. Possibly to make an impression on an employer who had fired me and I had just lost a house that I once owned. All within three months' (Nechi Institute 1992: 21).

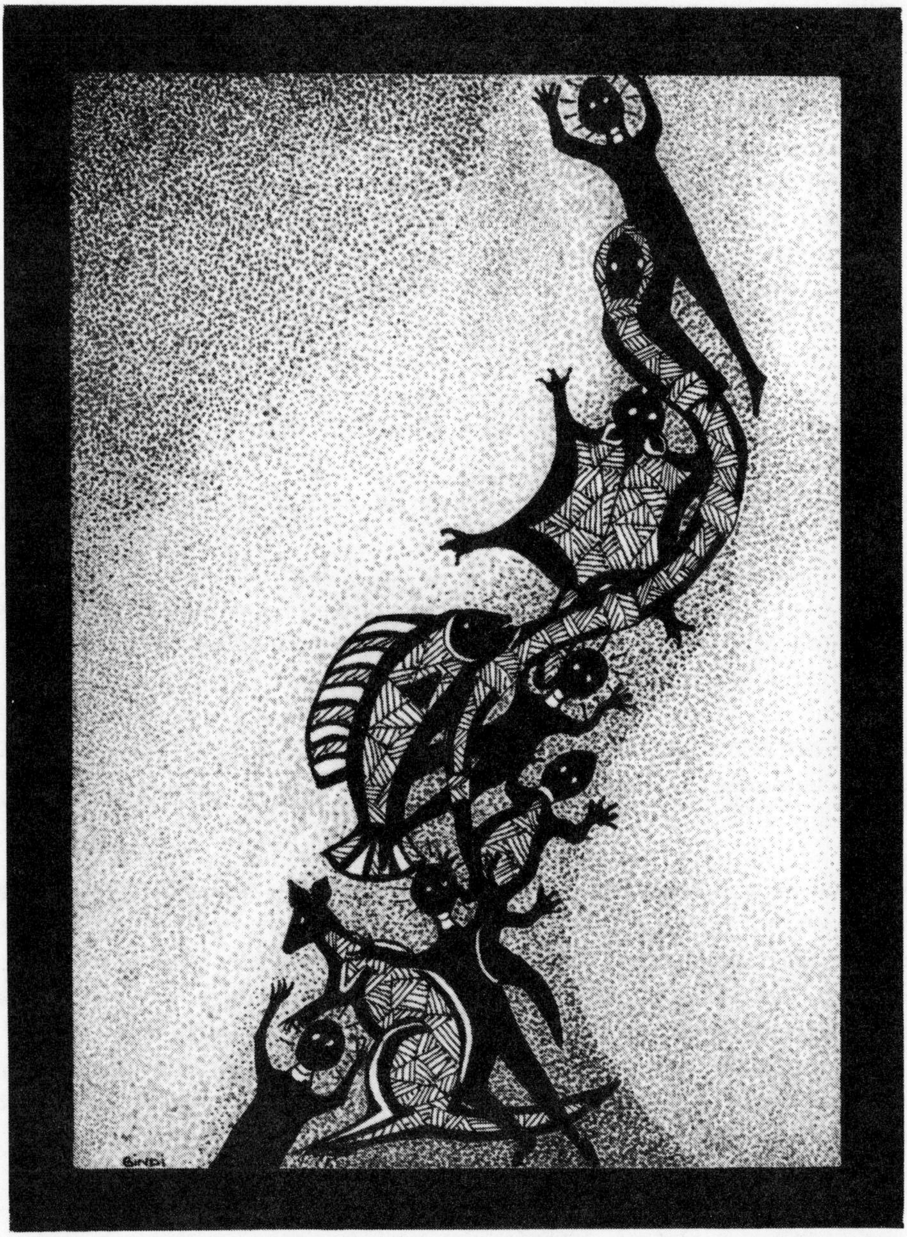
BINDI

RECOVERY ACTIVITIES

The Nechi study also examined the different kinds of formal and informal activities their respondents became involved in, as part of their recovery and aftercare.

In addition to Alcoholics Anonymous programs (47%), the most influential recovery activities participated in were: spiritual and cultural activities 27%; recreational activities 20%; therapy and counselling 16%; work and career 12%, training workshops 10%; activities with friends/family 8%, support groups 7%; community activities 6%, voluntary service 6%, church activities 6%; fitness, relaxation and nutritional activities 5%; and self-help books and tapes 3%.

Most respondents said they participated in two or more such activities to assist in their recovery. The most common, and apparently most powerful, carried a spiritual and cultural emphasis: such as, pipe ceremonies, sweat lodges, fasts, prayer, cultural ceremonies, and listening to the Elders.

KNOWLEDGE AND GROWTH

Many of the respondents indicated that Nechi training had a positive personal and/or professional impact upon their lives. About one third indicated that they were considering further education or post-secondary training. A similar number said they had participated in some other addictions-related program, workshop, seminar or conference after their Nechi training (Nechi Institute 1992: 51, 29–30).

Respondents indicated that Nechi training was not only important in promoting recovery, but also in providing a catalyst to personal growth generally. Nechi training 'was the beginning of knowing', said one respondent, 'not only for my job but also for my personal life'. For another it 'opened doors for new interests and information on all the possibilities to create positive change for myself and others and community'. This 'motivates me to continue, particularly in this field (of addictions)'; 'I realized I need more education to aid my knowledge in work' (Nechi Institute 1992: 51).

The study indicated increased cultural identity and pride in participants; an improvement in personal confidence and interpersonal skills; a strengthening of family relationships; improved knowledge of alcoholism, codependency and related issues; and improved communications with partners, children, siblings, co-workers, clients, and other family members. 'In conclusion, an overwhelming 83% of the respondents reported that the Nechi training had an important or positive impact on their interpersonal relationships'. Further to this, 48% described the training as having been important to their spiritual development (Nechi Institute 1992: 59–60).

'I felt at home, once I began to understand. The spiritual values and experiences I had at Nechi have become the foundation or source of energy for the rest of my life'.

'My cultural identity was paramount to my growth. I give thanks to Nechi for enhancing my spiritual development through the Elders that were available to me'.

'I now understand my role as a human being. My faith has increased and I now have a good relationship with God' (Nechi Institute 1992: 60).

Since 1974 Nechi Institute programs have gained increasing popularity. Nechi courses obtained formal accreditation with the University of Alaska, Anchorage, Alaska in 1989; and the University of Athabasca, Athabasca, Alberta, in 1989; and Keyano College, McMurray, Alberta in 1993. By the end of 1993, 3,200 people had participated in Nechi training.

When asked about formal recognition of Nechi addictions training, 78% of the respondents described accreditation as 'Very Important' or perceived it as having a positive result. Some saw accredited Nechi training as the beginning of a university career, or as another opening for further education and employment. Others felt that accreditation enhanced the status of the training in the eyes of prospective employers, with existing and potential funding sources, with governments, and with the wider community (Nechi Institute 1992: 74–5).

RECOVERY-RELATED EMPLOYMENT

Perhaps most significantly, the Nechi study revealed that at the time of their training many of the participants were already in, or later moved into, positions of community responsibility — particularly in fields concerned with addiction services, family and community health, or child welfare services. The highest represented occupation of Nechi participants was in the field of Addictions Counselling (Nechi Institute 1992: 48).

THE RIGHT PEOPLE — THE RIGHT IDEAS

The underlying philosophy of so many successful Canadian and American Native addiction programs was the development of treatment and rehabilitation programs which were in tune with the culture and values of Native people, and which were able to heal social and spiritual problems specific to the indigenous experience.

Intrinsic to many of the recognised problems in Native communities — ill health, poor housing, poverty, unemployment, and social pathology — was the complex disease of alcoholism. There also came the realisation that the extent and intensity of the alcohol and drug problem for Native people was the result of critical differences between Native and non-Native people, both individually and as collectives, and that effective treatment and rehabilitation would require recognition and some resolution of those differences (Poundmaker's/Nechi Centre, leaflet, [ca. 1988]).

The development of a strong philosophy has been an important contributing factor to the success of this program. Central to its philosophy is the commitment to service and a professionalism among alcohol counsellors and care givers. Poundmaker's and Nechi staff are expected to act as role models for clients, and for the whole Native community. Since total abstinence is the only solution for the Native client, staff cannot just 'talk the talk', they must also 'walk the walk'. It is absolutely vital that staff themselves support the program in both body and spirit (Poundmaker's/Nechi Centre, leaflet, [ca. 1988]).

In a talk entitled 'An Issue of Life or Death' delivered on 21 November 1991, Maggie Hodgson, Executive Director of Nechi Institute, related the words of one of her Elders: 'Our culture is the way we live today'. We must take care of how we live today as being something we want for our grandchildren.' At Nechi employees are encouraged to be role-models of sobriety to their people. Alcohol workers must be 'the wellest of the well to treat the sickest of the sick', she said:

> The issue is: how can we choose to role-model addiction to drugs and alcohol to communities who pay attention to our behaviour, before they pay attention to what comes out of our mouth. As our cultural norm is to teach by role-modelling, if we speak in one way and act in another, then we choose *death* instead of *life* for our people — it is as simple as that.

◆ ◆ ◆

[1] The Indian sweat lodge (or 'sweats' as the ceremonies are sometimes called), is a closed in, humpy-like construct which is heated by fire to produce a sauna effect. In Indian culture the sweat lodge experience, and the prayers and rituals associated with it, represent and symbolise both physical and spiritual purification, and are actively employed in the process of healing.

Chapter six

ADDICTION PROGRAMS

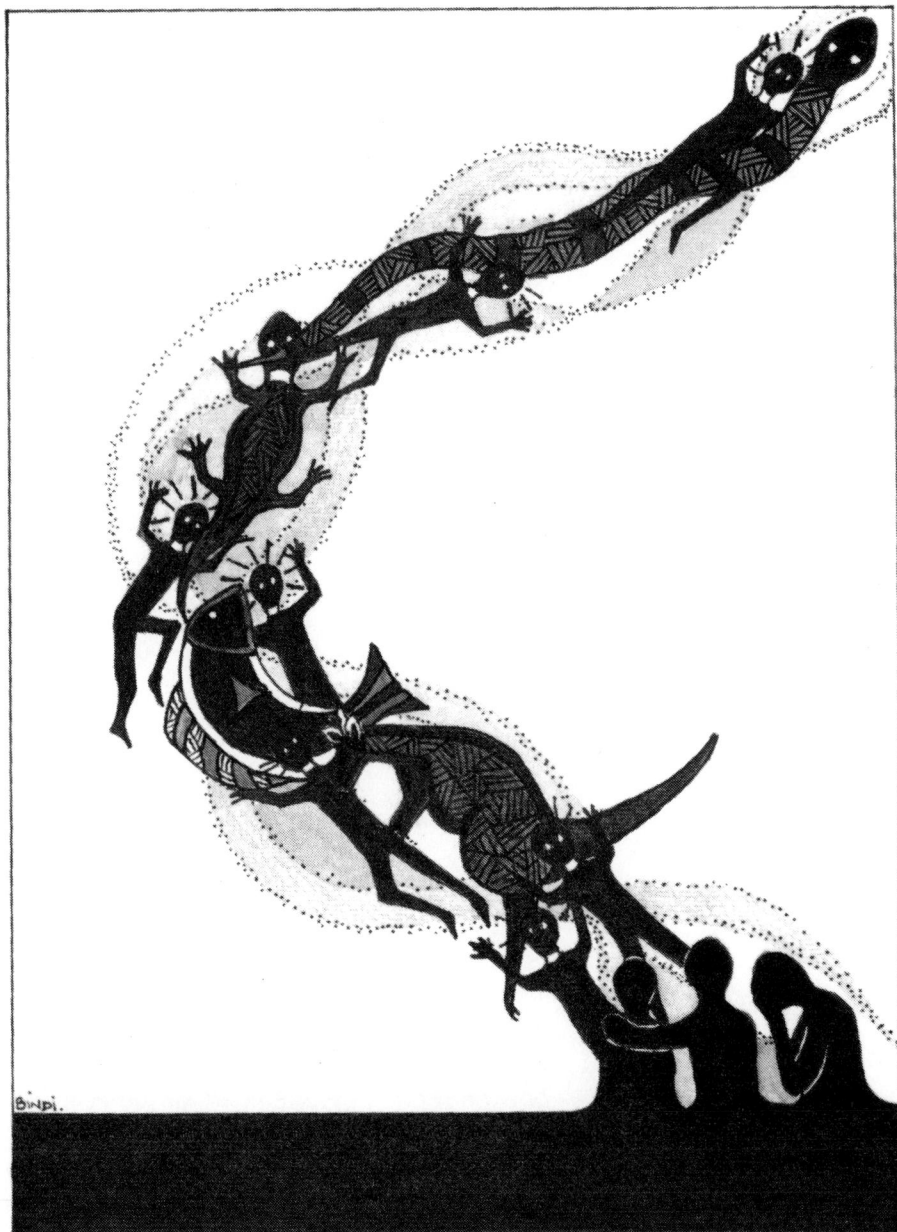

They've got to make their own place clean. And
make the petrol sniffing place a good place, clean
place, no grog, no petrol sniffing, strong family,
strong culture (Bertha Nakamarra, Ernabella HALT
1991: 16).

IS THIS THE RIGHT TIME?

Is this the right time for a program for community detoxification for Australia? An examination of our best solutions — namely 'Dry Areas', 'Sobering-Up' centres, and Nursing Stations — provides the answer to this question.

Although we admire those people who have striven so long in this area we must now seriously consider their effect. In fact, to their credit, most of these workers will say that what has been achieved is simply not enough, that more is needed. Existing approaches have only displaced the problem. Many thousands of dedicated hours have been spent bandaging the wounds, resetting the arms, and conducting futile battles to regenerate destroyed livers and other organs. They simply have not succeeded in getting significant numbers of people 'off the grog'.

After his study of one of our 'best' solutions, namely, 'Restricted' or 'Dry Areas' in the Northern Territory, d'Abbs concluded:

> Ultimately, success in overcoming Aboriginal alcohol abuse problems will be a function of the capacity of Aboriginal people, individually and collectively, to exercise control over their social environment in general and the use of alcohol in particular. Restricted area policies which do not promote this capacity are unlikely to make a significant contribution to solving the problem. Insofar as some restrictive area policies promote such a capacity, they have a useful role to play as Aboriginal alcohol control policies (d'Abbs 1990: 132).

Alcoholism is so high in some Aboriginal communities that between 60% and 80% of adults either drink regularly or have a member of their family seriously addicted (Hunter, Hall and Spargo 1991b: 39). Nothing short of a massive program for community detoxification will reverse this trend. In Australia today there is no more widespread or critical need than the introduction of properly designed and fully equipped detoxification treatment centres, where addiction can be treated as a serious public and social health issue, rather than as a criminal offence.

Thinking that there is a half-way solution in getting off the grog is like the idea that we can be 'a little bit addicted' or 'a little bit violent'. The Aboriginal experience of alcoholism has been particularly devastating. Yipati Munti of Ernabella, Northern Territory, describes how it has affected the people:

> A lot of people drink grog. They go hungry — no food, no shelter, no family. They get sick. Some die from lack of food and from drinking too much. They catch diseases, then go and stay in rubbish places.

> Some people might go hunting for meat and they'll get a lot, as well as quandongs, desert raisins, and wild figs. When they live in their own country, the children rarely get sick, and adults are healthy, too.

> But people drink grog and get sick or die. They get really depressed from not eating anything. These people ought to leave grog alone and sit down in their own place where they'll be happy and healthy ...

> Aboriginal people ought to leave grog alone and instead, camp with their relations — parents and grandparents. It will make them feel better to eat plenty of fresh meat and have access to bush food (HALT 1991: 30).

Taking the bull by the horns over alcoholism seems to be the one thing which we have not been really good at in Australia. Those brave projects for Aboriginal detoxification, where they have occurred, have received miserable support from governments.

AA AND OTHER ADDICTION PROGRAMS

The first and best known programs in the world for detoxification were those developed by Alcoholics Anonymous (AA) for dealing with individual alcoholics. Over many years, millions of men and women have participated in AA programs (for those suffering from addiction to Alcohol), Al-Anon (for families and partners of alcoholics), Al-a-teen (for youth), ACOA (for adult children of alcoholics) and many other related programs for addiction (drugs, overeating, gambling) or emotional disorders. Many elements contribute to the success of AA programs: their organisational flexibility, their volunteer nature, and their emphasis upon anonymity, and non-professional and non-profit association.[1] In spite of recent challenges to their claimed effectiveness the testimony of thousands remains unrefuted.

THE AA TWELVE STEPS PROGRAM

The purpose of the Twelve Steps program is to awaken faith and trust in a 'Higher Power' by which a person might have victory over addiction (or any other affliction), and attain freedom, happiness, and personal serenity. This forms the basic principle of AA and related programs. It is stressed that AA is not a religious program, but it is a spiritual one, based upon the underlying wisdoms of love and compassion common to the world's major religions, and upon fundamental principles of human psychology. For this reason it is easily adapted to any social or cultural situation.

The AA 'Twelve Steps' (see Workbook 7) provide a map or a guide to personal, emotional, and spiritual growth which, while originally used to assist people to attain sobriety, can also be adapted and applied to a range of emotional and mental ills — anger, insecurity, alienation, abusive behaviours, codependency, indecision, and fear common to alcoholic families and experiences.

They constitute a program for changing lives and situations through a process of changing attitudes. But they require an admission that this is a task which cannot be done alone. Those suffering from addiction, or some other emotional disorder, need help. Help, firstly, from a Higher Power in Whom they are encouraged to place their confidence and trust. Help, also, from other 'seekers' who will understand, nurture, and share with them their 'journey' of self-discovery.

Through regular meetings participants discover and learn to make use of their internal resources and powers of reasoning. They learn to make peace, first with themselves, and then with those whom they have hurt over the years. They will learn to forgive those who have hurt them. By overcoming the obstacles of denial, guilt, shame, anger, and self-deprivation, 'the individual' is given — in some cases for the first time — the opportunity to emerge, flourish, and seek full potential. *Recovery begins with self-awareness.*

ADULT CHILDREN OF ALCOHOLICS

People who have grown up with alcoholism frequently become alcoholics themselves, may marry an alcoholic, or may continue to see alcoholism among other family members. Each situation exists separately, and has its own sets of problems characteristic to itself.

Growing up with alcoholism injures and hampers personal growth in children and, if it is not addressed, will result in suffering throughout that person's whole life. Support groups for Adult Children of Alcoholics provide a safe environment in which these experiences can be shared, burdens can be lifted, and injuries can be identified. Sharing childhood experiences can be frightening and painful. For many it may be the first time they have broken the conspiracy of silence of repressed feelings.

Through sharing, support groups have discovered a range of characteristics common to the experience of growing up with alcoholism. Adult children of alcoholics, for instance, have no frame of reference for what is a 'normal household'. In order to live beyond their chaotic day-to-day life, they must use fantasy to imagine what life would be like if their parents were sober. Or they may use self-deception and lies to believe that 'there is nothing wrong in our house'.

Adult children of alcoholics often lie when it is just as easy to tell the truth. Lying and denial become the norm in a family seriously affected by alcohol. These children grow up with many inconsistencies, broken promises, and masquerades — where the family keeps up the pretence that everything is alright at home. When it comes to the family against the world, members in the alcoholic home demonstrate extreme loyalty towards each other.

Criticism and feelings of guilt are also a part of growing up. Children are frequently made to believe that their family would be better off without them, or that they are personally responsible for all their parent's troubles. 'It is you kids who drive me to drink'. High levels of emotional blackmail are common in such families.

Not being able to do anything about the family's problems, these criticisms are frequently internalised. Never feeling good enough, always falling short of the mark, feeling responsible for the bad behaviour of others, are common among adult children of alcoholics. Negative self-feelings, self-loathing, and guilt haunt them from childhood into adulthood. Blaming behaviour becomes part of the family and individual personality system.

Constant attacks on the personality and worth of a person in childhood intrude upon, and breach, the individual's personal boundaries. Adult children of alcoholics have difficulty developing a sense of their own separateness, or individual selves. They may never learn to be self-reliant. This makes them particularly vulnerable to the development of dependent personalities.

Negative self-feelings may include:
- feeling isolated and afraid of people
- fearing authority figures
- feeling guilty when other people become angry
- never standing up for oneself
- an over-developed sense of responsibility and concern for others
- or becoming completely irresponsible
- constantly seeking approval from others
- confusing love with pity
- always wanting to 'rescue' or to be 'rescued'
- living the life of the victim (self pity, worry, dramatisation of victim role)

- anger, jealousy, apathy, and despair
- becoming vain
- being angry
- becoming controlling or possessive
- developing a compulsive personality
  (e.g. workaholic).

Those who have had traumatic childhoods often lose the ability to feel, or to express their feelings to others. This includes good feelings as well — such as joy and happiness. Life in alcoholic families is a very serious, angry business. It is no wonder that children in these families have difficulty being spontaneous and having fun. Many have difficulty socialising with other children or may not be able to respect or relate to adults.

Alcoholic families also have difficulty in expressing love. Children may seldom see examples of happy, caring relationships between adults they know. Their own relationships with adults may be fraught with inconsistencies: 'come close, go away'. Feeling loved one minute and rejected the next is not the formula for a secure parent-child relationship. Rather, it engenders confusion and fear of abandonment.

Adult children of alcoholics have extraordinary difficulty in setting up, or maintaining, intimate relationships in their adult lives — even though these may be highly desirable. Childhood messages of being worthless, unlovable, and nothing special, are carried into adulthood. The sense of urgency and panic which childhood insecurities inject into adult relationships can smother partners and make trust between adults impossible to establish. Poor role models of loving parent-child relationships can also result in the repetition of cycles of physical and emotional abuse in the next generation.

Adult Children of Alcoholics may grow up with
- no experience of 'normal family life'
- denial that there is a problem
- self deception, lies, phoneyness
- conspiracy of silence and repressed feelings
- extreme loyalty to the family
- uncertain personal boundaries, confusion
- low self-esteem, self-loathing
- judgemental attitudes to self/others
- terror of rejection and abandonment
- emotionally dependent personalities
- difficulty in expressing feelings
- difficulty in having fun

- problems establishing healthy intimate relationships
- impulsiveness and perfectionism
- procrastination
- becoming super-responsible
- or becoming super-irresponsible
- compulsive personalities.

(Woititz 1986, 1988; Lerner 1988; Nechi Institute Workshops 1990; Friends in Recovery 1990; Alcoholics Anonymous 1976).

BOUNDARIES FOR CODEPENDANTS

Personal boundaries exist for our protection. They represent the barriers between ourselves and others — physically, intellectually, emotionally, and spiritually. They ensure that our behaviour towards others is appropriate. Without them we would be overwhelmed by others.

When our boundaries are intact we have a good sense of who we are in relation to others. Personal boundaries are healthy. They ensure the privacy and separate integrity of our thoughts and feelings.

Boundaries may be flexible, depending on how we feel about the people we are with. The act of becoming close to another person implies the act of *allowing* others closer, and the exercise of our free will in doing so. People without boundaries will not know when they are being physically, emotionally, or mentally violated. Without a good sense of ourselves, we also have difficulty respecting the individual boundaries and rights of others to their separateness (such as in cases of verbal abuse and sexual harassment or assault):

> This phenomenon is common to Codependants in general, and adult children of alcoholics in particular, which may account for why so many tend to remain in abusive situations (Lerner 1988:1).

Co-dependency refers to people who are involved jointly in the situation of alcoholism. For example: a drinker husband and his abstinent wife; alcoholic parents and their children; partners who both drink. *An essential part of recovery for codependants is the development of personal boundaries:*

> Nowhere is this more dramatically illustrated than in adult children of alcoholics. They need to understand and develop boundaries in order to fully recover and claim their identities (Lerner 1988:1).

When children say 'no' they are experimenting with and asserting themselves as separate entities from their parents. Healthy mothers and fathers will respect this as an important developmental stage and will not be threatened by it. In an alcoholic or abusive family the personal space and emotions of its members are constantly under siege. Children may learn that asserting their individuality, throwing tantrums, and saying 'no', leads to trouble. It may even be dangerous. The invasion of individual integrity, personal judgment and emotions leads to codependency. Children and adults in these situations have difficulty in knowing whose feelings belong to whom.

Attention is focused upon the alcoholic parent, not the children. If he or she is depressed, or feels sick, other members of the family must tip-toe around the house. Children of these families develop a strong sense of responsibility for the welfare of their alcoholic parents, the non-drinking wife for the alcoholic husband. They become as entrapped in the cycle of abuse, as surely as the abusers themselves.

The personal boundaries of individuals can be violated through neglect and emotional abuse, through physical violence and incest. Victims learn to deny, ignore, or distrust their senses and emotions, leaving their protective boundary systems seriously damaged:

> They often ignore bizarre events and treat crises as if they were normal ...
> When physical boundaries are invaded, the victim often feels a deep
> sense of shame. Ironically, victims of physical abuse or incest often
> remain loyal to the people who abuse them. When their physical
> boundaries are repeatedly violated, victims often feel they're betraying
> their abuser by setting up boundaries. Feeling responsible for this leaves
> the child with the idea that the intrusion was justified (Lerner 1988:4-5).

Self-blaming is a common feature of codependence, particularly among physically abused spouses and children. Abused children suppress their own anger, and may even internalise the rage of their abuser — dumping this on their own children or partners in adult life.

Unmet needs of childhood re-emerge to cause havoc later in life. Those who have been humiliated, criticised, and shamed will humiliate, criticise, and shame others. Bonding with others becomes supremely difficult.

If you love someone who is harmfully involved with alcohol or drugs, but are not addicted yourself, you also need support. Co-dependants have many common feelings of frustration, anger, rejection, confusion, and fear. They often feel 'second-class', ignored, replaced, or discounted.

Programs for codependants begin to repair and rebuild personal and emotional boundaries. They help people know who they are, and to feel good about themselves. This is where support groups play their greatest role. Some call this process 'reparenting'. It is a process where lost childhoods are returned. It is a process where the needs of childhood are honoured, and the confusion of neglect is dispelled through group recognition. By repairing damaged boundaries we attain a sense of wholeness and spiritual union.

INDIGENISING THE AA PRINCIPLES

Native people in North America have found the basic philosophical and organisational principles of AA to be an excellent starting point for their own programs. Native treatment centres, and many community-based support groups now being run in cities and rural communities, have adapted and indigenised the AA approaches for self-help and member support. These programs are shaped by Native cultural and spiritual values — with liberal sprinklings of 'tough love', compassion, and mutual support.

Meetings and groups are set up with the objective of avoiding typical organisational formality, excessive cost, and undesirable conflicting interests and jousting for power. AA also provides a ready resource of books and pamphlets, guidelines, non-sectarian prayers, and many cogent slogans — such as 'One Day At A Time' and 'Easy Does it', 'Keep it Simple', 'Let Go and Let God', 'Live and Let Live'.

AA sobriety treatment plans and follow-up programs are based upon almost one hundred years of experience. Where these can be adapted, Native people have found no reason to re-invent the wheel. They have also found many willing hands among AA members from outside the community who have helped Native people set up their own programs.

In recognition of the special needs of indigenous people, including the need for self-determination, Native directors and staff have significantly indigenised Native rehabilitation and sobriety programs to suit specific client groups — teenagers, adults, inmates, city dwellers, remote community reserves, and so forth.

Each program has its own characteristics. The versatility and crafting of programs to specific client groups has led to many exciting developments in Native sobriety. Some groups have published beautifully illustrated leaflets and other resource materials to be used in their programs (Weber 1976).

On reserves, regular meetings of support groups provide a caring and secure environment for the expression of problems between community members who seek sobriety together. Annual Pow Wows, or special 'self-discovery' traditional camps in peaceful natural surroundings, enable people from other reserves and other provinces and states to come together to share their culture, experiences, and discoveries.

The Poundmaker's Lodge has a community feel within the treatment centre itself. The directors will tell you that the bedrock of the program is AA. But its extensive cultural, educational, life-skills, counselling, and recreational components which draw upon the essence of Indian socio-spiritual thinking and practice, make it unique.

Round dances, handgames, sweat lodges, pipe ceremonies, and Pow Wows were dying, until they were reintroduced by Poundmaker's. Part of our course was to teach these again. We used Elders all along in this (Eric Shirt, Poundmaker's Lodge, interview 20 September 1990)

Native ownership of programs generates commitment and enthusiasm among staff, workers, and participants. Those who have worked with these programs say they have 'changed their lives'.

The cultural aspect of Native sobriety initiatives has also proved to be a great strength in American Indian programs. On a recent visit to Australia, 'Grandmother Kitty' (tribal name: Deek Keel She Wa), a graceful white haired elder of the Lakota Sioux tribe and founder of one of the first alcohol counselling program for Native Americans shared these ideas. Treatment, she explained, needed to focus upon cultural identity. A knowledge of tribal values and traditions restored self-esteem which had been lost through addiction.

In a series of seminars in Sydney and Brisbane on the teachings of the Wolf Clan Lodge of the Senca people 'Grandmother Kitty' said:

Alcohol was controlling me, I wasn't controlling it.

I knew in my centre that there had to be another way and that way meant getting back to our roots, getting back to our traditions and our ceremonies, being just who we are. The problem lay in me trying to be someone that I was not.

We get back to the basics, we get back to the fact that each one of us is a sacred being, that we are related to all things, that we need to purify our bodies, we need to get off the concrete and be aware of that which is around us, the way we grew up.

The Wolf Clan Lodge, she said, is not a religion, but a way of life. 'It's so people can tap into their own knowingness and not depend on others'. It is teaching people 'the pathway of peace' (Bogle, *Australian*, 11 April 1991).

THE ALKALI LAKE AND O'CHIESE RESERVES STORIES

In 1975 a revolution of community detoxification began in Alkali Lake, an Indian reserve of about 500 people in northern British Columbia, when a small girl told her mother she didn't want to go home with her because her parents drank too much. For fear of losing her daughter that mother, Phyllis Chelsea, decided to sober up. Over a fifteen-year period most of that community turned to follow.

The detoxification of Alkali Lake occurred through a long and sometimes painful process of learning, rehabilitation, and mutual support. Cultural revival, community-based healing workshops, and support group formation, were an important part of whole-community recovery. Alkali Lake become a model community and paved the way for many other North American Native communities. When new people left the reserve to undertake treatment, community members gave them every support. They looked after their children and even fixed up and painted their homes, so they could look forward to a new and positive environment to come home to.

In January 1985 Chief Theresa Strawberry, inspired by the Alkali Lake story, decided to give up drinking and enrolled herself in Poundmaker's Lodge where she learnt to help herself through the understanding of alcohol abuse. On her return home to O'Chiese reserve, Alberta, she threw herself into encouraging other members towards the path of sobriety. After only two years 85% of the people on O'Chiese reserve had become involved in sobriety programs. Here is her story:

> After returning from treatment [Chief] Strawberry began to study the problem of alcohol abuse in an effort to find a way out of the alcohol trap. Previously she tried to solve the problem through creating jobs and economic development projects. But again, in the long run alcoholism affected the success of these new ventures. Strawberry began to realize she had to attack alcoholism head on.

Chief Strawberry formed a team made up of a social worker, alcohol program director, the band council manager, a psychologist, and other band members. They met with the directors of Nechi and Poundmaker's Lodge, the chief of Alkali Lake, and Paul Hanks, a pioneer in a mobile treatment program:

> Strawberry and the team decided the mobile treatment was their goal as they felt the reserve could not afford to wait for admission into regular treatment programs. During the team meetings, the new team began to learn peer support and develop a group vision as well as focusing energy on wellness. Then chief and council passed a band council resolution prior to their own election which stated all council members must go for treatment within six months of their election.

The council felt that it was essential that leaders became sober and healthy role models for the rest of the community. For several months Poundmaker's Lodge representatives came to O'Chiese to support fledgling AA groups. Children needing treatment for inhalant abuse were identified. An Al-a-Teen group was set up. The mobile treatment began with sweat lodge ceremonies for both men and women. Other community members assisted by organising baby-sitting, cooking meals, and running a bus service. To celebrate the opening of the mobile treatment centre a sober dance was held. Almost everyone who attended stayed sober.

Thirty people graduated from the first mobile treatment program. Follow-up treatment and after-care facilities, to reinforce sobriety, were organised. A range of community development, training, and educational programs was planned with the objective of building a 'mentally, physically, and spiritually healthy' community. A video of the O'Chiese experience, entitled *A Love Stronger than Poison*, was released in November 1987 (Crossingham 1987: 6).

'EVERYBODY'S PROBLEM'

Everyone of us has been affected in some way or another by alcoholism and drug abuse — even if we do not have a problem ourselves. Our liberty and the quality of our life, the way we regard strangers, our relationships with neighbours and family members are tainted by alcohol and drug problems within the wider community.

If we live in a 'high crime' region, or if we are surrounded by patterns of recurring violence, our entire outlook on life is restricted. It is not safe to go for a walk after dark. It is not safe to invite people into our home. It is not safe to talk back to family members who are drunk. The kids aren't safe around a particular individual or group of people.

Personal accounts of these experiences paint a dark picture of the life of the alcoholic, and of those who have lived with, or grown up with, alcoholism. We read posters and leaflets down at the council office, or at the doctor's telling us how drugs and alcohol affect our body. We personally know of young lives which have been wasted or lost through alcohol-related accidents or violence. We are familiar with the long-term effects of abuse. We may have stood by helplessly and watched the health and happiness of a loved one or friend gradually decline. How we suffer personally and spiritually, and how this affects the soul of our people over time — all this saddens us.

It is exciting to hear about communities which are learning to pull together for community healing. Some Aboriginal and Torres Strait Islander groups have set up Sobriety Societies. We hear about North American Indian programs — like Poundmaker's Lodge and the Nechi Institute in Alberta — which concentrate upon holistic healing and alcohol awareness training. We see video documentaries of whole villages — such as Alkali Lake and the O'Chiese reserve — which have restored health and well-being to 85–90% of their people through community detoxification programs.[2] When we hear of these things we are given the opportunity to turn our despair into a vision of victory. The first step is to recognise that we are not alone. For every community problem there is a community solution. It starts with caring about each other. As one community worker at Alkali Lake said:

> The message which has gone out is loud and clear: 'The condition of the soul of our people is everybody's problem'. 'Alcohol abuse and violence is everybody's problem ... *Everybody's Problem*'.

◆ ◆ ◆

[1] There are many books and booklets available on the subjects of Alcoholics Anonymous, Co-dependency, Adult Children of Alcoholics, Families and Alcoholism, Physical and Emotional Abuse, and problems related to addiction which affect people's lives, such as work, love, health, intimacy, marriage and children. ... (see resource Materials sections at the end of this book.)

[2] See the videos: *Honour of All — the Alkali Lake Story*, Part I and II; and *A Love Stronger Than Poison*, which document the stories of Alkali Lake, British Columbia and the O'Chiese reserve, Alberta.

Chapter seven

'BREAKING THE CYCLE': SETTING UP ALCOHOL TREATMENT PROGRAMS

The women who came to the workshops had no
historical reason to trust. As children they had
learned that their trust would be taken advantage of.
And yet in the groups, they trusted (Bass and Davis
1988:14).

SETTING UP A TREATMENT CENTRE

Towards the end of 1990 I joined members of ATSIC in discussions with officials of the National Campaign Against Drug Abuse (NCADA) for the hiring of Eric Shirt to conduct a feasibility study for the setting up of an Aboriginal Treatment Centre in the New South Wales south coast town of Nowra.

During his second trip to Australia in April 1991, Eric Shirt urged communities to run 'proposal workshops', where people could learn to develop good proposals to put forward to governments demonstrating the need for alcohol treatment. Following this, he believed, funding for 'feasibility studies' was vital. Such studies would investigate and present statistical evidence upon current social situations, states of health, and size of the addicted population expected to be serviced by the programs. Feasibility studies should also commission the architectural planning, siting, and facility needs of a suitable centre designed to meet these needs.

Thirdly, Shirt felt the communities needed to create their own action teams, and support groups, which would implement their project. This involved networking with government and health professionals, indigenous peoples, and community leaders in the setting up of comprehensive and culturally relevant alcohol counsellor training programs. Programs in counsellor training should continue to evolve, as a function of staff input and experience, once a treatment centre has been established.

The key to the success of the Poundmaker-type model is twofold. First, it was an indigenous initiative; and secondly, in Canada it attracted the *sustained commitment of governments* (both federal and provincial) to culturally relevant programs for community detoxification. The Poundmaker's experience has demonstrated that *only rigorous and high quality programs of treatment* will achieve this end.

Treatment centres need to be set up, staffed by, and run by Aboriginal people, for Aboriginal people. They should facilitate the development of sophisticated and effective programs of treatment. They should be housed within newly constructed, well equipped, and fully funded facilities, which allow for ongoing exploration, development, and training in addiction counselling techniques.

Aboriginal people should not even entertain a project for addiction treatment and rehabilitation if it means that two or three semi-trained counsellors struggle to provide services to too many clients from a tin shed or abandoned hostel.

Under no circumstances should treatment centres double-up as alternative, overnight detainment facilities for drunken persons picked up by police. (These facilities are needed, but they are not the same thing). Treatment comprises the *voluntary* submission of individuals to a highly concentrated process of personal, emotional, and spiritual healing. A nightly inflow of unwilling drunks would be extremely disruptive to this process. Sobering-up services must be provided from a different venue.

DOONOOCH SELF HEALING CENTRE, NSW

Since 1989 there has been growing interest in the setting up of Aboriginal Treatment Centres throughout Australia. Aboriginal representatives from several states have either visited Canada to look at similar Native-run programs, or have met and spoken with Canadian Indian alcohol workers on their visits to Australia. As the Native Canadian history and situation parallels the experience of Aboriginal and Torres Strait Islander people, there is much to gain from this exchange. Some communities have been so keen that they have raised their own funds to seek more information. Several Aboriginal individuals have undergone treatment or training at Poundmaker's Lodge and the Nechi Institute, and other Aboriginal organisations have brought Indian representatives to Australia to consult with them on the development of programs here.

The independent action taken by the Nowra, NSW, people produced the 'Doonooch Self Healing Centre' — an alcohol and drug healing and rehabilitation program based upon Aboriginal spirituality, culture and community healing approaches. A central figure in this activity was Bobby McLeod, himself a recovered alcoholic:[1]

> Bobby worked quietly for several years with Aboriginal people to help them to get off their alcohol and drug dependency. In mid 1990, with the assistance of his brother and several Aboriginal people, all of whom gained stability through Bobby's efforts, Bobby formally established the Doonooch Self Healing Aboriginal Corporation and started a residential treatment facility for drug and alcohol abuse in Callala Beach. This facility closed in November 1992 due to the lack of consistent and sufficient funding. Doonooch moved its administration to the South Coast Aboriginal Medical Services and finally re-established its operation

at its current location in May 1993 when funding was obtained through
ATSIC (notes provided to the author, Benson 12 June 1993).

Between 1990 and 1993 Doonooch received 'tremendous' support from national and
international organisations, such as World Vision, World Indigenous Science
Network, Community Aid Abroad, Uniting Church of Australia, Qantas Airlines, and
ATSIC. Doonooch also sought out expert advice and training from a number of
private indigenous organisations, such as Poundmaker's Lodge, the Wolf Clan Lodge,
and the Native Counselling Services of Alberta to help them develop culturally
sensitive and Aboriginal appropriate programs in the areas of treatment, corrections,
and social services.[2]

The six founding members who set up this program the director, Bobby McLeod,
explained, had themselves 'experienced a profound transformation into a healed,
positive lifestyle, having been caught in negative lifestyles such as alcoholism,
violence, and other sorrows' (McLeod 1992:1). By June 1992 some 30 people had
found healing through the Doonooch self-healing methods. The centre also claimed a
'100% success rate' in continued commitment among its staff, Board of Directors and
participants, and was attracting the attention of several outside agencies:

> The success of our Centre is being recognised by public hospitals and
> courts, with a growing number of referrals, and the Centre's capacity is
> constrained only by physical resources. We will be able to accept referrals
> once basic facilities are constructed (McLeod 1992:1).

Doonooch has now turned to government and charitable organisations to fund the
purchase of 550 acres of land in the Budawang ranges, southwest of Nowra, for the
development of a major healing and rehabilitation facility which could meet this need.
Negotiations with ATSIC for the funding and construction of an alcohol and drug
treatment program in Nerriga are currently being finalised.

In addition, Doonooch is seeking to develop a minimum security forestry camp
for Aboriginal offenders to be jointly managed by Doonooch and the Native
Counselling Services of Alberta (NCSA). With NCSA'S twenty years of experience in
Native-run corrections (Hazlehurst 1993), the partners are seeking to develop a
'Treatment through Healing Correctional Program' specifically for Aboriginal people.

Those involved in Doonooch believe that these programs, along with other
initiatives presently being explored — such as parenting programs, midwifery, job
creation, economic development, court work and justice panels — will lead the way
towards Aboriginal people gaining greater control over their own futures (Benson
1993).

CAAAPU TREATMENT PROGRAM, NT

After arranging initial training sessions, the Central Australian Aboriginal Alcohol Planning Unit hired Eric Shirt as a full-time consultant and actively sought the establishment of Aboriginal alcohol treatment and training programs in Alice Springs. Since October 1992 the CAAAPU Treatment Program has offered a four weeks residential treatment program. An Aboriginal alcohol training program is also in place. These two programs are headed by the visionary Aboriginal alcohol workers, Doug and Lana Abott. Initial funding of half a million dollars was provided by ATSIC, with the Northern Territory government providing salaries for the six alcohol counsellors and four other staff involved in this project. But the goal of CAAAPU, since it started on this course, has always been to raise at least five million dollars for the establishment of a major Aboriginal Treatment Centre in Alice Springs.

The enormous interest which the CAAAPU initiative has sparked throughout the country is an indication of the urgent need and the readiness of Aboriginal people for the establishment of Aboriginal alcohol treatment centres in every state and territory. The time has never been more right for the support and implementation of such a strategy. Support should be sought from every quarter — the community, state and federal governments, health, education and employment agencies, the private sector, businesses, private foundations, charities, and churches. Australia, now, certainly has reached the stage of having *The Right Place, the Right Time, the Right People*.

PLANNING AND ORGANISING A TREATMENT CENTRE

The fundamental structural components of the treatment programs being run in North America are as follows:

- Group supports
- Lectures
- Behavioural change exercises
- Counselling
- Personal growth and self knowledge
- Dynamics of attitudes and relationships
- Empowering experiences
- Recreation
- Leisure
- Information

The success of addiction programs will also depend upon whether there is a network of support waiting for these persons on their return to their communities. In the Alkali Lake experience, some strong individuals were even able to get off alcohol without treatment, so long as they received therapy and support from within their families and communities. But few are likely to remain sober, even after an excellent program of treatment, if they return to an unsupportive home environment — particularly where non-drinkers are seen to be 'traitors'. Ideally, both treatment centres and a concentration of community support towards sobriety must be present. Working to secure commitment at both levels is critical.

OVER-COMING NEGATIVE THINKING

> … no one should glorify himself over another; … no one should look upon another with scorn and contempt and no one should deprive or oppress a fellow-creature. All must be considered as submerged in the ocean of God's mercy. We must associate with all humanity in gentleness and kindliness. We must love all with the love of the heart ('Abdu'l-Baha 1922/1982).

Indian communities have shared something else with Aboriginal people: that all too common problem of jealousy and mean spiritedness, where the efforts of individual Aborigines or groups are sabotaged by the criticism and malignance of other Aboriginal people.

In a reference to problems of negative thinking and petty mindedness Eric Shirt had a favourite saying — I heard him use it many times: 'If five hundred thousand people all say the wrong thing, it's still the wrong thing'.

Eric Shirt shared with the *Healing Our People* conference how a change of attitude has had a powerful effect in reversing this trend. Focusing on alcoholism as the common enemy had helped to galvanise people into a positive force. But, further to this, Canadian Native people are now beginning to hold each other accountable for giving mutual support to Native efforts. It is a case of reminding people that 'Hey, we're all on the same team', he said:

> Alcoholism kills … This illness removes everything. It removes your culture, it removes your family, it removes your jobs, it removes your health and finally it removes your life — no 'ifs' no 'buts' about it. It is the number one killer and you have some very concerned Aboriginal people in this community that want to start up treatment in this country.

But Aboriginal and non-Aboriginal people need to support these people:
to say, 'listen, let's give you a hand, because we would like to see people
get well, because we want them to be contributing members in their
community, and we don't want them to be dying on the river banks just
outside of town!' [3]

I would encourage everybody to support these people, because treatment
centres are about saving human life ... But if you bad mouth that centre
... We have a saying among us alcohol workers. Those who don't help,
but who just sit back and criticise we treat this as *high treason*! You don't
criticise people who are saving our people's lives (Eric Shirt, video taped
interview and notes from the *Healing Our People* forum, Alice Springs,
April 1991).

Ten years earlier, in *Walkabout to Nowhere*, Doug Milera also pointed out the
importance of Aboriginal rehabilitation and treatment, and the need for the Aboriginal
community to get behind those people who were running these programs, or
attempting to set them up:

The operation of some places may prove difficult, but the difficulties
could be overcome. I believe that finding sobriety is as easy or as hard as
the individual decides for himself, [but] *for those who are trying — don't
knock them* (Milera 1980: 36).

Why *do* people 'knock' those who are trying to save lives by overcoming
community problems? Probably the most powerful reason for this is the *habit of
negativity*. Addiction can come in many forms. We may think we are more intelligent if
we are not addicted to alcohol, cigarettes or drugs. But we might be just as addicted to
hate, blaming of others, and negative self-images. Self-deception can be even more
insidious.

The concept of 'life force', is common to many indigenous societies. From the
perspective of one healer:

The life force pours out of you through the holes you create in your life
through what I call addiction ... Usually the worst are emotional
addictions, such as addiction to sadness, to chaos, to a feeling that we're
not good enough ... I believe that all beings on this planet want to
become enlightened, one way or another. Yet at the same time it's the
thing they're most afraid of, usually unconsciously ... The reasons you
have the addiction is to bleed off the life force, so that there is no danger
of ever becoming enlightened (Andrews 1989:44).

The best way to overcome the grip of negativity is to analyse and to dismantle this habit. In one of their first exercises, working groups may wish to explore the historical source of some of this negativity. Knowing *where we have come from and where we are now* is an important step in making empowering decisions for the future. 'Healing comes through unlocking the stories, and letting them be told in their entirety — rewriting the true history' (NCSA 1993: 37).

But the process should not stop here. It is paramount that the connection between 'taking back control' and 'taking responsibility' for our actions is made. When it comes to family violence, wrote Esther Supernault, in her NCSA manual *It's a Family Affair*, the blaming has to stop.

Responsibility for our actions sometimes frightens us, especially when it forces us to face our own inadequacies, insecurities and dishonesty. How much easier it is to blame, to point fingers away from ourselves. Then we can settle back and away from commitment.

> But in the end, we lose. We never grow or learn. We stay stuck in the rut of indecision, filled with muddied thoughts that block the free flow of our own creative spontaneity (Esther Supernault in NCSA 1993: vi).

But 'how freeing it is to grasp that vehicle Change', continued Esther Supernault:

> How exhilarating it is to pick up speed, upward and onward, the freedom winds on our faces, our eyes clinging to the distant horizon. It matters not what it holds for us; only that we get there, and grow, and learn, and love and laugh along the away. As we should, as we were meant to do (Esther Supernault, NCSA 1993: vi).

When we are confronted by the dark night of our despair, unable to find our only way home through this fearsome darkness, self-responsibility is the torch lying at our feet. It is there — for the taking. We only need pick it up. After we have charted a course, we can show others the way we have come.

> Healing is a holistic approach beyond generations involving the individual, the family, the community and nation (NCSA 1993: 37).

LIFE-STYLE ISSUES

On the subject of alcohol and drug dependency two Aboriginal participants at the *'Window of Opportunity'*, First National Congress on *'An Intersectoral Approach to Drug*

Related Problems in our Society', held in Adelaide 2–6 December 1991, made these observations:

> Why do Aborigines drink? They've got to be given reasons *not* to drink. We can't do it on our own. We need all the help we can get (Maureen Smith, Staff Development Officer, Department of Community Services, Sydney).

> We need to talk about the pain. We need to share the pain. We need to heal our inner selves — and help to heal others (Jean Jans, Community Resource Officer, Department of Family Services and Aboriginal and Islander Affairs, Gulf of Carpentaria).

People suffering from alcohol, illicit or prescription drugs, or substance abuse share similar problems. It is common for them to have feelings of isolation, detachment from reality, personal alienation and loss of trust towards family members. They need more comprehensive treatment than simply 'drying out'. Programs will need to focus upon needs for social reconstruction and social reintegration. Alcohol and drug workers themselves will need to understand the life-style issues underlying patterns of addiction. They will need to develop special skills for dealing with these processes.

LOCAL INTERVENTION

For many Aboriginal individuals and communities, alcohol use may have become the primary coping response to a range of personal, social, and economic stresses which surround them. Added to this, is the learned drinking behaviour of family and friends and the powerful pull of peer group drinking.

Any project for intervention into the cycles of addiction will need to begin with a good analysis of the background of local drinking, and its current patterns. We need to know 'what's in it for them', in order to develop a program which will meet those *same needs and motivations* in a less harmful way. Here is an example of a community analysis of their particular problem:

People in this community drink because

People are saying	*Problem Analysis*
• 'life is boring here'	• something to do
• 'parents/brothers drink'	• learned behaviour
• 'its exciting/fun'	• social stimulation
• 'want to be with friends'	• brotherhood/belonging
• 'my friends expect it'	• peer pressure
• 'people relax'	• escape from stress
• 'makes me feel good'	• low self-esteem
• 'makes me feel important'	• feeling downtrodden
• 'I feel strong'	• feeling powerless
• 'to show white fellas'	• stating opposition

Community-based programs should respond to all of these identified needs and issues. They should provide a sense of belonging, and a sense of purpose to people's lives. They should raise people's self-esteem and help to empower individuals and communities. Programs should also be fun and exciting, informative, enriching, and forward thinking. They should help teach people about themselves, their illnesses, their cultural strengths, and directions for well-being.

Community-based programs have the added advantage of sustaining the emotional and spiritual needs of a people. Once people are sober, these initiatives will surely lead to other developments within the community. In their examination of public health issues Torzillo and Kerr were certain of a 'critical link' between health service planning, community development, and political action. In their work they could see a direct relationship between initiatives which 'enhance identity and cohesion, increase the community skills base, provide economic development and strengthen political power' and Aboriginal health improvement (Torzillo and Kerr 1991: 332, 327).

Eric Shirt explains how this, in fact, occurred in Alberta:

> ... twenty years ago there were no businesses on our reserve. There were no people with any kind of university degree. There was high unemployment. Our culture had died. Our ceremonies had died. Our power had died. There was very very low activity. Just alcoholism and death — that was the destiny of our reserve.

> And then we started getting our people well through these treatment centres. Now on that reserve twenty years later we have Indian people that own businesses, gas stations, pool halls, restaurants, school bus companies, construction companies, farms. And we have over 70 people

with university degrees on our reserve of 3000 people — every thing
from teachers to lawyers. That's in 20 years. Why? Because if we get
people well they want to improve. They want to contribute in their
community. They want to be helpful ... but they can't if they're ill.

... when we get our people well they take care of their housing problem.
They take care of their child problem, take care of their employment
problem. They take care of their education problem, because that's the
nature of the human being — that's the nature of Indian people *to take
care of things* (Eric Shirt, video taped interview, April 1991).

In the long run, the option of alcoholism cannot compete with the attraction of
individual and community empowerment. Community awareness, and education
about these options, is an important part of intervention. As alcoholism represents a
'vicious cycle' of despair, violence and ill health, which can affect several generations,
intervention should begin at *several* points at once. There is no *one way* of doing things.
An action team may wish to start with the adult men, the women, or the children and
youth. They may wish to involve health workers, the school, community police, youth
workers, the church, the Women's Resource Centre, or the community council.

It is true that the best prevention of alcohol and drug abuse is 'DON'T START'.
Therefore, an action group might decide to begin with young people. They may like to
develop teaching programs, videos, posters, recreational outings, or cultural programs
for children in schools. Or a group might decide to kick off their prevention program
with a big *Community Care* education campaign — such as a series of drug awareness
days, getting outside agencies to contribute.

Individual intervention is, perhaps, the most critical and the most complex strategy.
This is where community support groups play a most powerful role, and why
effective alcohol treatment programs will be essential. The Mountain View
Rehabilitation Centre, Pennsylvania, USA, outlined some steps to individual
intervention. Addicted persons, they say, need a safe place, a forum to meet and to
discuss together their disease:

Interveners should show genuine respect and concern for the addicted
person while they show them the truth of their situation. Wherever
possible, evidence should be linked directly to the drinking or drug-
using. The tone of the confrontation should be non-judgemental.

The evidence should be presented in explicit detail to give the addict a
clear overall view of his or her behaviour during a given period of time.

The purpose of the presentation of this material is to have the alcoholic see and accept enough reality about his condition so that, however grudgingly, he or she will accept help (Mountain View [nd]).

'WALKING THE WALK'

The staff motto of Poundmaker's Lodge is that people must not only 'talk the talk', they must also 'walk the walk'. At Alkali Lake, and other communities which have begun community detoxification, Chiefs and Community Council members are asked to set an example to their people. After a program has begun they are given six months to seek treatment for their alcoholism, or to resign as community councillors. This is not only drastic, it is also a powerfully effective strategy. It soon shows up those leaders who have a personal or financial investment in the continued misery and addiction of their people.

Leaders committed to the 'bad old ways' will soon fall away. New leaders, those men and women with a real commitment to the future of their people, will soon emerge to take their place. Even a small action group can take this courageous stand — so long as they stick together as one voice. Just watch things start hopping after such an announcement!

A NEW IDEA OF HEALTH

In the splendid book of Anangu Pitjantjatjara Lands paintings and thought, *Anangu Way*, produced by Healthy Aboriginal Life Team (HALT 1991) it was pointed out that the English word 'health' has become associated with the doctors and nurses who have provided medical services to communities:

> In this way, 'health' has become closely linked to concepts, practices and institutions of Western medicine ... At one time people came to think of 'health' as exclusively the business of medical workers: synonymous with the practices of preventing and treating diseases and injuries (HALT 1991: 2).[4]

This assigning the business of disease, injuries, and death to a specialised group of outsiders has not been particularly 'healthy' for Aboriginal communities over the years. It has formed a powerful component of welfare dependency and conditioning, apparently absolving Aboriginal people from personal and community responsibility. According to HALT this 'narrow view of health has recently been reappraised by many people, both in and outside the professions':

A new idea of health is emerging which embraces many facets of life, and
extends its business far beyond the province of medical professionals. It
requires a different language: suggesting that health is neither an entity
nor a state; but a process of living. The passive recipients ... become
themselves the principal agents of its achievement within the alternative
paradigm (HALT 1991: 2).

The Anangu concept of health, shared so beautifully in *Anangu Way*, draws upon a
rich reservoir of traditional ideas and practice as guidelines to healthier living. It uses,
as its 'core metaphor', the concept of the life *'journey'*; integrating references to diet,
hunting, parenting, ceremonial celebrations of life, grief in death, and of Aboriginal
kinship with the land and all species of plants and animals. It affirms the integrity and
autonomy of the person, individual ownership of the 'story-line', the profound bond
between 'countrymen', the expression of kindness to one another, and the sorrows of
parting.

Several of the paintings illustrate, explicitly, how illness has arisen from
Aboriginal exposure to the invasive influences of Western society, and unhealthy
choices of alcohol abuse, petrol sniffing, and eating processed foods. *Anangu Way* calls
upon traditional skills and cultural understandings which advance a life-world filled
with meaning, potency, and vitality. It also reflects the treatment/prevention debate
challenging health and social service practitioners today:

The message of the paintings is, rather, the canny insight that health will
be better promoted by affirmation of the skills and concepts that advance
it, than by emphasis on the factors that impair it. ... Such Anangu ideas
pervade the paintings: statements of an ideology of health which is
integrative and whole (HALT 1991: 2-3).

PARTNERSHIP, EMPOWERMENT, AND PEOPLE OF VISION

For Aboriginal and Islander communities to take responsibility for, and control of,
problems of ill health, addiction, crime, and violence, for them to become masters of
their own destinies, is a revolutionary concept. It is of great interest to Aboriginal
people, but does not sit well with some of those in authority — despite their protests
to the contrary. This is understandable, as many government agencies which deal with
Aboriginal people are still inherently paternalistic.

But it is particularly disheartening when the debate is dismissed by those in
authority with the assertion that, by 'community control of community problems',

Aboriginal people are suggesting that they provide all health care for themselves.

The authoritarian and patronising manner of some hospital staff in remote regions is one area of Australian race relations which has been among the last to be challenged. Threat or no threat of withdrawal of services, the 'old colonials' of the medical profession will simply have to review their attitudes and manner towards their Aboriginal clients. No doubt, as Aboriginal people seek community control over the very social pathologies which result in medical problems, there will be some churlishness and feelings of intrusion in some part of the medical profession.

Australian government agencies have wielded enormous power over the lives of Aboriginal families and communities in the past, but have not been answerable to them in any democratic sense. Bureaucracies and institutions which have held such authority have little experience in *releasing* power to the people they have managed for decades. In the Bjelke-Peterson period in Queensland, for example, requests and appeals from some Aboriginal community councils to the Department of Justice to legitimate the changing and consolidation of council by-laws, were still unanswered after six years.

After so much lethargy, indifference, and rhetoric, the only acceptable condition for joint problem solving between white and black will be one that guarantees increasing arrangements for Aboriginal self-determination and community control of local problems. Most officials and agencies are sensitive to the history and background of this today, but they will need to do more than pay lip service to the principle of Aboriginal self-determination. *Self determination is more than a moral code upheld in principle by federal and international law. We have to work towards giving the principle 'hands and feet' at the community level.*

When public servants or other workers find themselves leaving communities feeling disappointed after yet another brilliant proposal has been rejected — convinced that Aboriginal people 'don't want to help themselves' — then maybe some element in the transaction is missing! When communities see the need to take back control over their own lives, and are given the means and the motivation for becoming strong and autonomous, only then will genuine offers for partnership be made. Why would anyone want to stand in the way of this process?

The destructive aspects of the culture of opposition, so much a part of the Aboriginal psyche today, will not be easily replaced without some powerfully compelling incentive. It must be the kind of incentive which fulfils goals for autonomy more effectively than existing sets of relations and practices. It must be a replacement which arouses the Aboriginal will to survive. It must satisfy the longing for liberation and dignity, and strengthen the presently fragile filaments of culture, identity, and social cohesion.

The movement for community empowerment does all of these things. If the excitement aroused by workshops and seminars already held in Queensland and

Northern Territory is any indication, this approach promises to generate new levels of Aboriginal commitment and to produce new moulds of contemporary leadership.

Some social scientists may be critical of activities for social repair and regeneration — repudiating them as a form of 'social engineering'. But it was the earlier social engineering by settler, colonial, and welfare interests which so dramatically disturbed the physical location, culture, family, and community of Aboriginal and Islander people. What are we left with if we leave the present social situation to continue unattended? Soon, as Langton pointed out, there will be no Aboriginal culture or society left to protect (in Balendra 1990: 23).

Social engineering is a fundamental right which needs to be reclaimed by oppressed populations. It is a fertile, exciting, and empowering concept. If Aboriginal people wish to rebuild their society — knocking out the 'old rotten bits' and building up those aspects of their culture which *they* want to preserve — then let the designers, draftspersons, and workers be Aboriginal people of the greatest capacity. Strengthen them with new skills in community healing, negotiation, team-work, and action planning. Let these 'engineers' be people of vision.

> In the past we were happy and free from sickness; and in the future we will become strong and healthy again (HALT 1991).

◆ ◆ ◆

[1] 'Doonooch, meaning Owl or Keeper of the Night, is the sacred totem and protector of the Monaro Tribe. Some ten years ago Bobby McLeod, a Monaro who was a chronic alcoholic and always in trouble with the law, went through a healing process with the help of Elders and Aboriginal spirituality, and a return to his Aboriginal culture and values. He learned to direct his energies toward developing a self healing concept focused at promoting individual, family and community health. In 1986, Bobby committed himself to assisting other Aboriginal people experiencing difficulties similar to those he went through' (notes provided to the author, Benson 12 June 1993).

[2] During 1991 and 1992 Eric Shirt from Poundmaker's Lodge acted as a consultant in the setting up of the program. In April 1991 the Native American elder, 'Grandmother Kitty', visited and gave advice. By mid-1992 Alan Benson, Assistant Executive Director, Native Counselling Services of Alberta (NCSA), was a regular adviser with Doonooch Self Healing Corporation.

3 During his six week stay in Alice Springs in 1991 Shirt was shocked to hear of the death of ten Aboriginal people on the Alice Springs river banks where most of the drinking occurred. 'Do you think those people wanted that?', he asked a gathering. 'Do you think those people wanted to die alone, in fear, sick and in pain? I know from experience that every time we've set up Indian treatment centres ... people come to them because they *want* to get well ...' (Eric Shirt, video taped interview, April 1991).

4 The paintings and stories recorded in the *Anangu Way* come from the land inhabited by the Pitjantjatjara, Yankunytjatjara and Ngaanyatjarra people (Anangu), Northern Territory.

PART 3

Chapter eight

'THE JOURNEY TO WHOLENESS': SETTING UP COMMUNITY HEALING PROGRAMS

[O]ur highest duty is to follow wholeness, peace and the kindness of our being, to treat others fairly, and to help where we can help ... Healing is therefore accomplished through love and *is* love (Hugh Prather 1989:13-14).

A SPIRITUAL SOLUTION

In her presentation to the Domestic Violence Conference in Adelaide, May 1990, the Maori speaker Meri Balzer said that: 'If we are denied spiritually, it will have a domino effect. It will eventually affect our mental health, our emotional well-being and our physical health':

> Until we understand 'health' in its many facets, we will never understand abuse. Communities need to look holistically at those things which will make them healthy. Doctors, professionals, social workers look always at ill health, and try to solve it. This is hard work. We need to look at good health issues (Meri Balzer, Domestic Violence Conference, Adelaide, May 1990).

The special bonus of *healthy living programs* is the resurgence of traditional values and culture. According to Hopi legend: 'The Indian people will be in our night time and we will come into our daytime and become leaders when the eagle lands on the moon'. For many years this legend was a riddle which no one understood. Then, when in 1969 American astronauts landed on the moon, they sent back their first message to earth: 'the eagle has landed'. During that week the first Native alcohol rehabilitation program was opened in North America and 'the concept of alcohol treatment which involves the whole community spread like "wildfire" throughout the continent' (*Windspeaker*, 13 November 1987).

> This resurgence of Indian people was prophesied in the Hopi legend many years ago and it's coming true now. Not only have these communities turned their backs on alcohol, but they have returned to their Elders, they have reintroduced their culture, they participate in the sweat lodge and have again become the people the Great Spirit meant them to be (Editor's note, *Windspeaker*, 13 November 1987: 3)

FINDING THE 'WARRIOR' WITHIN

> The prophecy is that we would go to our Elders in this time of rebirth.
> But they would be blind, their mouths sewn together, and have not ears.
> It's true. They have been brainwashed and struggling to come back. They
> still have to be healed (Vera Martin, Elder, NCSA 1993:34).

Finding solutions to the 'too hard' issues of alcoholism, violence, and child abuse, requires more than courage and strength. It requires a deep sense of caring, a heightened consciousness of spiritual principles which apply to all people and to all living things, and a powerful belief in the future. With a full awareness of who we are, and where we are going, we can assault any problem — directly, at its source.

Community development and innovative preventative programs need not be expensive, but they do need regular support. In terms of human suffering, and measured against the costs of running police and prison services, they are extremely cost-effective and have both short-term and long-term gains. Throwing more money at the criminal justice administration will, in the end, do little to reduce family breakdown or crime. What is needed is a brave and assertive community response.

There are definite links between negativity and failure, between positivity and action, between planned action and success. If we want to take action we need to harness our personal and community energies. We need to overcome negative attitudes and behaviours and nurture, in their place, positive thought and action. With a strong conviction of our future we are less likely to allow negative thinking to get in our way.

Perhaps what men and women need now is a 'Warrior's heart'. Moore and Gillette (1992) said that the Warrior is a part of everyone's psyche or soul. Not for the expression of aggression or rage, but for the expression of courage, honour, chivalry, and nobility. Peaceful Warriors are needed to 'pledge their loyalty to their workplace, communities and families':

> The Warrior within encourages every man and woman to take up his or
> her sword and fight to preserve, to provide for, and to extend the things
> and the people he or she cares for and believes in (Moore and Gillette
> 1992: x–xi).

> Native men, and women, can stand for what they believe is right,
> protecting their children and honouring one another's gift of life and
> renewal to the community and nation (Supernault 1993: 39).

Once we have found our Warrior's heart, all the opposition in the world will not deter us from our chosen path. We will have the clear sight and vision of the Peaceful Warrior, and we will be able to measure the relative worthlessness of this opposition. We will recognise 'noise' when we hear it, and we will move on to create better things in our lives irrespective of this 'noise' of opposition. In time, the sheer powerfulness of this philosophy will attract many others (See Workbook 8, 'The Warrior Journey: Dance-Meditation').

BECOMING A 'HEALER'

In their manual on family violence, *It's A Family Affair* (1993), the Native Counselling Services pointed out that, in communities, 'the healers have to heal themselves *first*, before they can help anyone else'. Most elders, community counsellors, social workers, para-professionals, and community members have all been caught up in the history and trauma of residential schooling, loss of family and culture, alcoholism, and violence. Eric Shirt, founding member of Poundmaker's Lodge, spoke about the need for caring people in their programs. Treatment ultimately hinges upon participation in the human experience of caring, sharing, and helping, he pointed out. He outlined the essence of this important role:

> I want to give you one word of advice. And it is the best advice
> I can give you.
>
> It will make you better as a Native person.
> It will make you more effective in your role as a HEALER.
>
> It will improve your standing in your community,
> And it will even advance your career.
>
> • *That is, that you care,*
> • *That you do this work with your heart.*

(Eric Shirt, 'Healing Our Youth', First National Conference on Adolescent Treatment, Edmonton, 17–20 September 1990).

There is nothing more limiting to our ability to enjoy personal growth than a harsh, internalised, attitude of self-loathing. The first step in healing is learning to appreciate and love ourselves. Without this we cannot appreciate or love others. Nor can we deal honestly with those behaviours which are self-abusive, or abusive of our families or the wider community.

Healing can begin, both individually or collectively, simply by creating an atmosphere in which people can change their unconscious beliefs. Within a positive, supportive, and loving environment people can be aided to change their image of themselves, and of the potential of those around them.

Both individuals or groups have the capacity to create a powerful atmosphere for healing. There is no one technique. Programs for attaining a deeper inner growth might include techniques of laughter and games, prayer, dance and song, yoga and exercise, group-support work, service to others, creative expression, or educational and recreational activities. When these activities are conducted in an atmosphere of caring support they become 'a way of opening the heart to Being, to Love' (Hugh Prather 1989:15).

'LIFE-SPRINGS' PROGRAM

In their quest for community detoxification and community healing the Alkali Lake people found that programs for personal growth were extremely important. They were initially prompted by the many 'New Age' inspired, self-discovery kinds of workshops proliferating in Vancouver during the seventies and eighties. 'Life-Springs' was one of the first programs experimented with.

Life-Springs programs sought to help people address their social and personal disorders and to rebuild their lives. During an early group session the Alkali Lake people discussed some of their discoveries about this process:

> A person has to want to develop. They've got to make a conscious effort to grow. And that effort can't be in just one area. It has to cover that person's life: the physical, the mental, the spiritual and the emotional.

> We see what our potential is. We see our abilities, and what we have to do to get there. No-one is going to do it for us. Each person has their own strengths, their own gifts, and they have to start just wherever they are (*The Honour of All*, Part II, video, 1986).

ALKALI LAKE, 'NEW DIRECTIONS' PROGRAMS

In addition to setting up specialised support groups, Alkali Lake began to develop their own programs for personal and community healing. The 'New Directions' Program was originally based upon a series of workshops developed to meet the needs of the Alkali Lake people to overcome individual and community addiction. But as the Alkali Lake band members grew closer together through sobriety they discovered that there was a great need to share and to heal childhood and adult experiences, to develop personal awareness, and to stretch people beyond their self-imposed limits. These workshops became safe and embracing venues for freeing people from burdens of pain, and exciting avenues for personal discovery and growth. They were both liberating and empowering.

In response to requests for assistance from other communities the Alkali Lake band developed a range of training programs and workshops. The philosophy and purpose of their approach was explained:

> Our premise that strong communities are made up of strong individuals brought about the development of culturally specific training which balances the physical, emotional, mental, social and spiritual aspects of our lives.
>
> Within the intensive group settings participants learn basic living skills, reaffirm self-respect and increase self-confidence, thereby relearning how to care for themselves and others. This type of education assists in the development of quality relationships and the enhancement of communication skills.
>
> We believe that when each individual is balanced and in harmony with themselves and their world they have a positive impact on society, beginning with themselves, their families, their communities and ultimately with the family of man ('New Directions' Program, leaflet, Alkali Lake 1990).

The Alkali Lake *Personal Development Intensive Training* program is described as a five day and four evenings (60 hours) intensive training workshop in personal development:

> The purpose of this experiential training is to assist people to form a positive attitude towards all aspects of their lives. We become aware of, and deal with, our emotional blocks and our false images. We learn to acknowledge, accept and resolve past ugly experiences generated through alcoholism, drug abuse or emotional neglect. We focus on changing the negative feelings, beliefs and attitudes to positive and life serving ones.

We learn to move rapidly from problems to solutions by learning how to heal ourselves before letting go of the past, and look toward a healthy future.

We answer the question, 'Who am I?', and experience our personal power and the unique and special gifts that each person has within. When we begin to love ourselves, our families, and our people unconditionally we can move toward the future with confidence, creating a peaceful and harmonious world ('New Directions' Program, leaflet, Alkali Lake 1990).

The *Healing the Hurts* program is described as an intensive four day workshop which focuses upon negative experiences of Native people and their communities. Workshops include: understanding our past, internalised oppression (how we hurt ourselves and one another), the impact of family separation, healing physical and sexual abuse, accepting and forgiving, healing the shame that binds us, and the fulfilment of Native prophecies.

The workshop processes include: large group presentations, small and large group healing circles, laughter and play, peer counselling, mediation, guided imagery, role playing, and ceremony ('New Directions' Program, leaflet, Alkali Lake 1990; see also 'Healing the Hurts', 1989, video). Other Alkali Lake programs listed were:

- Elders Training
- Sexuality Workshops
- Communication Workshops
- Alcohol Awareness Training
- Cultural Awareness Training
- Share the Alkali Experience Workshops.

In the 'New Directions' Training leaflet (1990) the Alkali Lake band advertised that all its programs were 'culturally aware' and could be 'adapted to local needs'. They could also be modelled for suit different age groups and training levels — adult training (ages 19 and over), youth training (ages 7 to 18), advanced training and so forth.

An important achievement of this, and other programs, occurred when arrangements with some Canadian tertiary institutions resulted in the accreditation of Native-run courses.

THE CULTURAL COMPONENT

> Culture is really important to our unity
> (*The Honour of All*, Part II, video, 1986).

The Poundmaker's Lodge holds that the Native client will respond best to a specialised treatment approach which combines Indian cultural awareness and aspects of professional treatment and the philosophy of Alcoholics Anonymous. A central component of the Poundmaker's treatment program involves the strengthening and renewal of 'Indian culture'. An elder works full-time at the Centre, holding pipe ceremonies, sweat lodges, and other sacred ceremonies. With meditation, prayer, ceremonies, and elder counselling, patients are given spiritual assistance in overcoming their afflictions.

The centre also has hand games, native singing, dancing and occasional Pow Wows. Every summer, Indian Days are held on the Poundmaker's grounds. This 'rich tradition' makes the Poundmaker's experience unique and powerful for its clients:

> Alcohol and drunkenness have never been a part of Indian culture and it is the rich heritage of native culture on which the Poundmaker's program is based ...

> It is our belief that in seeking spiritual development, we may find the strength we need to gain and keep our sobriety (Poundmaker's Lodge 'Alcoholism and Drug Abuse Treatment Centre, leaflet, 1988).

The Poundmaker's Lodge philosophy rejects any natural connection between alcohol and aboriginality. It treats alcoholism as a disease, which has reached epidemic proportions among Indian people.

Treatment includes an *'Educational'* component whereby participants learn about the disease of alcoholism and its effect upon the health, personality, and family life of the person. *'Counselling'* sessions help participants to get in touch with their feelings, past hurts and experiences, attitudes and behaviours — laying a foundation for emotional growth. A *'Skills Development'* component helps to introduce and develop skills for sober living through a series of structured activities, such as self-awareness, assertiveness, communication, and problem solving.

THE HEALING CIRCLE

We have to help each other find our vision
(*The Honour of All*, Part II, video, 1986).

The healing circle approach is the most fundamental of all approaches to community well-being. It is salve applied by the people at the community level. The people diagnose the problem. *They* decide the appropriate treatment. *They* administer the healing. As Judy Atkinson explains:

> *The healing circle approach means owning our own healing.* We need to link all the issues together — alcoholism, family violence, child abuse, rape, incest, unemployment, and health. Healing programs are effective because they take a holistic approach. They treat not only victims, they also treat the perpetrators. In 99% of the cases of violent assault on Aboriginal communities perpetrators have themselves been victims of some of the most terrible forms of assault when they were young. They need healing too (Atkinson, personal communication, 6 January 1992).

'Healing circles', or 'sharing circles' as they are sometimes called, have the simple objectives of caring, sharing, and mutual support. They can be set up for any group of people in need. When they are specialised — that is, when they are focused upon a particular sector of the community — participants can more easily relate the problems common to the group. The experiences of love and comfort which healing circles engender can be quite transforming to participants.

After one or two ice-breaking exercises, and perhaps a prayer or a sacred song for unity and assistance, the group sits down together in a circle of a manageable number (up to about thirty for initial introductions, and about ten for specialised group activities). During healing sessions a symbolic item — a rock picked out from the country, a wood carving, an eagle feather — is handed around from one person to another. The person who holds the item has the authority to speak about his or her personal experiences. Others in the group listen and give their support, love, and sympathy. The emotions which healing sessions arouse can be extremely powerful and there will be few dry eyes in these sessions. People will often share good experiences, information about helping, or solutions which they found to a problem similar to one described by another member of the group. Sometimes healing sessions will lead to decisions and maybe some form of support group action.

SETTING UP SUPPORT GROUPS

Support groups can be therapy-oriented or action-oriented. They provide a place for support and problem-solving within a secure and loving environment. Initially, when dealing with people in crisis, specialised support groups offer enormous therapeutic value. People with like experiences, from similar backgrounds, have the most to share and understand.

Specialised support groups can be set up to meet the needs of specific sectors of the community — alcoholics, co-dependants, victims of abuse, young mothers with problems, habitually violent men, gamblers, married couples, youth and children can be very effective. Women's groups, men's groups, and youth groups are particularly successful at responding to the special needs of each of these groups of people. For example, the Indian-run 'Hey-Way'-Nogu' centre in Vancouver ran Men'sSurvivor of Family Violence Groups, Women's Survivor of Family Violence Groups, Support groups for twelve to eighteen year olds (male, female), and Co-dependency Support Groups.

Sometimes the function of a specialised support group will evolve. A women's support group, which may have started out as a support group for victims of domestic violence, may become an agent for the promotion of family-life skills and community development. A men's support group may develop into a 'Men Against Violence Group' and may spearhead 'tough love' forms of community action.

Mixed groups can also be set up to discuss the concerns of a cross-section of the community — men and women, young and old. Mixed groups tend to work best when they are action oriented ('Crime Prevention Working Groups', 'Child Protection Teams', 'Healthy Living Teams', 'Youth Drug Prevention Teams'). Focusing on a target problem which concerns everyone can give purpose and direction to a working group or action team.

Support groups require the minimum of organisation and little cost. In the first instance, all that needs to be planned is *when and where* meetings will be held, and whether people will require refreshments. A regular time and day is easier to remember. Gatherings can be held anywhere, of course — inside or outside. Some groups enjoy experimenting with locations — like organising a sharing circle under a big tree on a nice day.

Support groups provide a haven in which the process of personal growth and healing can begin. As one participant said: *'When strangers loved me, when I was incapable of loving myself, I began to trust. Self-abuse stopped as self-esteem began'*.

Supports Groups will

- respect the specialness of each individual
- reduce feelings of isolation

- give support and encouragement
- show that 'it's O.K. to be me'
- teach self trust
- increase self esteem and confidence
- help dispel anger, hurt and shame
- affirm and validate an individual's feelings
- help identify dysfunctional patterns
- encourage reality-testing
- teach problem solving
- foster positive decision-making
- assist with goal setting.[1]

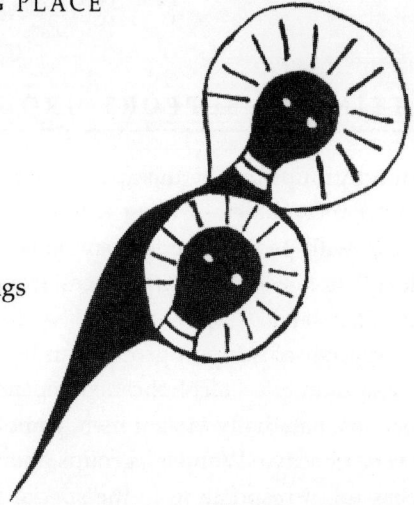

Community development and expanded opportunities are just some of the many wonderful fruits of community healing. Many support groups become the catalyst for the organisation of 'fun activities' for the young and not so young — picnics, sports, recreation and community awareness days. They often involve the local talent of community workers and elders for the introduction of cultural or preventative education into school programs.

People involved in recovery will begin to feel well, strong, and happier in themselves. People who feel loved and supported, will have more love and support to offer others — particularly their families and friends. Support group experience, and team-work action, represent *highly visible and valuable skills*. People who acquire these skills will be more effective in inter-personal communication, planning and organisation, problem solving, and decision-making. These skills can be applied to many levels of community action in the future (see 'Support Groups' in Hazlehurst 1990: 33-8).

Group support is the beginning of the journey to wholeness. The second step is personal growth and community training.

'HEALING OUR PEOPLE WORLDWIDE'

The Poundmaker's Lodge and Nechi Institute have become world leaders in the field of progressive addiction treatment and training. As the transforming influence of caring group activities upon the lives of individuals and communities became apparent, these successes were shared with Native people throughout Canada and the United States. The ideas were first passed on by word of mouth and through Native newspapers. Detoxification/personal growth workshops and consultancies took programs to other regions and provinces, involving many other communities. As Pow

Wows and conferences began to attract the interest of hundreds of participants, the international implications of the Native detoxification movement were considered. 'This has meaning for the whole world', said one excited participant at the *'Healing Our Youth'* conference in Edmonton in September 1990.

In 1992 the Native people of Alberta hosted an international conference in Edmonton. Recognising the potential of indigenous people to lead the world in social and spiritual recovery Nechi and several other Native organisations collaborated as hosts of a world indigenous gathering promoting addiction-free lifestyles. The *'Healing Our Spirit Worldwide'* conference, 7–11 July 1992, was co-hosted by the National Native Association of Treatment Directors, Nechi Institute on Alcohol and Drug Education, Poundmaker's Lodge, and the National Association of Native American Children of Alcoholics. Australia was not untouched by this exciting development. About 300 Australians joined the 3000 delegates from 17 countries in Edmonton to explore the holistic treatments which have liberated thousands of Native people to enjoy addiction-free lives, and to reclaim their language, culture, and spirituality.

For Australia there were two important fruits from this Edmonton conference. The aboriginal Co-ordinating Council Cairns, conceived the idea of holding the first national indigenous alcohol and drug free conference dedicated to healing. On 22–26 May 1994 the 'Healing Our People' conference with the theme of 'Breaking the Denial, and Letting the Healing of Our Prople Begin' was held in Cairns. It was hosted by ACC and their newly established 'Bama Healing Centre' (an organisation set up to deal with areas of alcolhol and drug abuse). At the same Edmonton conference it waas also decided that the second 'Healing Our Spirit Worldwide' conference would be hosted by the australian Aboriginal people, and held in Sydney on 14–18 November 1994. These were exciting breakthroughs in direction and emphasis for Australia, and represented proud moments in the cause of self-dtermination for the leaders who look up this challenge.

GETTING THE MESSAGE ACROSS

In addition to residential programs and workshops the message of the Canadian Native healers is spread in a number of other ways.

Newsletters and Newspapers

The *Windspeaker* is a bi-weekly newspaper, published in Edmonton. It is one of several which promote an alcohol and drug-free future for Native people and their children. The *Windspeaker* reports on alcohol and substance abuse prevention activities and events occurring in Indian country throughout Canada. Communities are encouraged to send in information about their activities. Workshop programs, Pow Wows, and poster competitions for school children are just a few of the events which it publicises. The newspaper communicates that there is growing support among Native people for substance-free lifestyles.

'Super Shamou' Comic Books

A new comic book hero 'Super Shamou' is a friend in need. Comic book stories of this substance abuse fighting superhero, who rescues kids from disastrous situations, has become so popular that print runs of over 85,000 (in English, Cree, Inuktitut, and French) have not met the demands.

National Addictions Awareness Week

In 1987 the third week of each November was proclaimed 'National Addictions Awareness Week' by the Canadian Minister of Health and Welfare. With the assistance of various sources of funding, Nechi Institute adopted the theme 'Keep the Circle Strong', and took a leadership role in the promotion of the alcohol and drugs awareness week. The goal was to heighten public awareness of addictions within society; to celebrate and support the efforts of those working towards addiction-free lifestyles; and to invite others to join an ever growing circle of friends, family, and communities across the country in this campaign.

A variety of activities organised to promote awareness in drug and alcohol issues were reported in the Native newspaper *Windspeaker* (see 1987; 1990). Community supported activities for this special week have included 'Celebrate Life' and 'Say No to Drugs' presentations at local schools, essay contests, discussion groups, and community feasts. Local dignitaries were pressed to join the activities. During the celebrations in one year a mayor opened a feast, RCMP officers flipped pancakes at a breakfast for over 500 at the remote community of Rankin Inlet, and elders told stories to the children. Promotional materials — buttons, stickers, posters, newsletters, a media package, children's colouring-in books and other materials were produced. A local organiser reported that: 'It makes it a real positive experience for the kids when adults jump on board'.

In a full page advertisement, the Nechi Institute urged people to become a part of the celebration by sending in their declaration to 'Join their Circle':

> This is an opportunity for everyone to share the dream of an addiction-free future for themselves and their children ...

> ... join a growing circle of friends, families and communities across the country who have chosen a lifestyle free of alcohol, drug and solvent abuse. Everyone is invited to join in the spirit of caring (*Windspeaker*, 31 August 1990).

Organisers of 'National Addictions Awareness Week' activities held at the Nechi Institute mailed out an official declaration of intent to communities throughout the country. The declaration read:

> As people gather completing a circle of life, filled with hope and love in our tomorrows, founded on our traditions, and a growing circle of friends, and communities which have chosen a positive lifestyle free from alcohol and drug abuse, let us grow strong each day, together to *Keep the Circle Strong*.

Nechi coordinator Louise Mayo, declared in 1990 that, since its introduction, National Addictions Awareness Week had strengthened bonds within the communities and between neighbouring communities. In the previous November, 1989, a great circle of several hundred Native people and their non-Native friends was formed in front of the Alberta legislature to show this support for sobriety. 'This tremendous achievement shows the leadership of Native people in recognising and promoting alcohol and drug awareness through the week and throughout the year' (*Windspeaker*, 31 August 1990).

In 1987, 25 communities had joined the project. In 1989 this had increased to 405 communities (over 18,000 people). By 1991 1,165 community-based groups, a total of 405,879 people across Canada, participated in the campaign and celebrations (Nechi Institute Annual Report 1991/92).

THE NEED FOR 'NEW VISION' LEADERSHIP

For two centuries Aboriginal people have been fighting a battle for survival: physical survival in the first years of European contact and cultural and spiritual survival in the decades that followed. The strong voice for human rights and social justice which was raised by protest activists from the mid-1960s onwards sought to repair the cultural foundations of community groups, and to broaden the indigenous identity generally. Generic references, such as 'Koori', which have been quite widely adopted in New South Wales and Victoria, 'Murri' (in Queensland) 'Nunga' (South Australia), and 'Nyungar' (Western Australia), have encouraged a sense of regional unity between diverse Aboriginal groupings.

Contemporary leaders have fought at both state and federal levels for Aboriginal land rights, a fairer share of local government resources, and the means for social and economic development. They have taken the human and legal rights campaign as far afield as the United Nations and other forums of international law.

A quieter and perhaps not so public leadership has also been emerging from among the middle-management Aboriginal professional sector and from within communities themselves for the restoration of family and community life. Often the vanguard of this new movement has been middle-aged women. These women have become increasingly vocal in trying to raise community and government awareness about social conditions. They have also gained support from some of their men folk — community leaders and elders — and from outside professionals in this endeavour. The immediate concern of this leadership has been to tackle the horrendous problems of family violence and crime associated with alcoholism which are destroying Aboriginal families and communities.

Visionary leaders will be the key to community healing in the future. They see the need to revitalise and repair the broken spirit. They want their children and grandchildren to live with dignity and confidence. But they recognise that many Aboriginal people are ill-equipped in many ways, and need help to do so.

Often holding back visionary leaders is the state of the local community. Communities themselves are at different stages. Some will need to resolve deep and long-term conflicts between families and clans before they are able to develop cohesive, community-wide programs. In this case, conflict resolution may be the first step forward in healing the rifts and *making a community.* Where there are no serious divisions, preventative approaches will take root more easily.

Support groups, however, can be established by only two or three people as a nucleus of healing, no matter how terrible the situation. As they expand to embrace more and more people their positive emphasis upon unity and mutual support will shield and uphold people living in families or communities in a state of chronic disruption. Groups should seek outside help to assist them in discovering techniques in personal and group healing, and to find ways of dealing with personal and inter-personal crisis.

'RENEWING THE SPIRIT' IN AUSTRALIA

Native workers say that 'Only by renewing the human spirit can the process of regeneration begin'. 'Heal the spirit of indigenous people and you will heal the social problems'. Aboriginal people have been hearing this message from their brothers and sisters in North America. This is a message which has 'hands and feet' — practical applications and ways of being achieved. Community healing can be started by just two or three people who meet together to talk and share. If this support group meets regularly, with the purpose of healing the hurts, giving families support, or of overcoming violent or self-destructive behaviours, it can become a powerful tool for rejuvenation.

An association or organisation could be formed for the purposes of formally developing training programs for community members and workers in areas of alcohol and drug awareness, violence prevention, child protection and care, suicide prevention and so on. As such work is greatly needed, government grant applications from an organisation with community healing objectives should receive a favourable response.

At the end of 1993 Australia's first private, Aboriginal-run, organisation for personal and community healing was set up in Rockhampton, central Queensland. The founders of 'We Al-Li', which literally means 'Fire and Water', took this name for their new organisation because these two fundamental elements are seen to balance each other, and because in nature and in traditional thinking they are seen as cleansing agents, and as agents of regeneration. There is an irony in this name, also appreciated and mentioned by the founders. 'We Al-Li' — 'Fire and Water' — will be used to combat the devastating effects of 'Fire-water' (alcohol) upon Aboriginal lives. The Mission Statement of We Al-Li is:

> To develop a program and place for healing the individual, family and community dysfunction of family violence and the pain of mind, body and spirit resulting from violence and oppression.

The stated purposes of We Al-Li are to:

- establish a program for healing, sharing and recreation
- promote individual, spiritual, cultural, physical, emotional and mental well-being
- strengthen families and communities through personal, group and community development within natural environmental settings
- develop retreats and holistic Aboriginal health programs
- establish a training and skills development centre.

The organisation plans to start off slowly. Its first program will be developed through group workshops with invited participants. In order for the organisers to plan and structure the program, workshops will be focused upon specific topics of healing. However, they will be flexible enough to allow participants — who may be in crisis at the time — to express individual needs and for the group to respond with a listening ear and loving support.

The first workshop planned for 1994, 'Lifting the Cloaks of Oppression', is on the topic of dispossession trauma. It will encourage participants to share negative experiences of class, race, gender, age or self-oppression which continue to hold them in the state of victimisation. The next workshops planned for 1994 are 'Health and Self', 'Anger, Boundaries and Safety' and 'Grief and Bereavement'. Other themes to be developed include Healing from Sexual Assault, Alcohol and Drug Abuse, Family Relationships, Stress Management, Sexuality, Physical Health, the Environment, Job/career, and Spirituality.

While experiential workshops will be the mainstay of its healing program, We Al-Li also hopes to offer a range of camp-out retreats, community activities, training materials, seminars, and conferences to help reach a wider audience of need throughout Queensland and Australia. To ensure its continued growth We Al-Li has incorporated a evaluation element into its program.[2]

THE ROLE OF GOVERNMENTS

It is clear from the accounts in this book that caring people are already beginning to seek training and to develop programs which will lead to Aboriginal community healing and renewal. But they need the full-hearted support of those who control the resources and services essential to community well-being. It will be innovative and clear-sighted officials, among today's bureaucracies and agencies, who will help local people carve a workable path for future community healing.

With the exception of alternative dispute resolution, we have not done too well in proactive or preventative areas in Australia. This has been largely because we simply have not known a way forward. We have not had the skills or techniques for the development of effective preventative programs. The experiential field for social regeneration, in the hands of those who most need it, is one which offers enormous promise. This will be the time for the government to 'let go the ropes' in order for communities to take up the responsibility. It will be the role of federal and state Departments of Justice, Welfare, Health, ATSIC and other relevant government agencies — as well as regional and local Aboriginal bodies such as Land Councils and Community Councils — to recognise and to offer *unconditional support* to communities wishing to take back control over personal and inter-personal problems.

This is a new time of testing for Australia. It is a test of our country's commitment — indeed practical and humanitarian grasp — of our stated pledge to indigenous self-determination. Experience suggests that the necessary understanding and disposition is not yet there in either government or in contemporary Aboriginal political circles, which are largely occupied with other battles. Despite this, some very real and substantial innovations have arisen from the vision and autonomous courage of smaller community collectives. It may take some years for these developments to demonstrate their worth to wider interests. In the meantime, it will be up to community healing and preventative action groups to get on with the job — with or without this support. Perhaps, in the long run, this will be a blessing. First, it will ensure *absolute indigenous invention* in healing techniques; and second, the development of *non-political programs* which are accessible to *all* in need — irrespective of family, clan, or regional affiliations.

Brooke Medicine Eagle, a Native healer, writer and dance performer shares with us her earth-centered teachings:

This attention towards oneness, or wholeness, is what my tradition names *holiness*. As we become whole, holiness extends out, just as we might extend our dance circle metaphorically to include all other human beings ... [animals, plants and fishes upon Mother Earth].

This holiness is the essence of healing, which means to manifest wholeness in spirit and bring it into our bodies, our families, our communities, our world. We heal by beginning to consciously embody the Spirit that lives as one with us and in all things. Thus the function of a healer is to embody and manifest that wholeness of Spirit in such a way that he or she can guide those who have fallen out of rhythm, who have stumbled into dis-ease, and help them to reestablish their balance and rhythm (Medicine Eagle 1989:60).

◆ ◆ ◆

[1] There is a wide range of reading material on programs for adult children of alcoholics and co-dependants (see Woititz 1986, 1988; Lerner 1988; Grateful Members 1977; Friends in Recovery 1990).

[2] Judy Atkinson and Coralie Ober, who registered for graduate studies with the author at the Queensland University of Technology in 1993 and 1994 respectively, were two of the founders of We Al-Li, and will be devoting their higher degree work to the creation, implementation, and testing of community healing programs under this organisation.

Chapter nine

'GIVING SOLUTIONS HANDS AND FEET': INITIATING THE COMMUNITY REGENERATION PROCESS

The day will come when, after harnessing the winds, the tides, and gravitation, we shall harness for God the energies of love. And on that day, for the second time in the history of the world, man will have discovered fire (Teilhard de Chardin in Carlson and Shield 1989: xvii).

SHAPING A VISION OF THE FUTURE

> Imagination is the art and practice of producing ideal creations and forming clear mental images. Your imagination is your future. It is the only place the future exists (Terry Lynn Taylor).

There is an old Chinese proverb that says: 'Before a thing of beauty can be made in the material world, first it must be conceived in the heart and the mind'. It is in the realm of ideas that we will first empower people. Practical solutions will proceed from the liberation and the creative release of the mind. Dysfunctional communities, particularly, will need to be freed from the collective mind-sets which are destructive and self-defeating.

In his famous self-help book, *You'll See It When You Believe It*, the American author Dr Wayne Dyer wrote:

> Every man-made creation starts with a thought, an idea, a vision, a mental image. The thought is then applied in some way to form a new product ... We all go through this process thousands of times every day. The ultimate in becoming a transformed person is seeing ourselves as unlimited by our form (Dyer 1989: 26).

'What would our communities be like if there was no violence or addiction?', Judy Atkinson asked in her journey around Australia between 1989 and 1990. This is one of the most important questions a community can ask of itself. If we do not ask 'imagine if' kinds of questions we deny ourselves opportunities for happier, healthier life styles. Totake control of our own destinies, we need to develop a *vision* of the future. We need to understand:

- where we have come from;
- what is happening to us now; and
- which direction we would like to go.

Choices we make in life are strongly influenced by self perceptions — how we think of ourselves, whether we believe in ourselves, and what aspirations we have for our future. When a committee or gathering of concerned people wish to reduce interpersonal aggression, for instance, they need an image of what their families and communities would be like *without* these problems. Shaping a vision for the future is the first stage in reaching this goal. What would life be like for our children in a safer social environment? How would our men feel when they are free from violence? What sort of life would our women have? Questions like this help shape our plans for violence-free communities. The steps between 'where we are now' and 'what we would like to become' seem immediately clearer and more manageable. The *Crime Prevention for Aboriginal Communities* manual outlines this process:

Desire + Ability + Opportunity = Realising Our Vision

We *see* what is possible, then use our *desire* to become what we see. We use our *ability* to become what we desire. And we use our desire and ability to provide *opportunities*, in real life, *to realise our vision* (Hazlehurst 1990: 3, 26).

Over the last two hundred years Aboriginal society has been subjected to enormous pressures for change — derived mainly from sources beyond their control. Denial that certain problems exist has allowed outside authorities and others to intervene and impose their solutions. 'And history shows, their solutions just become our future problems', Atkinson observed:

By acknowledging the problem, and looking for reasons why, we are developing ownership of the solutions. Once we understand what is happening we want to find answers because we can see what it is doing to us (*Beyond Violence* 1990: 6).

Communities which are weighed down with problems of alcoholism, inter-family fighting, juvenile offending, and widespread despair and negativity produce a people without a sense of future. Shaping a vision helps communities to take control of their own destinies. It is an empowering process, fuelled by the energy of positivity. Positivity is a source of energy which is free and available to all. As history has shown, the will to survive, and to succeed, can give a people resilience against the most determined forces of destruction — including war, natural disaster, famine, poverty, and oppression. *The greatest danger to survival is loss of heart.*

COMMUNITY REGENERATION AND PRIVATISATION

Research in both Canada and Australia has shown that, for large numbers of indigenous communities, the process of social disintegration is extreme. They suffer disproportionately from virtually every social problem known to humankind.

Native workers explain the multiple impact of their clients' life predicaments. Problems, which arose from enforced residential schooling, widespread alcoholism, family violence, offending, imprisonment and poor parenting, have had a cumulative impact upon maturing Native adults and a cyclical effect upon the next generation. Faced with catastrophic community decline, Native organisations have sought to respond with a multi-service, multi-interventionist approach.

Since the early 1970s Canadian Native people have taken a lead in areas of community reconstruction and regeneration. This has been achieved by a collaborative process of innovative programming, and by fee-for-service contractual arrangements which have allowed privately run Native organisations to develop and administer a significant proportion of service delivery to Native people.

The objective of these programs has been to heal Native individuals and to heal whole communities. To enable Native people to take charge of their own lives, a range of new coping skills are offered in problem-solving, crisis intervention, dispute settlement, team-work building, action planning, and professional development. Programs are particularly directed at offenders, or 'at-risk' populations, such as youth. They are delivered, with equal energy, to those undergoing terms in correctional institutions, as well as to urban residents and rural communities.

Community development is not seen as a single process but as occurring within an overall environment of positive change. If the causes of Native over-representation in Canadian prisons are multiple and interactive, workers say, solutions themselves must also be cumulative, and can have a multiple impact over time.

Prominent among the private Native organisations, delivering these programs, is the Native Counselling Services of Alberta (NCSA), Edmonton. As mentioned earlier, the Family Life Improvement Program (FLIP) is one NCSA program which is conducted in a support-group setting. Through the process of group discussion, role playing, story-telling, and personal sharing FLIP assists people to explore issues such as family relationships, drugs and alcohol, sexuality, domestic violence, divorce and separation, the emotional development of children, further education and personal growth. Participants are taught how to seek out positive life opportunities, how to access public information, and how to deal with government agencies (NCSA 1985a).

NCSA'S Youth crime prevention programs combine education, with recreation, and esteem-building activities. Healthier lifestyles are actively sought through youth sports and outdoor activities, personal counselling, family workshops, cultural participation and spiritual renewal, employment training, addiction prevention, fun-

drives, and other public education campaigns. The social environment surrounding youth offending is worked on, not just the individual. At family workshops parents and youth are invited to discuss family life, alcohol addiction, and other problems which they share. Programs which set up youth teams, and which tap youth talent for community problem-solving, are particularly popular (NCSA 1985b, 1987, 1991; Hazlehurst 1994a, 1994b).[1]

COMMUNITY OWNERSHIP AND PRIMARY PREVENTION

In Australia the primary prevention approach has also begun to impact upon identified community problems. Juvenile offending, for instance, has responded quite dramatically in one northern Queensland community. At Weipa community workers report that their community has almost eliminated youth offending through the establishment of a range of diversionary activities generated by youth teams and youth programs. 'They are all much to busy doing more exciting things' said Jean Jans (personal communication, 10 June 1992).

By early 1994 the Weipa community, with the assistance of youth workers and the full support of the Weipa Aboriginal Council, had established a Youth Centre. The Centre, which was jointly funded by the mining company Comalco and the Weipa Council, is open between 1 pm and 10 pm. It has its own library and acts as an alcohol-free zone, recreational haven, homework centre and disco spot for the young. The youth program has also acquired a youth bus and a boat, which is used to take children and youth on recreational outings in the local area.

Through courses and workshops Weipa is now working on increasing the skills of local workers in the areas of grief counselling, budgeting, suicide prevention, and individual counselling in order to extend help to the adult members of the community. 'Over a three year period we have been trying to build up our community resource base', explained Jean Jans. 'People are now working much better together and are much more supportive of each other' (personal communication, 24 January 1994).

Part of the primary prevention approach has been to help communities overcome denial, blaming, and powerlessness. Through practical crime prevention work, action groups can explore means by which new skills, taught at the community level, can empower people to take ownership of, and responsibility for, local problems. Taking ownership begins by teaching people how to analyse their particular crime problem, and by giving them new tools for action. With the assistance of crime prevention manuals and workshops people learn how to set up and run action teams and community support groups, and are trained in the related skills of mediation, team-work ability, and action planning.

Action teams for crime prevention may be self appointed, or they may be nominated at a community meeting. Team representatives may work with a number of other agencies, such as police, schools, medical and service agencies, and local organisations. After analysing the crime environment from the point of view of both the community and the offender, they may choose to run public education campaigns, develop offender and victim rehabilitation programs, refuges for women, post-release schemes, youth team activities or any number of prevention strategies (Hazlehurst 1990: 10-32).

In order to be really effective the community needs to think about prevention in the longer term. We need to introduce preventative measures *before* problems have taken hold, particularly where young people are concerned. Thinking about prevention and taking early action is called 'primary prevention'.

In her work over the years as a drug and alcohol counsellor Jean Jans has used and adapted the 'primary prevention' approach in many Aboriginal communities. In the video, *Primary Prevention for Community Wellbeing: An Interview with Jean*, she outlined the practical application of primary prevention:

> Primary prevention is when a community decides to do something about their problems. It focuses upon the social and personal factors which lead people to abuse alcohol, tobacco, drugs and petrol fumes.

> Primary prevention focuses on *good health issues*. It focuses on developing and maintaining healthy life-styles. This program goes hand in hand with all other areas of community development.

> Local people identify their own problems, and are responsible for finding their own solutions. If we have ownership of problems we have control of our own destiny (Hazlehurst 1989a).

Many activities, Jans stressed, are 'problem-oriented'. They are focused upon poor health and problem areas. We need to think about *'well-health'* issues and *'positive growth'* areas as well. By becoming 'solution-oriented' in our approach we concentrate on changing the underlying emotional and spiritual environments in which unhealthy life styles, negative attitudes, and violent behaviours are cultivated. Promoting environments which nurture balanced, happier outlooks can become the central focus of our work.

'Community care' and 'community responsibility' approaches are the foundation stones of all preventative programs. Empowering solutions need to be tailored to the immediate social environment. That is, they have to have 'good social fit' by responding to the precise context and nature of local problems. Good social fit will be achieved by ensuring that local people have the dominant role in the planning, design, and implementation of these programs, and in their later evaluation and improvement. Community involvement, and information gathering, ground solutions in the immediate social environment, and increase confidence and capacity in groups to design relevant programs for early intervention.

'Primary prevention is not just about stopping something', said Jean Jans, 'it's also about making good things happen in the community as well'.

USING A HOLISTIC APPROACH

A holistic approach to problem-solving aims at responding to all aspects of the human condition. Treating the 'whole' person and the 'whole' community produces the most fruitful results.

Our behaviour reflects what is going on inside us. Positive or healthy behaviour reflects a healthy balanced life. Negative behaviour shows that inside we are empty, angry, and confused. As individuals, or as communities, things have become unbalanced. Negative attitudes and unhealthy ways set-in, and life quickly becomes unbalanced. Violence and abuse hurt us fourfold. They hurt us physically, emotionally, mentally, and spiritually.

In examining our personal or community problems we need to consider what is missing in these four aspects of our lives. When we look at vandalism among young people, for instance, we need to consider in what ways the community is 'short changing' its young people. We need to ask why is life so dull for our young people that the vandalism of community property is seen as a sport? Here are some questions which the community may wish to ask themselves regarding youth needs.

Youth lifestyles: what is really missing?

- Are young people being helped to make healthy lifestyle choices?
- Are we setting a good example to our youth?
- Why are dangerous lifestyles still more attractive?
- Are our youth being equipped for future family and community responsibilities?
- Are there enough educational and recreational programs for youth?
- Are programs relevant to the local social environment?
- Do our programs stimulate young people mentally and physically?
- Can they relate to these programs?
- Do young people value adult approval?
- Do they have the opportunity to enjoy adult approval through programs which encourage personal achievement?

- How can we encourage cultural and spiritual awareness, increase pride in Aboriginal history, nurture artistic and athletic talents, and enhance personal qualities and leadership skills?

The same steps can be taken when analysing problems concerning young mothers, middle-aged men, elderly women, young men, and children. Holistic solutions which address 'what is missing', as well as 'what is wrong', will be based upon a clearer understanding of the issues, and will have a far-reaching impact upon the community's future.

GATHERING INFORMATION

It is not always necessary to undertake lengthy research to get a good sense of what is going on. Information on problems can be gleaned from surveys of local opinion, from community meetings, focused workshops, or just by talking with people. When they know that their views will be taken seriously, and may help others, community workers, professionals, victims and perpetrators are often very willing to share their experiences. Police, hospitals, and government agencies can provide useful indicators of social disadvantage, local offending, and patterns of ill health, injury and accident which have resulted from alcoholism or violence.

Reliable information helps action groups decide where to focus their activities — the *target issues or target problems*; to identify who are the perpetrators — the *target offenders*; and who are the most likely to be hurt — the *target victims*. Further analysis leads action groups to understand the *social and environmental circumstances* surrounding these problems. For example: when they occur, how they occur, and why they occur — providing a much sounder basis for the development of socially and environmentally relevant solutions.

Unless the action group is well informed on all aspects of the problem they will be handicapped in designing workable solutions. Having a good sense of the territory will bring clarity of thought and confidence to problem-solvers. The key is to understand the problem from the point of view of the perpetrator as well as from that of the victim. We must try to understand the *'what's in it for them'* aspect of the problem.

An informed action group should be able to predict with considerable accuracy how things will unfold when changes are introduced, from where opposition might come and why, and where there is a need for greater community involvement. When the action group sees how positive programming can replace 'what is missing' in community life, they will know best how to 'sell' it to their target recipients.

Agroup which is determined to develop workable and socially relevant solutions will need to identify the:

- target problem or issue
- target victims
- target offenders
- 'what's in it for them'
  (offenders' motives, areas of deprivation)
- environment and circumstance
- 'what's missing' in the community

DEVELOPING HEALTHY LIFESTYLES

Individual and group decisions impact upon those around us. Noisy, disruptive, and violent behaviour affects the peace of mind and sense of well-being of relatives, friends, and neighbours. People are often disruptive in groups. Those who drink moderately give up and join the heavy drinkers — taking an 'if you can't beat 'em, join 'em approach'. Drinking cultures are particularly powerful in this respect.

By the same token, healthier lifestyles *start with the choices of one or two individuals* — that is, people who are committed to shaping a new vision for their community and sharing it with others. The choice of one individual to stop drinking in Alkali Lake, for example, led to the detoxification of almost a whole community. At first individuals sought the knowledge and support of outside specialists. An AA officer was a central resource to the early development of their first alcoholics' support group on the reserve. Workshop leaders from as far afield as Vancouver were invited to give occasional workshops on positive thinking, self discovery, and group healing. Old friends from the churches and interested academics lent their hand. A visiting psychologist continues to play an important role in their addictions support groups. Wherever the resources were, the Alkali Lake people sought them out and applied them in their own way to help their people. And it did not stop there. Over several years many other communities, and thousands of Native people, became committed to the detoxification movement.[2]

Remember, if the problem is group oriented — such as alcoholism — then the best solution will also be group oriented. The healing of an individual will begin the process of healing the *whole community*. Individuals who work together to improve the quality of life in the community can have a powerful influence upon those around them. Their example will in time persuade others to join them.

> The word *action* implies activity. Doing something. And we are doing something. That's why we called ourselves the TWAL Action Group (Weipa South, Queensland *Beyond Violence* 1990: 9).

Action Groups

IT ONLY NEEDS ONE PERSON TO START

Forming an action group

Developing healthy lifestyles in the community is both an individual and a group responsibility. An action group is a group of people who meet and work together to develop focused plans of action. Here are some of their functions:

1. *Action groups are community-based:* Much of their thinking is fuelled by local knowledge and experience.

2. *Identifying problems:* The function of action groups is to identify matters of local concern. They may set up public meetings, conduct personal interviews, or run small workshops to encourage the community to face problems and to discuss them together.

3. *Shaping a vision for the future:* The role of action groups is to give 'hands and feet' to community aspirations. Based upon the information they gather, and their own analysis of the problems, action groups can help to shape an *informed, inspired, and realistic vision for the future*. They share this vision with their community andtry to interest others in it.

4. *Seeking empowering solutions:* Action groups take responsibility for the development of solutions to the problems which have been identified. This may include asking for community ideas, looking at what other communities have done, inviting service agency input, reviewing resource materials, or adapting new or unique approaches which may be appropriate.

5. *Action planning:* The next vital step in this process is the mapping of a plan for action. This will involve deciding what we want to achieve, who we will need to talk to, and what resources we will need to call on, to achieve our goals.

6. *Establishing support groups:* Action groups can focus their attention on the needs of young mothers, on developing programs for youth, on healing for victims, on help for violent offenders, on detoxification for the whole community, or any other target area through the establishment of specialised support groups. Support groups are excellent vehicles for beginning the healing process and for developing alternatives to addictive and non-violent life styles. Social and recreational activities run by these groups can be a lot of fun!

7. *Crime preventative programming:* Through their preventative activities and liaison work, action groups open the way to honest dialogue between the community and outside agencies, reduce fear through access to better information, explore options, and bring a great deal of satisfaction to participants. Small successes will lead to later, more significant ones.

8. *Monitoring and evaluation:* It is important for the action group to allow time to monitor its own programs. Evaluation is a healthy approach which helps the team to nip problems in the bud, make necessary adjustments, and give programs the opportunity to mature and develop. Community feedback helps in this monitoring process. Criticism and self-examination will make the team strong.[3]

Growth is positive
A realistic action group will also not expect too much too soon. It may take years to turn a long-standing problem around, but the pleasure of success *can* be enjoyed in bite-size portions!

'Stepped goals' bring surer rewards and they also help us develop and monitor estimates of how much time and patience will be needed. Later, new visions for the future may arise.

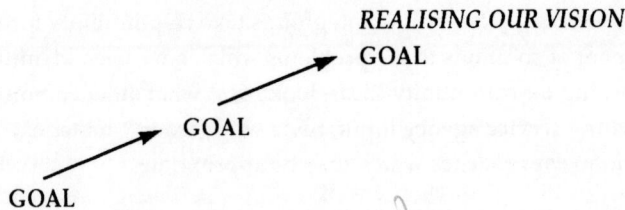

REALISING OUR VISION
GOAL

GOAL

GOAL

Experienced workers say that there should be plenty of room for growth and learning. Make all members aware of the importance of flexibility. Try not to get too attached to pet ideas. Make a point of separating community personalities from action plans. This way individual egos will not be hurt when a team decision is taken to try a new direction. As a solution must have 'good social fit' there needs to be room for growth. An earlier analysis may not fit new or developing situations. When planning the next stage of the program, subject the problem to a completely new 'holistic analysis'.

Members of the action group need to be kind to themselves and to each other. They should never be disheartened when a program does not achieve overnight success. It takes time and patience to sell a new idea to the community — especially where there have been many disappointments in the past. *Persevere*, give each other lots of support, and invite others to join. These are themselves positive developments, and other things will grow from them. Even if programs are not perfect, they will be close to the mark. Give the community the time it needs to become interested and for programs to take shape. Action groups should frequently compare their achievements with their vision for the future — just to remind themselves of how far they have come!

Native workers have found that the history and evolution of the problems of disempowerment, addiction, ill-health, violence, and imprisonment have produced a complex and inter-related cycle which impacts upon the individual and upon the generations. From their experience, the only effective *treatment of multifaceted problems is multifaceted solutions*. As the nature of any cycle is circular, there is no logical or single point of entry. Intervention should occur at as *many different points* as possible. It takes some practice to suspend dearly held commitments and beliefs about the 'right way' of doing things. But there is always room for the expansion of ideas and action. Do not be surprised when things take a new direction or turn out differently than was originally planned. *Growth is positive — for individuals, for groups, and for societies.*

KEEPING OPEN OPTIONS FOR CHANGE

Here is a broad example of the need to keep open our options for change. Some years ago concepts of 'autonomy' and the need for local control came into mode. Anyone worth their salt upheld this principle. However, many communities did not have the resources or know-how needed to set up programs on their own. This was particularly true in communities fraught with high levels of crime, social tensions, inter-family fighting, poverty and so on. Community workers and volunteers were already exhausted and over-worked. While government agencies were insisting upon the virtues of local autonomy, community members were crying out for training, support, encouragement, and assistance.

Professional support need not be cast as 'outside interference', as long it is offered with respect for the needs for local management, achievement, and growth. On the other hand, to deny requests for outside help would do local people a great injustice. New action resources and community skills are the means to autonomy.

The game has not exactly changed, but the stakes have been raised. With an awareness of the need for self-determination has come an awareness of the need for management and community development skills. When black and white people look to *working together* for common objectives, their activities need not be mutually exclusive. Caring people can join forces. Overseas prevention models have shown that joining community talents with those of receptive government agencies and respectful professionals can produce powerful and effective results. If the community wishes to pursue genuine partnership, as a stepping stone toward community control, it should not be prevented by the 'ideological' argument that partnership, or outside involvement, undermines self-determination. This need not be the case at all.

It is important to be clear about our history of ideas — where we have come from and where we are going. During the late 1960s and 1970s protest politics played a significant role in challenging bureaucratic paternalism and in stimulating the decolonisation process in Australia. Through a series of inquiries and representations, the indigenous rights debate was raised to the national and international level during the decade of the eighties. But the 1990s began the period of 'coming home'. It represents a period of making tangible the promise and the obligations of liberation. It is the *constructive phase*, where goals for community renewal and self-management will take shape through the conversion of administrative structures, procedures, and power relations.

During this phase it will be increasingly recognised that 're-empowerment' means governments letting go control, on the one hand, and Aboriginal people being enabled to take up control, on the other. In large-scale development projects or economic enterprises, communities can only act as equal partners, or as autonomous agents, when they are given not only the *opportunity for partnership* asbut also the *skills for that autonomy*.

◆ ◆ ◆

[1] NCSA also has developed a range of justice program alternatives, including Native-run offender rehabilitation and treatment centres, which are worthy of examination (Hazlehurst 1994a; 1994b).

[2] See *The Alkali Lake Story*, listed under 'Resource Materials' section at the end of this book.

[3] For an outline on evaluating a program see *Crime Prevention for Aboriginal Communities* (Hazlehurst 1990: 39-43).

Chapter ten

TEAM-WORK IS TERRIFIC!

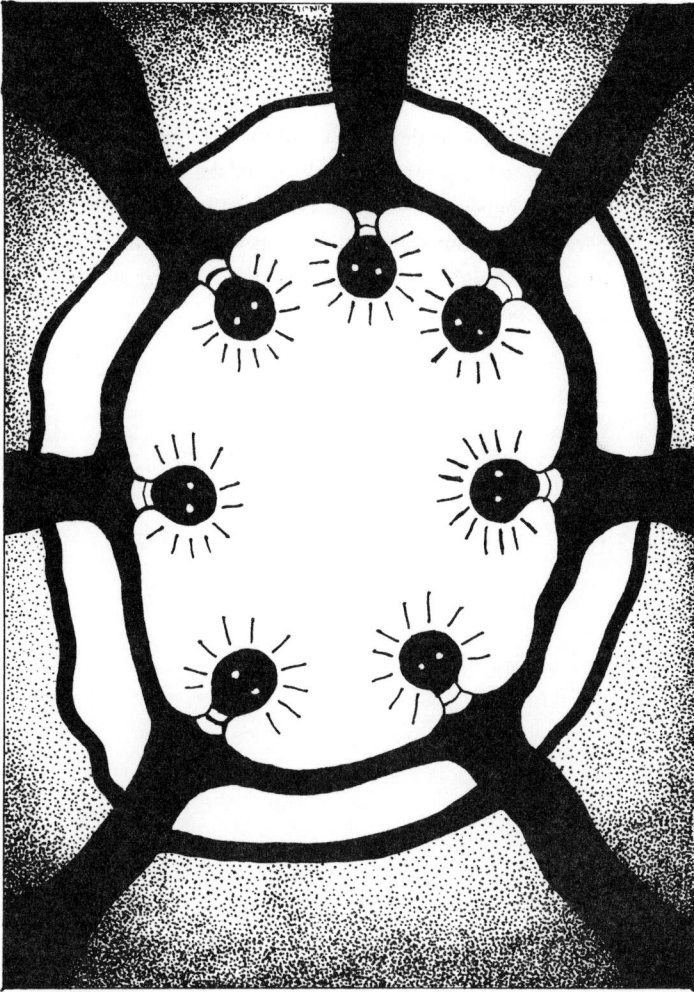

When we walk to the edge of all the light we have
and take the step into the darkness of the unknown
we must believe one of two things will happen —
there will be something solid for us to stand on, or
we will be taught to fly (Claire Morris in Wong and
McKeen 1992:43).

TEAM-WORK ABILITY IS A POWERFUL SKILL

To be effective the community must have new tools and new skills at its disposal. The first and most important of these new tools is the ability to work as a team. In a team-work situation people's efforts are more structured. They learn to appreciate the talents of other members, they become more involved, and they have more enjoyment working things out together. Team-work improves the confidence and experience of action groups, strengthens the community-base, and contributes to the personal growth of individuals.

Each member of the team is unique and will have different thoughts, ideas, and talents to offer. Team-work gives everyone a chance to be personally involved, and to hear other views. The principles of equality and fairness will be important to the smooth functioning of a team. If this can be achieved, it will set a good example to the rest of the community.

If there are fights and feuds affecting some participants, they can be asked to 'leave this baggage at the door' when the meeting begins. Tell them they can 'pick it up again' when they leave. Some groups go through an exercise of having members remove an imaginary backpack from their shoulders when they enter the room, especially when they are still learning how to function as a team. The effects can be hilarious, but effective. In time, members will *not want* to pick up their negativity again!

Team-work is completely different from power politics. It is based upon strong principles of equality, positive thinking, and strength-in-numbers. The 'team' should always be stronger than the individual. Remember, no one is here to win fame or fortune. If they are, they are probably on the wrong committee. For this reason, credit for activities should be accepted *on behalf* of the action group, not by individuals. This way, everyone feels good about group achievements. (Likewise, criticism should be shared and not personalised). The interests of the *team* should always come *first*.

Perhaps the action group will be responsible for helping the community achieve a violence-free (or addiction-free) environment. Team-work ability is a *vital tool* in this direction. The action group provides an excellent role model of balanced and harmonious relations, and can demonstrate the fruitfulness of a more positive approach. At an early meeting discuss how members can learn to communicate and work more effectively as team players. It is well worth trying to organise team-building sessions for participants.

LETTING GO BAD HABITS

The first task of an action group is to defeat bad habits of back-biting and jealousy. Team members need to be able to recognise negative behaviours. Unless they are identified (given a name), understood within the context of local history (depersonalised), and set aside by participants (defused as a potent force), they will destroy the solidarity of the group before it has even got started.

When a problem arises within an action group, identify the exact nature of the problem, so that it can be discussed honestly and constructively. Once analysed, it is much easier to overcome. Don't let problems fester. They will still have to be handled, only the longer they are left the bigger they will become. This is a special skill which a team will acquire through practice.

Recognising the *'small bone syndrome'* is an important step in the process of developing objectivity. Long years of subjugation to governing administrations, inadequate resources, and situations of poverty, keep people in a state of constant competition with each other. Certain families and personalities become embroiled in inter-personal battles which undermine the strength and cohesion of the community for decades.

Negativity, jealousy, bickering, and blaming behaviour should be avoided at all costs. *Don't accuse each other for everything wrong in the community!* Conflict makes unified efforts impossible. Through team training it is possible to 'throw over' these bad habits. Problems are much less elusive once they have been broken down into their component parts. If our *villains* are 'cycles of domination and poverty', 'urban migration and sudden growth', 'limited access to education and employment', or 'alcoholism and family fighting', then *these* issues can be tackled *directly*.

Learning to name our villains can be a painful process when problems are deep rooted. So members need to show a lot of kindness towards each other during this period. But if the focus is on the higher goal of team-work action, and the greater good of peace and security for all, this can also become a very empowering process. When groups are not caught up with accusation and counter-accusation, defence and counter-defence, they are free to get on with the job of making healthy change. Look around — is this where our community's energies have been going all these years?

Having also experienced these difficulties the Alkali Lake people made 'The Honour of One is the Honour of All' their central theme. People started to take pride in each other's achievements. From the very beginning team members can make this project *special*. It can be designed to bring people together, rather than to introduce another element of competition and jealousy.

Once a community understands the history and background to local problems, and develops support groups for its suffering members, it will be able to take comfort in sharing each other's sorrows and successes, disappointments, and victories. *'Sharing and Caring' become the new face of liberation.*

> There is no such thing as false hope. Optimists live longer. Pessimists have a more accurate view of the world, but they don't live longer (Dr Bernie Siegel).

SETTING UP SUPPORT GROUPS

Programs which focus on *risk reduction and health promotion* will work best when they are established close to the community base. Support groups are one of the best vehicles for achieving the objectives of personal growth and community healing.

Support groups are a collection of caring people who share common experiences: such as alcoholism, child abuse or family violence, or who have a common interest in, for example, the well-being of youth and children. They provide a loving and safe environment for people to share these experiences, and to learn how to cope with the effects they have had in their lives.

Support groups are forums of compassion for those who are suffering or who are in need. They offer a listening ear, emotional comfort, new direction, and practical help. They are also excellent environments for building self-esteem and for replacing negative self-images with positive ones. They work at developing alternative behaviours and non-violent life styles.

Support groups are 'specialised' because they focus upon, and respond to, specific areas of need. Here are some examples:

Victims' or Elderly Support Groups

A victim support group may focus on helping anyone who has suffered from violence or other crime. It is often not realised that a victim can go on suffering long after the event of a crime. Victims, particularly the elderly, can become fearful and may lose their self-confidence. They may become bitter and blaming of others around them. Adults, who were victims of violence as children, need to learn how not to perpetuate cycles of violence into the next generation. They need special help and support to *understand and to unlearn* those patterns of violence which were impressed upon their psyche at a young age.

Support groups set up to help people suffering from cycles of addiction, family violence, or childhood experiences of abuse, can take several roles. They can play a powerful healing role through simple group discussion and interpersonal exchange of experiences and feelings — even when these events occurred many years ago.

Victim support groups can also make a public statement of disapproval of violence (an important step in getting the community to refuse to tolerate this). They bring to public attention that there are always *victims* of violence, and that individuals, families, and whole communities suffer.

Support groups can provide a catalyst for the setting up of refuges and shelters for victims of family violence. They may act to defuse domestic disputes by helping to talk people through their differences. The development of a new range of crisis intervention skills, mediation, or dispute resolution services may grow out of these activities.

Women and their Families Support Groups

Women and their Families Support Groups provide a forum for 'Women Helping Women'. They assist women to cope on a day-to-day basis with their lives. These groups concentrate on healing the hurts and identifying the needs. They build up the confidence of women through shared activities. Sharing ideas for healthier living can be a lot of fun (arts and crafts, cooking classes, sewing activities, foraging for native foods, information exchange on matters of child care and family health, education upgrading, and new skills training).

Women Growing Strong kinds of activities will, sooner or later, affect the whole community. Strong groups can stir up the courage and conscience of the community to tackle difficult problems. The central message of these support groups is to teach people that: 'no-one deserves to be beaten and abused!'. 'Everyone has a right to feel safe!'.

Children can also share a vision for violence-free environments. They can have lots of ideas about how to deal with kids' problems and in many ways can be more influential in reducing childhood offending. With adult support Kids Teams and Youth Teams are particularly good at setting up popular entertainment for young people — such as bush camp outings, regular sports, fashion, music and dance, arts and crafts, bike tracks, alcohol-free discos, and other safe activities. With team training, youth and children are quite capable of seeing the advantage of planning 'healthy futures' strategies for their peers. Exciting projects will aim to link young people back into the community through their experiences of adult support and adult approval.

Violent Men Support Groups

Support groups can also focus on the needs of violent men. Men's Support Groups can help offenders recognise the origin of their personal conflicts and to cope with them without resorting to hurting themselves or others. They teach new patterns of behaviour in a constructive and safe environment.

It is vital that people who suffer from deep rage and frustration are helped to channel these feelings, and to deal with them effectively. A Men Against Violence committee (a kind of 'AA' for violent men) or similar group, will focus upon the problems of men who are habitually violent and will provide the support of other men who will listen and understand. Understanding how violence is learnt, and how to replace it with alternative behaviours, is an important phase for offender healing and violence reduction in the community. Just having an avenue to 'talk out' frustrations can defuse tensions and save others from injury.

ROLE PLAYING

Role playing is a useful technique for practising new skills: for instance, in a personal crisis, in the event of a dispute, or in the handling of a violent situation. Participants need to see that they have behavioural options. Rather than raising a fist in an escalating argument, they need to discuss ways of defusing conflict. They need to *rehearse other ways* of handling anger. Role playing exercises are particularly useful for participants. During a support group session people can play-act a situation, explore behavioural options, and practice non-violent skills. In a conflict there are other things a person can do, besides raising a fist. As the experience of members expands, communities may like to investigate ways of building crisis intervention and conflict resolution services into the community infrastructure. some groups have written and performed plays on these subjects.

ENNOBLING THE TASK

It is important that we *ennoble the task* of building alternative behaviours. That is, that we show people the importance of what they are doing through their support groups. Take some time to consider a name for the group. Create one that captures the *essence* or *spirit* of what we hope to achieve — our vision for the future.

At a crime prevention workshop I ran in 1989 in a northern Queensland community, an action group was formed on the second day. After a lot of discussion about what the group wanted to achieve, the name 'Abmelgorr' ('People Coming Together') was suggested by a participating elder. Everyone was very pleased with this beautiful name!

'Men Against Violence' is a name which draws attention to the role this group wishes to play in changing attitudes, balancing personal relations. It highlights the vital role of men in bringing about peace and security to their community. Violent life-styles are terribly difficult to break, and every effort to do so is of value. The aim of any perpetrator program should be the absolute and permanent cessation of violence. *'The Cycle Stops With Me'* is a noble goal!

If a man achieves nothing else in his life, but stops the cycle of violence at his generation, then he has achieved something of great worth. He will certainly have saved lives. Anyone who participates in such a group has reason to feel proud of their efforts, because they are building a safer place for the children of the future.

To involve people in a support group will not only give them the help they personally need, but will also give them a new purpose in life. Some of the best supporters of programs are those who have been helped themselves. Once they have learnt new skills for non-violent behaviours, ex-offenders often become excellent role models and credible counsellors. After experiencing the benefits of a support group, some participants become enthusiastic and committed helpers of others with similar problems.[1]

SETTING UP ACTION GROUPS

A cluster of keen individuals who wish to identify and to target particular problem areas within the community, and to plan a course of action to tackle these problems, can set up an action group. Action groups may be composed from any sector of the community depending upon group priorities. A community might set up youth teams, men's teams, women's teams, or even mixed teams of youth, elders, adults, and children. Common goals of the action group unite team members no matter how different their background. It is surprising how many hidden talents there are in one locality. Elders have told me that they are 'just *waiting* to be asked to do something'. Often a program is activated by the efforts of just two or three individuals, but eventually expands to involve the whole community.

Another consideration for the team is to decide whether it wishes to invite representation from service agencies or other professionals. This is entirely up to the group. With the abilities and resources that many agencies offer, it is a good idea to at least have the support of professional workers for preventative programs rather than their sulky indifference or opposition. By involving or liaising with representatives from service agencies, communication will improve, and energies can be pooled in solving community problems. This way we are making the most of every resource available to us. If certain agencies or individuals want to dominate the action group, welcome their assistance, but explain to them the importance of community ownership of community problems, and community ownership of community solutions.

The size of the action group will depend upon how many people in the community are interested in contributing, and how many people from agencies are invited to assist. It is not important whether the action group is five or six people, or ten or twelve people, as long as the job gets done. If there are a lot of people wanting to join the team, form specialised action or support groups according to people's interests and talents. Some will want to work with youth, some with women, some with sports, some with addiction, and so forth.

Draw up a list of those people who might be called upon to help implement plans of action. This list might include a cross-section of elders, youth, housewives, counsellors, school teachers, child welfare workers, legal aid officers, nurses and health workers, police-aides or energetic adults who enjoy sports, hunting, gathering, or fishing. This exercise will help the group understand the infrastructure of the community and to identify available resources in or around the community.

Action groups may meet irregularly, according to the project needs. But support groups, because of the important healing work and emotional support they provide, should meet at a regular time, at least once a week. Public meetings with the general community, or meetings with agency representatives (if they are not actually participants), will usually be held less frequently. Meetings should be helpful, freindly and pleasant to attend, not another chore! Spread the burden through mutual support.

The social and recreational activities run by these groups can be very enjoyable. Action groups and support groups can work together on big projects, share ideas, congratulate each other on every achievement, and give each other lots of rewards and encouragement. This is very important for everyone. It helps to draw the community together.

NEW SKILLS TRAINING

Action groups will benefit if the talents of their members are enhanced with new skills training. This will not only empower individual members, but will go a long way to producing a unified team. New skills training provides a selection of tools which will maximise the ability of action groups to respond to community needs, and to handle the current and changing pressures of community life.

Workshops with an official trainer could be arranged. Alternatively, informal 'learning by doing' kinds of activities, based on manuals, videos, and other resource materials, can be an equally powerful method of group learning. Team-work training, for example, could include topics such as:

- Power politics verus teamwork
- Positive thinking and positive action

- Communication and cooperation
- Setting up Support Groups
- Setting up Action Groups
- Problem identification and analysis
- Primary prevention
- Action planning
- Program implementation
- Program monitoring and evaluation
- Crisis intervention
- Conflict resolution and mediation
- Negotiation
- Networking.

New skills will help to make an action group special. By being an example of unified action the team could become a role model for other groups, and a source of inspiration to other communities.

ACTION PLANNING

Action planning is simply the planning and staging of action towards desired goals. With our vision in mind, we can map a path, pinpointing a series of stepped goals along the way. This will give a general outline of our plan for action. To achieve our first goal we will need to decide who we should talk with, who needs to be involved, and what kind of program we want to set up.

It is the action group's responsibility to recruit volunteers, work with the natural leaders of the community (elders, community counsellors), invite agency assistance, find funding (if this is necessary), delegate responsibilities, rally community support, gather resources (posters, white-boards, video machines, tools, vehicles), set up community days, organise workshops and seminars, develop funding submissions to government or any other essential task required to implement our plans. It is always better to do one thing well than to be too ambitious in the early days of program development. Dividing work up into smaller stages, and deciding priorities, makes a program more manageable.

Team-work, problem analysis, and action planning are the three most important skills of any action group. A well thought out plan will carry a team through the rough patches in the program, particularly at the early stages when they are experimenting with techniques and gaining confidence. Many people are naturally good at action planning and will find they have been doing this all their lives!

COMMUNITY AWARENESS THROUGH PARTICIPATION

An essential part of an action group's responsibilities is to *communicate* regularly with the community, to listen to their concerns, and to seek their participation and support. In planning its activities the community remains a rich and relatively *untapped resource* for action groups. Individuals from diverse backgrounds can contribute their personal time and enthusiasm to help promote a wide range of preventative activities. Working closely with other community members is central to the successful implementation of these programs.

Community days, or even whole weeks, can be organised along particular themes and can involve everyone. Different organisations can set up information booths, kids' arts and crafts displays, personal safety demonstrations, and recreational activities.

If, for example, the theme of a community day is 'Caring for Ourselves' some of the displays might include demonstrations on first aid and personal safety put on by the school children, a 'Drink Safe' and AIDS awareness booth run by the local nursing station, an accident and fire fighting display manned by the police, a search and rescue video show provided by the emergency services, a 'Safe Families' information booth run by the Women's Action Group, a hunting and fishing safety demonstration put on by the Men's Action Group, and a 'Seeking Sobriety' program put on by the local Sobriety Group. Other popular themes for community days are 'Caring for Our Kids', 'Family Days', 'Arts, Crafts, and Traditional Activities Days', 'Sober Discos', alcohole-free 'Music Festivals', 'Sports and Recreation Days'. Food stalls and lots of fun activities as well make these days enjoyable for everyone.

In 1989 local government, service agencies, and community members got together to run a 'Care for Kids' week in Woorabinda, Queensland. Through voluntary labour a range of low-cost 'fun' activities were organised, including a swimming carnival, talent quest, fashion parade, kids' posters, food fair, a children's street march, and various stalls and events run by different service agencies. At the same time daily community workshops were held to discuss serious issues — such as sexually transmitted diseases, AIDS, family violence, caring for kids etc. This very successful and relatively inexpensive project helped to draw families and the community together and to increase awareness of the needs of children (Atkinson 1990: 22).[2]

WORKSHOPPING SOLUTIONS

Workshops are a powerful tool for community problem solving and action planning. Here are the results of one brain-storming session by the Aboriginal participants at the Adelaide, *National Forum on Domestic Violence Training*, April 1990. The workshop was asked to imagine they were an action team. In examining 'solutions' the workshop identified seven domains for action:

Areas for community action

Families	Children and Youth
Women	Men
Prisoners	Service Providers

Community Development and Training

Suggestions for action in each area were written up on the white-board by the group leader. For families it was proposed that 'Parenting Centres' be set up to provide information, training programs in family living, and a range of support group programs suitable for family members. Inexpensive recreational and creative programs should include special activities for whole families.

Women were seen to need shelters, resource centres, communication workshops, empowerment workshops, and their own support groups. The workshop felt that communities should not be getting service agencies to do all the organising for them, but should seek to initiate and run programs themselves.

The workshop was asked what community resources were available to help young people and children. It was decided that young people, adults, and grandparents could all provide resources. Grandparents could teach hunting, fishing, and other traditional skills and could pass on cultural values through story-telling. Educational and personal development programs were needed. A youth 'Drop-in Centre' with its own youth workers was highly desirable. Child Support groups and teen teams could provide similar programs for the young in the meantime.

The needs of men, and their lack of access to information on a range of subjects, were discussed. Men's resource centres were proposed. The emotional and personal needs of men are often neglected. It was agreed that support groups for men were a high priority. Men who have the courage to stand together could support each other, and help others to overcome alcoholism, violence, and despair. Men needed to take back their role as protectors of the family. Some participants said that men would like to contribute by organising sports activities and camping trips for children. It was suggested that men working on CDEP schemes could design and build playground facilities for children rather than simply sweep up leaves.

People were not happy with community life generally. There was a need to 'stop the fighting between factions'. People needed to 'open their homes up'. They needed to 'sit down together'. 'Common projects would get people talking' and would 'improve everyone's self esteem'. It was suggested that the government should be petitioned to allow hunting and fishing on traditional land. This would help ease social rifts and economic hardships in communities. It would stimulate the transmission of traditional knowledge to children.

Communities could also become involved in the development of prisoner visitor schemes, prisoner information services, prison cultural programs, and other training which would help both prisoners and their families. Service providers (including police and magistrates) needed cultural awareness training. Wherever possible Aboriginal people should staff, or be directly involved in, service delivery and in the cultural education of service providers. The participants felt that, in order to 'make sure we're getting the best out of programs', an exchange of ideas and resources should be encouraged between communities and agencies.

It was proposed that existing programs be utilised where possible for the seeking of funds, and that efforts in the development and extension of programs be coordinated. Health services, for instance, could be invited to help communities run regional and local 'healthier lifestyles' forums. There was an emphasis upon culturally relevant programs and options which reinstate community responsibility and community control.

'Community days' were thought to be a great idea for bringing adults and young people, families, and communities together. Projects should be imaginative rather than expensive. Being able to generate action without heavy dependence on outside resources liberated people and empowered them to get on with the job. Every new project should be launched with a ceremony or a celebration to mark the occasion, to make people feel proud of their achievements!

A brain-storming session on possible areas for community education and training produced a long list. Here are just some of those ideas:

Areas for community education and training:

- team-work building   • releasing anger
  - family violence workshops
- communication skills   • cooperation
  - negotiation and lobbying skills
- administration skills   • programming
  - dispute resolution and mediation

- personal development
  - understanding the system
- assertiveness
- family-life skills
  - independent living skills
- stress management
- cultural development
  - understanding mental health
- work skills
- preventing addiction
  - drug and alcohol education
- codependency
- forming support groups
  - adult children of alcoholics
- counselling

Programs like this could be organised and run by any community using local talent, with the help of manuals, handbooks, and outside specialists. In a video filmed in 1989 at Alkali Lake during a 'Healing the Hurts' workshop the commentator said that, at the end of their workshop, the participants were all aware of the enormous commitment they were making to 'break the cycle of hurt and shame, to forgive, to regain our lost powers'. This was best expressed in the words of this elder:

> We have to sit down and speak the truth to each other and make a peace amongst each other. That people will bring unity and with unity there is strength. And with the strength of unity we will have the love and respect to walk in harmony with all life (Elder, 'Healing the Hurts' video 1989).

◆ ◆ ◆

[1] Canadian Indian organisations have found that ex-offenders are often the best role models when it comes to teaching boys and teenagers how to stay out of trouble with the law. Given the opportunity, committed ex-offenders can become an enthusiastic resource in guiding others away from lifestyles of crime. The Native Counselling Service of Alberta requires its prisoner counsellors to have had personal experience of the prison system, simply because these counsellors have the most credibility with offenders.

[2] According to Atkinson the 'Care for Kids' Week cost the community $3,600 (Atkinson 1990: 22).

The following Workbook section provides practical ideas and techniques for team building, healing circles, action workshops, healing exercises and games, and for developing proposals.

Speakers comments from the Healing Our People Conference, Aboriginal Co-ordinating Council and Bama Healing Centre, Cairns, 24 May 1994

ALCOHOLISM

Alcoholism is the number-one health problem. We need Aboriginal controlled, Aboriginal staffed, Aboriginal developed treatment programs
(*Doug Walker, CAAAPU, Cairns*).

Alcoholism is a disease. It is a treatable illness from which people want to get well. Our people do not choose to die at 29. Its their basic human right to recover from this illness
(*Eric Shirt, CAAAPU, Alice Springs*).

Drugs may promise you a lot, but they may deny you your reason for existence
(*Val Carroll, Benelong's Haven, Kinchela Creek*).

CHILDREN

Under-aged drinking must go. Binge drinking must go. Morning drinking must go. If we cannot do these things then alcohol must go. If we cannot keep a drug from our children we should not use it
(*Val Carroll, Benelong's Haven, Kinchela Creek*).

Honour the children. The pain of the child of the alcoholic is that no-one sees their pain. We need to set up groups to help the children
(*Phil Diaz, Miami*).

TREATMENT AND TRAINING

Alcoholism doesn't respond to research! It doesn't respond to videos, posters or moderate drinking programs! Alcoholism responds to systematic treatment
(*Doug Walker, CAAAPU, Alice Springs*).

My heart is set on training our people to become alcohol and drug educationists. Once we become aware, we can become the agents for change. To make healthy communities we need good role models
(*Leslie Baird, ACC, Cairns*).

We've been pushing for an Aboriginal sobering-up centre for about eight years. It seems that they won't give us one while these other services exist
(*Basil Sumner, Aboriginal Sobriety Group, Adelaide*).

LEADERS

We have to make sure our leaders are sober because we need them. If they're to speak properly for us they have to be strong. Not weak and drunk
(*Doug Walker, CAAAPU, Alice Springs*).

LAND AND CULTURE

As we become sober, we can get back to the culture. Learn the language, come back to the land. As we start to get back to the land it will become a place of peace
(*Leslie Baird, ACC, Cairns*).

When I drank my life was in the pub. I've been sober now for four years. I'm going to get my people sober, and we're going to get our land back
(*Doug Walker, CAAAPU, Alice Springs*).

In the spiritual matter of land rights the Aboriginal people and its leaders met with some success. That was the enemy without. Alcoholism is the enemy within
(*Val Carroll, Benelong's Haven, Kinchela Creek*).

SPIRITUALITY AND VISION

All development must come from within. No vision, no development. Culture is the mother of vision. It is the vision-bearers who break the cycle
(*Phil Diaz, Miami*).

WORKING TOGETHER FOR HEALING

You can be the architect of your own healing
(*Paraiare Huata, Central Institute of Technology, Auckland*).

How can we break the cycle? By letting go. By recognising that we are co-dependent. By seeking a support group. By just working with what we have. When we let go we are afraid. Its scary. But its also like dying and beginning a new life
(*Mercy Baird, Juyuga Ministries, Yarrabah*).

Martin Luther King said: 'Unarmed truth is stronger then evil triumphant'...We need to be spiritually connected. Working to heal the individual and the family go hand-in-hand with the development of the community. These are all inter-related
(*Phil Diaz, Miami*).

There is a gathering of forces. We all have our story. Its important to tell it, so we can tell our children. Here comes the truth. It is time
(*Anna Latimar, Executive Director, NANACOA, Seattle*).

'Let the Healing Begin'
(*conference theme*).

WORKBOOK 1

PERSONAL DISCOVERY EXERCISES

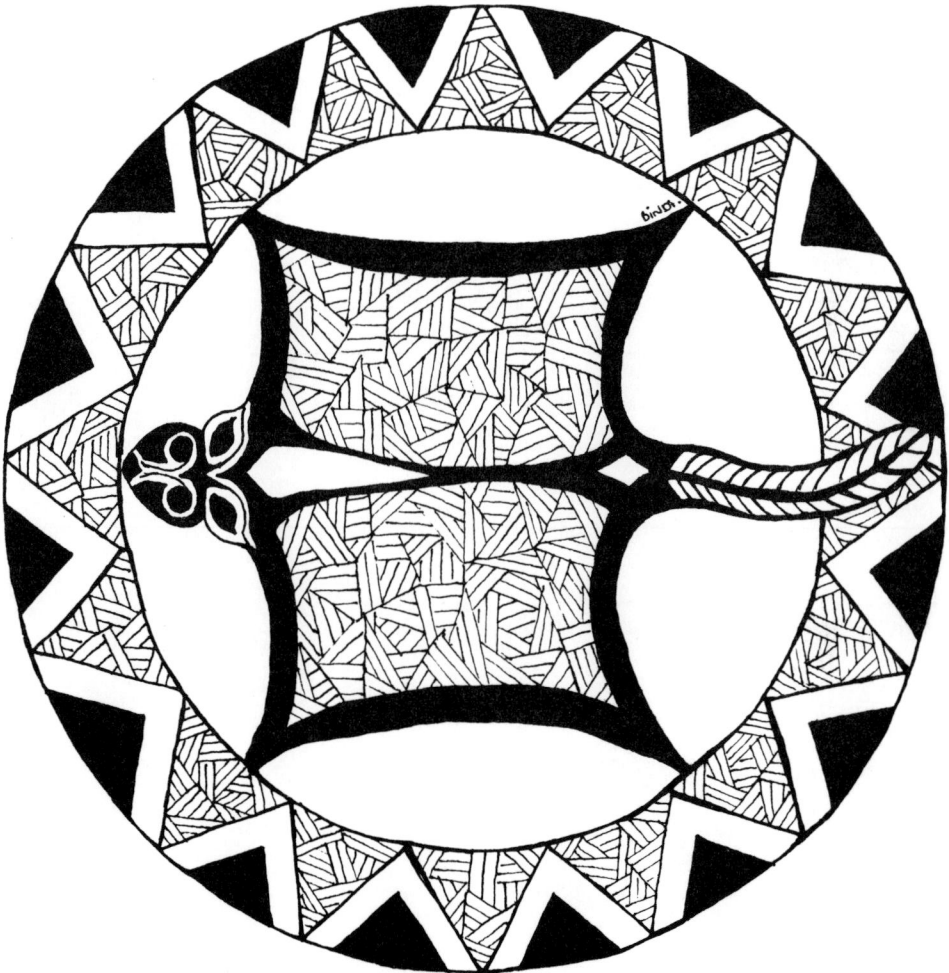

... everyone wants to become whole, to fulfil their potential ... we all, like seedlings or tadpoles, intend to become our full selves and will do so if we are not thwarted. People don't need to be forced to grow. All we need is favorable circumstances: respect, love, honesty, and the space to explore (Bass and Davis 1988:14).

THE PATH TO SELF-DISCOVERY

Learning to look at ourselves, perhaps for the first time, can be very painful. This is necessary, however, in order to move people from habits of dependency and shame to new levels of self esteem. Just as we need to understand the physical effects of alcohol abuse, we also need to understand the social and psychological effects of negative thinking upon our lives, and how to replace them with happier and more healthy outlooks:

STEP I: RECOGNISING SELF-ABUSIVE BEHAVIOURS

Dishonest or blaming behaviours stand in the way of a person's recovery. These are most common:

- repression — forcing yourself to forget
- projection — blaming others
- denial — not admitting you have a problem
  self-hate — blaming yourself, low self esteem
- withdrawal — silence
- rationalisation — making excuses

- fantasising — day dreaming and dramatising
- intellectualising — speaking from your head, not your heart
- procrastination — putting things off
- reaction formation — faking your feelings
- deflecting — laughing it off
- rescuing — stopping another from feeling.

STEP II: RECOGNISING COMPULSIVE PERSONALITY TRAITS

Here are some compulsive personality characteristics which we might suffer from on a regular basis or occasionally experience at different times of our lives:

- neurotic, fearful, insecure
- irresponsible, denial
- dependent, terror of abandonment
- loss of self, low self esteem
- guilt, self loathing
- self pity, worry
- people pleasing
- perfectionism, vanity
- excessive loyalty
- possessiveness, jealousy
- impulsiveness, recklessness
- phoneyness.

STEP III: SHARING, CARING, AND GROWING

Through the process of group interaction, participants learn to acknowledge their feelings, accept them, and express them openly and honestly.   After recognising that their lives have become *unmanageable*, participants are urged to seek strength from a Higher Power — to develop their spirituality; and to accept the support and caring of others in the group — to develop their trust.

Most people do not have all the tools for self healing.   But with faith in a Higher Power, and trust in others we can gain access to a richer pool of resources.   'Sharing your tools for recovery with others will help you recover', wrote Woititz (1986: 14).

During our sharing times each one of us will gradually learn wonderful new skills of sharing, caring, and growing.   We will learn these by:

- opening up slowly — being honest about our feelings (using ' I feel [sad/confused]' sentences)
- listing problems — overcoming denial
- sharing experiences — feedback and solutions
- listening — hearing, being non-judgemental
- testing solutions — developing realistic expectations
- expresing care/concern/love — for self and others
- identifying the positive — acknowledging beautiful things, simple pleasures, feeling good about our selves and our achievements, (using ' I feel [happy]' sentences).

STEP IV: HOW TO RELAX WITHOUT ALCOHOL

There are many practical things, and exercises, which can be used to help us relax and attain better health, including:

- managing stress
- releasing anger
- learning to let go of 'problems'
- looking at beautiful things
- sharing our achievements
- keep fit exercises
- relaxation techniques
- organising ' fun' activities
- music used in healing activities
- games, sober discos.

STEP V: FINDING THE ' WARRIOR' WITHIN

In every one of us there is a strong, confident, and courageous person. In every one of us there is a *man or woman of spirit*.   As we slowly remove the barriers our *Warrior Heart* is released from the cage of self oppression.   Signs of our true selves and new ways of finding ourselves will be found in:

- prayer and meditation

- increasing self awareness
- self acceptance and forgiveness
- self confidence and self esteem

- feelings of belonging
- detachment and personal serenity
- being at peace

- awareness of others
- listening skills
- loving ourselves and loving others
- communication and assertiveness skills

- problem identifying/solving capacity
- positive decision making
- leadership training
- taking assertive action

- commitment, completing what is started
- involving friends or family members
- helping, accepting, forgiving and loving others.

EXERCISES

'I Trust' exercises
As a group exercise, Dr Woititz suggests that we write on a board or on butchers' paper words ' describing what *trusting* feels like'.

When I trust, I feel

safe	scared
close	relief
serene	warm

wonder	calm
fulfilled	secure
liberated	connected

Trust may feel different to different people.   The group can share ways in which they can work on building up trust (Woititz 1986 :15).

GROUP RULES

Learning to work in a support situation, with a group of people with needs just like ourselves, is a special privilege.   In the process of healing ourselves, we will also be learning the skills of the ' healer'.

A true healer has great compassion for others, as well of self understanding.   Our first step in becoming sensitive towards the feelings of others' is to let go of our bad habits of blaming and denial. Some good ground rules shorten this process right away.   Discuss them and have the group agree to them first.   Here are some suggestions for group rules:

- be honest about your feelings
- speak for yourself, use ' I' statements
- be present — no popping in and out of the room
- pay attention — so you won't get the wrong idea
- silence is OK — time to think before talking
- no fights — leave your prejudices by the door
- confidentiality — what goes on here stays here
- courtesy — do not interrupt when someone is talking
- fairness — do not hog all the group time
- observe — listen — learn
- no hiding or fiddling — hats, dark glasses, with articles on the floor.

WHAT IS FEEDBACK

Feedback occurs during group discussions and sharing times. It is a problem-solving process.   The purpose of feedback is to share, not to counsel and advise others.   It is to help others find their own counsel and guidance *within*.   'I share my thoughts, problems and experiences with you'.   'You share similar experiences which may throw some light on my problems, or solutions which you found worked for you'.

Feedback should be given in *non-judgemental* statements. 'I noticed that you (describe behaviour or attitude). As a result, I feel that ...'. This is better than: 'You were wrong to (behaviour/attitude), you should have ...'.

When receiving feedback it is important that you listen to what the other person has to say. Do not become defensive or try to explain yourself when people comment. 'Yes, but...' indicates that a person may be becoming defensive. This may be a good time for the group to help that person by pointing it out to him/her. This may be painful, but recognising denial and self-justification leads to self-acceptance and growth. Being sensitive to each other's feelings, and not being too hard on each other, however, will avoid over-stepping personal boundaries.

EXERCISES

The 'I Feel' exercise
The group is asked to express their feelings about a sad subject (alcoholism, child abuse, my life in general, an emotional issue, how I feel about myself). They are then asked to express their immediate feelings in one word on this topic. These are written up on a big sheet of butchers' paper or a board in front of the group.

The same exercise can be tried a little later with the group on a happy subject (my favourite place, a walk in the sunshine, the support I get from this group, how I see my future). Keep the old list and compare the different feelings.

Here is an example of feelings people may offer:

The 'I Feel' list

angry	surprised
annoyed	hopeful
disgusted	cheerful
disturbed	delighted
disconnected	energised
jealous	content
frustrated	balanced
resentful	glad
shocked	aware

lost	excited
impatient	thrilled
helpless	fantastic
troubled	warm
bitter	happy
mixed up	calm
scared	loving
trapped	peaceful
hostile	pleased
unhappy	proud
hurt	relaxed
sorry	relieved
rejected	satisfied
empty	thankful
desperate	understanding
disappointed	together
miserable	sensitive
depressed	alive
bewildered	confident
unloved	grateful
betrayed	wonderful

(Ideas above were drawn from the 'Sharing Room' at the Poundmaker's Lodge, Edmonton, September 1990.)

'How To' exercises

The focus of group discussion is very important.   Identifying the problems is the first stage.   Knowing the solutions is the second. Learning how to build a bridge between the two — the ' *How To'*— of problem solving is where real growth occurs.

For example: Dulcie has a problem of trusting.   She feels isolated and afraid of people.   The solution is to learn how to trust, and, therefore, to become less isolated.   The question is: *'How can we become more trusting?'*

The Support Group share their recovery tools to help Dulcie.   They share their own problems and experiences of trusting.   They help to build a staircase for Dulcie, between her feeling of fear to new feelings of trust.

The group examines reasons why people choose not to trust. Someone illustrates a time when not trusting protected her from a dangerous situation. Others share experiences of when trusting others helped them.

Invite people to share feelings associated with trust.

'When I trust I feel':

safe and secure	relaxed
relieved	happy
free	calm
close to someone	warm inside
fulfilled	special
open to sharing	understood

The group discusses ways they can bring trust into their lives.

GAMES AND ACTIVITIES FOR TRUST

Games and activities can be built into a program to increase trust on one hand, and reliability on the other. The group might like to start with the *Circle of Trust Game* where participants learn to ask for help and learn to trust that they will receive it. This could be followed by *Message Game* where participants learn the importance of reliability, of being there for someone else. The *Picnic Game* shows the importance of communication and trustworthiness (see Workbook 2, 'Healing Games and Exercises'). Later the group might like to organise a real picnic or some other group activity in this way.

The group can share ideas on ways they could build more trust into their relationships with family and friends.

These things will help me to build up trust

- Communication is really important
- Learning to trust my support group
- Caring and sharing
- I practice trusting myself
- I make decisions and take little risks
- I try to believe that not everyone lies and cheats
- I try to be more optimistic about my life and future
- I try to be trustworthy myself

- I share my feelings (don't cover them up)
- I try to be realistic in my expectations
- I test my expectations with the group
- I transfer my new skills to my personal relationships
- I learn to laugh at myself and at situations.

Closing Prayer (optional)

THE SERENITY PRAYER[*]

God grant me the serenity,
To accept the things I cannot change,
The courage to change the things I can,
And the wisdom to know the difference.

Suggested topics for groups

There are many topics which our group may like to discuss. Explore some of these topics together and make a list for later gatherings. 'Learning how to' kinds of topics are a good place to start. Here are some ideas.

Learning how to

- ask for help
- say ' No' to friends
- be good to myself
- recognise my self-worth

- value others
- provide a listening ear
- respect other people's views

- organise my time
- take one day at a time
- plan my day
- finish what I started.

[*] The Serenity Prayer — Alcoholics Anonymous.

- make friends
- build self confidence
- be more patient
- be a good sport (play fair)

- lead a balanced life
- have more fun
- stay cool in a crisis

- improve my personal relationships
- not be judgemental of others
- not be too hard on myself

- relate to my family
- care for others
- support my family
- improve my family life skills

- do well at school
- use my artistic talents
- have a hobby

- develop coping skills
- manage stress in my life
- plan a physical exercise program
- meditate and/or pray;

- help to heal others
- introduce prevention to my community
- improve the quality of my life
- improve my character.

WORDS FROM PARTICIPANTS:

In 1987 a video entitled 'Poundmaker's Lodge: A Healing Place' was produced. Here is some of the narration, and some of the stories shared on this video:

'People can love you back to good health' — *Young mother*

I'd been up [awake] for about four days and I'd been partying over at a friend's place. We took a taxi to go downtown to a bar [pub]. We were just getting out and all of a sudden the taxi door opened and there was my mum standing there.

I was really surprised and I said, 'Mum, what are you doing here!'. I saw tears in her eyes and she said, ' what are you doing to yourself'. She said: 'Come, I'll take you home'. I said, ' No, I can't go back home with you'.

So I went running down the street and I hid in this apartment building. And you know, that jerked me back to reality. I thought, 'I'm not only destroying myself, but there are people who care about me'.

I guess I was so obsessed with the drugs and the alcohol that I had forgotten who loved me. I thought, 'I can't let these people down. I can't let my children down'.

Although at the time I never thought much of myself, when I look back — and to this day I believe — *that people can love you back to good health.*

'I've never seen love, until now' — *Young man*

What makes it hard for me, I've never seen love in my life. I've never even seen it in my childhood days. I've never had my mum come up to hug me. Maybe the odd time she'd come up and put her arm around me and tell me ' be strong'. The only time I've ever seen love is coming here [to Poundmaker's Lodge].

I went to boarding school in my younger days and when I returned back home there was lots of alcohol in my family. I can't forget how it was. I would be sitting outside and my dad would be inside swearing at my mum, calling me 'illegitimate kid!'.

I couldn't figure out why he didn't accept me.   My other, real dad, he deserted me at three.   These things, they're still in my mind.   I have to bring them out and learn to deal with them.

I'm a full grown man, and these things they're beating into me.   I try to drown them with alcohol, but that gets me into a lot of trouble.

I asked the Great Spirit to take them from me.   I believe that He watches over me.   I believe if I show Him I want to go the right way He will help me.   That some day I'll be strong enough to overcome everything.

The ancient sweat lodge — Narrator

At Poundmaker's the people take part in one of the most ancient rituals — the Sweat Lodge.   For thousands of years the Lodge has brought purification and comfort to those who enter.   The fire represents the sun, which gives life to all forms.   The stones represent Mother Earth, and the unending nature of the Great Spirit.

Ties with creation: that is my medicine' — Participant

As I enter the Sweat Lodge I am part of the circle of life and wish to be cleansed of the storms of terrors.   I feel spiritual ties to all creation.   As I walk out, and all is clear, that is my medicine.

'Peace and contentment by sharing' — *Young man*

Ambition to me is to be able to lead a good useful life. To be useful to my people. To find peace and contentment by sharing. That's ambition to me. We're champions! That we have that ability to make it in this world and still maintain our own society, our own beliefs, and our own values.

'A new vision of themselves' — *Narrator*

Since Poundmaker's Lodge began hundreds of people have walked away with a new vision of themselves. And a feeling of wanting to know something about the greatness and truth of the old traditions and values.

While there will still be hardships to face they have made a step forward, away from the miseries of alcoholism. Over the years not only have hundreds of people recovered their lives, but in time many have offered their love and understanding to others, both at Poundmaker's and in their home communities.

(*Poundmaker's Lodge 'A Healing Place'*, video,
Poundmaker/Nechi Centre 1987.)

WORKBOOK 2

HEALING GAMES AND EXERCISES

ICEBREAKER EXERCISE

Participants stand up and go over to another member to introduce themselves.   Each member of the group gives their FIRST NAME AND WHERE THEY ARE FROM.

Each participant tells the other member TWO THINGS THAT THEY LIKE, and ONE THING THAT THEY DON'T LIKE.   Move around the group until everyone is met.   *Think of something different to say to each new person.*   This should be brief, fun, light-hearted — even remember something from childhood ('*I like: watching sunsets over the sea, climbing trees.' 'I don't like: mosquitos, boring seminars, big dogs, noisy people*).

MISSISSIPPI RELAXATION GAME

Create a big circle with all participants facing each other.   Everyone takes an imaginary pen and screws it into forehead.   With leader, they draw the word Mississippi (dot each 'i').

Then take imaginary pen and screw it into the tummy.   Do again (jump up to dot each 'i').   This game causes much laughter!

STORY TELLING GAME

Create a small or medium circle (not too large so people can hear each other).   The leader explains that the group is going to make up a happy story to tell their grandchildren.   The leader begins a story about a girl and her magic basket (or some other subject).   Each person in the group adds a piece to the story and the story telling continues around

the circle from one person to the next.   This exercise helps people relax.
People will slowly become involved in the story and join in the fun.
(Smaller circles of between five and ten give more opportunities to
individuals to contribute).

CIRCLE OF TRUST GAME

Participants form small inner circle of about five people and a larger
circle of about ten.   The outer circle people are the 'givers' of help, the
inner circle people are the 'receivers' of help.

The inner circle people cross arms over their chests, and say quietly
to themselves: 'I need help and support'.   'I will trust'.   They then roll
back on their heels, falling backwards.

The outer circle people have positioned themselves behind — one
or two 'givers' to one 'receiver', depending upon size of that person
needing help.   As the ' receiver' falls backwards the 'givers' catch and
support them, gently placing them back on their feet. (Note: Do not wait
too long to catch the people in need of help! People are harder to catch
the further they have fallen.   To encourage trust, help should be swift!)

The outer circle moves around one person and the exercise is
repeated.   When each member of the outer group has supported each
member of the inner group, change places and repeat the exercise.
(The purpose of this exercise is to learn trust and to teach
supportiveness.)

THE MESSAGE GAME

Round I: Participants sit in a circle (about 10 in number).   A short
message is whispered from the leader to the person to their right.   (The
leader keeps a note of this message for later). The second person
whispers the same message, as best they can remember, to the next
person and so on.   The message travels clockwise until it has gone all
the way round.   The last person announces the message and it is
compared with the original message sent by the leader.

Round II: During the second round each person can alter *one* feature
only of the message before communicating it onwards.   When it
reaches the end messages are again compared.   (This is to show how

unreliable gossip can sometimes be, and how important accuracy in communication is.)

Try the exercise again, this time try a harder message.

THE PICNIC GAME

Materials needed: Butchers' paper and coloured pencils or crayons for everyone.

Preparation: The group will organise a 'paper picnic'. The group leader writes up two lists of food items for a paper picnic. (Each list should equal the number of people present.) The group leader sends one list clock-wise and the other list anti-clock-wise around the circle.

Each participant must cross off one item of food from each list. At the end of the exercise everyone will draw a picture of the items of food they will be bringing to the picnic. (People may improvise a little). Everyone brings these to the circle again and lays these out to see just what kind of picnic they will be having! Has anything been forgotten!

THE REPARENTING CIRCLE

Two circles are created — an inner and an outer circle of the same numbers. The outer circle bends forward and whispers something they have always wanted to hear said to them by their parents (e.g. 'I love you'; 'I am very proud of you'; 'I am proud to be an Aborigine/Indian/woman/man'; 'I am proud you are my son/daughter,). Wait a moment and allow the message to be received and accepted. Then the outer circle moves on one person and the message is given to the next person. The exercise is repeated, by the participants in the outer circle changing places with those in the inner circle. This can be a very emotional exercise. If it feels right, give each other a hug.

This was an exercise originally designed for children of alcoholic parents, but when adults enact the roles of parents and children it can be an excellent exercise for reparenting. It will help to heal the ' inner child' in any age group, and is an excellent teacher of parenting for adults.

THE SHARING CIRCLE

The sharing circle is a place for sharing and mutual support.   It provides a safe environment and a place to talk and exchange experiences.   Healing circle participants learn to give love and to receive love from each other.   It is a place where people learn to parent themselves, and to rebuild their lives, and personal relationships. Within sharing circles people learn to identify and to recognise their problems, rather than to deny them.   They can feel empowered by taking ownership of their problems with the support of others.

Sharing circles can be of any size, but smaller numbers will allow each person to have more time to speak.   Create a circle in a comfortable place — people may like to sit on cushions or mattresses, as these sessions can last quite a while.

Use an object which is meaningful to the group — such as an eagle's feather, a rock picked up from the land near the community or a sacred spot, or a wooden carving.   The person who holds this 'talking stone' or 'talking stick' may speak about any matter which is heaviest upon their heart.

Everyone has a turn to speak, and the item can go around several times.   People will often share their sorrows, memories, and unresolved hurts and difficulties, but they can often share their positive experiences, particularly when they see that this may help another member after they have heard them speak.

The 'sharing circle' has a special power with groups.   The positive experience of caring and sharing has a very positive energy and will create a real emotion in participants who are in great need.   It is important that this emotion is not suppressed as the airing of these feelings, perhaps for the first time in a person's life, has a cleansing and healing effect — as do the tears and sympathy which others express in support.

'I FEEL' EXERCISES

'How I Feel' exercises are a very important part of group work.   For instance, a healing workshop may begin with what people are feeling at the moment.   The leader may write up on the board ' What is Shyness'? Then she/he may turn to the group and say 'You tell me'. People will give many illustrations of how it feels to be shy, and of experiences they have had on buses, when dealing with government officials, or in the presence of other community members.

Seeing that list grow, and the different expressions of shyness helps participants become aware that they are no alone in their feelings. Understanding will give them a sense of achievement and confidence to tackle more difficult subjects.

If this exercise is practiced once every session people will become quite good at exploring and understanding their own feelings, and those of others. An 'I Feel' list might later be developed about a sad subject, such as 'How I Feel about Alcoholism', and about a happy subject. (For examples see 'Personal Discovery Exercises', Workbook 1.)

STEPPING-STONE WORKSHOPS

A community or group may wish to hold workshops on a range of subjects. These need not be difficult or complicated to run and can include the use of videos, healing games and exercises, the exploration of personal feelings, mutual support, and information sharing. The Family Life Improvement Program, run under the Native Counselling Services of Alberta (an independent, Canadian Indian organisation), put on the following workshops. These might give us some ideas for our own workshops.

Workshop I: Children Are People

Topics   Mothering
Children's feelings
Discipline and guidance
Children's self esteem

Workshop II: How Can I Take Care of Me

Topics   What is self esteem
Capabilities, responsibilities
Self-acceptance
Changes and personal growth

Workshop III: Violence In the Home

Topics   What is a battering relationship
                What is co-dependency
                Feelings
                Communication
                Breaking the Cycle

WORKBOOK 3

WORKSHOP METHODS AND TECHNIQUES

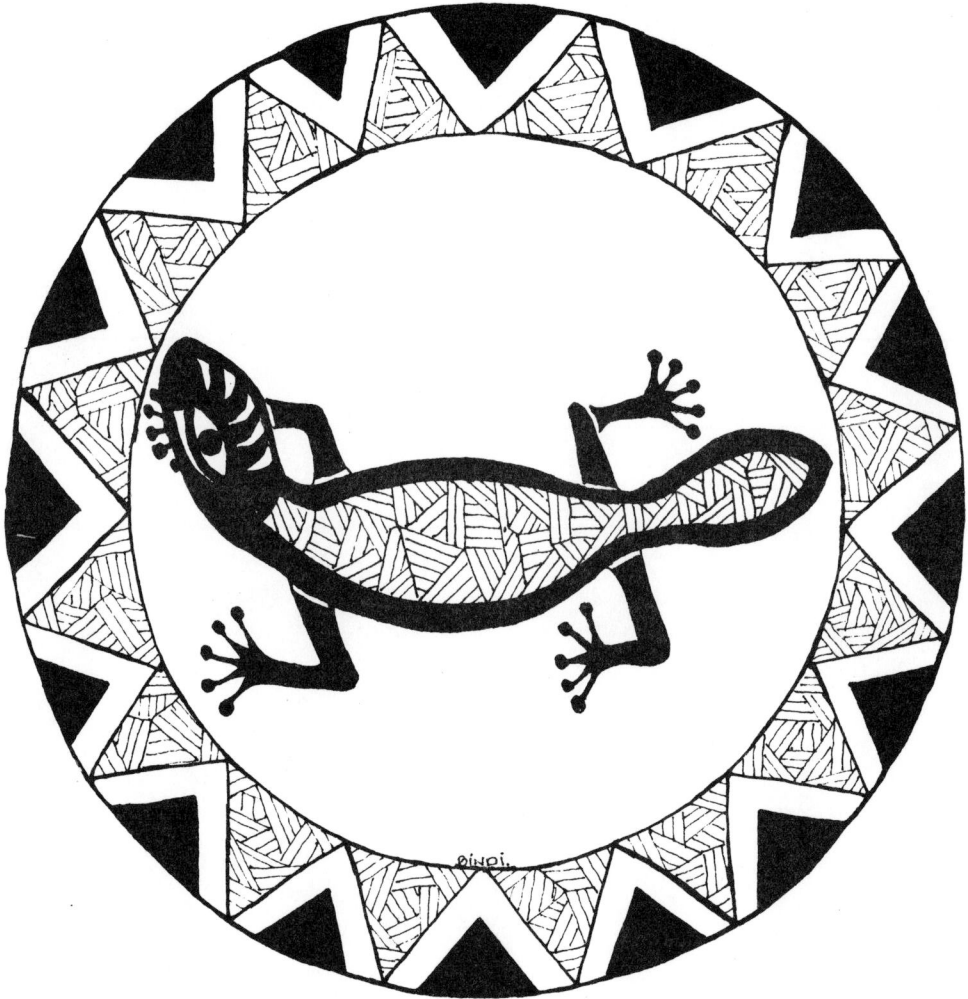

Here are some hints which group leaders can include in the running of community workshops. For convenience these have been divided into three main sections. People may like to add to these, or to make up their own exercises.

I EXPLORATION

In this section familiarise participants with each other and the purpose of the workshop. The basic principles of self–determination are established at the beginning, and some new concepts and new approaches could be explored.

1 Ice breakers:
Workshops should be fun! Especially so, when serious problems are being discussed. Find some good 'ice breaker' exercises to open the sessions. These can be a simple game, if people already know each other; or a light hearted ' getting to know you' kind of activity (see 'Healing Games and Exercises', Workbook 2).

2 Clear explanations and visual aids:
Start out the workshops with clear explanations and lots of practical examples to demonstrate what you mean. Visual aids are great for getting people focused. Use posters, boards, butchers' paper and lots of coloured pens.

3 Exploring new concepts:
Highlight the underlying principles of the workshop: such as 'Community Ownership of Community Problems', 'Community Ownership of Community Solutions', and 'Community Re-empowerment'.

Discuss *new concepts*.   For example: What is a holistic approach? What makes a balanced individual and a balanced community? Demonstrate the equal importance of *physical, emotional, mental, and spiritual* needs.

Outline the *objectives* of the workshop, such as 'Finding a Vision for our Community'.   In simple terms, explain what an action group is. Explore together the idea of teamwork.   Explain that the meaning of these new concepts will become clearer through the *'learning by doing'* process.

4 *Exploring new approaches:*

Videos are excellent for exploring new ideas.   Those which show new approaches being used by Aboriginal people in other parts of Australia, or by indigenous people in Canada, the United States, Greenland, New Zealand or other parts of the world are very popular (see 'Videos, Manuals and Other Resources' in the Bibliography Section).

When using a video allow plenty of time afterwards for discussion of what people saw and how they felt about it.   This is the time people's imaginations are most stimulated and it is a good time for sharing.

5 *Grounding discussions in the community experience:*

A genuine commitment to the principles of 'Community Ownership' is best demonstrated through the grounding of discussion in community experience.   Get workshop participants to discuss local issues.   Give ownership to their explanations and ideas by listing *their key points* on the board.   Continue this throughout the whole workshop.   This way participants can take pride in the way their thinking progresses and develops.

6 *'Naming Our Villains':*

In any community there will be many problems.   While we cannot handle them all at once, it is good to identify them and to give them a *NAME*.   To *know our villains* empowers us with the awareness that we *know what we want to change*.   Here is a list of villains which a group might feel are hurting them:

Alcoholism and ill health
family and community violence
child abuse and neglect

back biting, negative thinking
corruption in local officials (ignoring grog running
  or family violence)
boredom, nothing to do in this town
lack of caring for each other
loss of culture
loss of spiritual understanding.

Write your VILLAINS on a board.

Here are the key concerns listed by the Abmelgorr Action Group (meaning 'People Coming Together'), set up during a Northern Queensland community workshop in 1990:

Example:

Abmelgorr Key Concerns

- youth vandalism, homeless or neglected children
- young people walking around all hours of the night
    and missing school the next day
- the needs of young mothers and their babies
- family violence and the needs of men
- the needs of older women
- the needs of elderly people
- community policing
- sly grog, alcoholism, the canteen and the Council's
    attitudes towards all of these
- gambling
- community by-laws.

---

7 Shaping a vision for the community:
Ask the action group to shape a *vision* for the future for their community.   What would the community be like without these problems? How would our men be? What would the life of our women be like? What about our children — what kind of environment would we like to create for young people to grow up in?

If we had all the money and power in the world, what would be the best future we would want for our children and grandchildren? Get participants to *imagine* that they have such power for the moment. Help them to let their imaginations go. *Visualise* what the community would be like if these problems were removed.

Write these *New Visions* on the board. Then look them over together. Are some of these visions attainable now? Could others be reached in small steps over time? [*]

8 Setting up an 'Action Group':
Set up an action group and give it a name which reflects our special purpose and vision for the future. Prepare handouts based on developments in the workshop so far (for handout ideas see Hazlehurst 1990: 46-49).

The Abmelgorr Action Group explored what it would *like to see* for the community in the future. These were written on the board as general goals and aspirations.

Example:

Abmelgorr Visions for the Future

- *For the men:* more work, no boredom, security, pride, men's groups.
- *For the children and youth:* happy kids, kid's sports, no boredom, respect for adults, kids groups.
- *For the women:* young mothers' programs, family life programs, sewing classes and other recreational activities, support for women as family providers, womens' groups.
- *For the elderly:* nursing and retirement homes, community caring and support, respect.
- *For the community in general:* more sports weekends, alcohol free recreation, safe streets, safe homes, family pride.
- *Long -term goals:* A Youth Centre, a Daycare Centre, Alcohol Rehabilitation Programs, a Womens' Shelter, a Childrens' Shelter.

---

[*] This process is called 'Creative Visualisation'. There are quite a number of books available on this subject for those who wish to read more.

II SKILLS IN PROBLEM ANALYSIS

This section of the workshop seeks to develop skills in structured problem identification and analysis.

9 Targeting the problem:
For this exercise we will target *one problem* for analysis.   In analysing our problem we will need to identify the:

- *target problem*
- *target offending group*
- *target victims*
- *situational circumstances*
- *environmental circumstances.*

For example: if the problem is vandalism our community analysis may look something like this:

Target problem: *vandalism*

Target offenders: children between the ages of 9 and 12

Victims: the whole community

Situational circumstances: occurs after school, weekends and holidays

Environmental circumstances: children have nothing to do, and nowhere to play except around the town

Program focus: pre-teen action groups, community infrastructure, recreational talents of community members.

Ascertain those behaviours which are the most destructive or threatening to community health and general well-being; the age and sex of the offending group and of the victims; when and where the problems occur and related trends.

Describe the social situation and environmental circumstances under which the problems are most likely to occur (i.e. dark streets, around the canteen, after the club closes, evenings and weekends at home). From this analysis we can decide which are the key areas of focus for community healing.

If family violence is the target, we may decide to focus our initial program efforts on adult males, if they appear to be the main offenders, and upon adult women, if they appear to be the main victims. But to tackle such serious issues we will need a deeper understanding of the problem itself.

10 Creating a 'Problem Profile':

We need to create a *profile or clear picture* of the problem. Breaking down the component parts of the problem increases understanding and makes for holistic and informed solutions.

We need to know:

- *Ability:* how the problem/offence is committed
- *Opportunity:* when and where the problem/offence occurs
- *Desire*: why the offender wishes to commit the offence or indulge in the dangerous behaviours
- *Repercussions:* the physical, emotional, mental and spiritual repercussions upon individuals and communities;
- *Needs:* the physical, emotional, mental and spiritual needs. What is *missing* in individual lives and within the community
- *Resources:* available individual, community and agency resources which might help initiate intervention.

When looking at the *Ability + Opportunity + Desire* of offenders to commit the offence, give particular attention to the motives, reasons, and attractions behind the dangerous behaviours or disruptive events. List these on the board (for example: People drink because ...).

Ask the group to consider the *Physical + Emotional + Mental + Spiritual* dimensions of the problem, as it affects the whole community. Create a list under each heading. Can the behaviour of offenders be explained in terms of special needs in these areas? What are the repercussions of the problem upon victims/the whole community? What requires urgent action?

Knowing the problem from the point of view of the victim, the offender, and the community will result in more original, effective, and thorough solutions. Give this process of analysis the time it needs.

11 Creating a 'Goal Staircase':

Goals which our action group sets for itself should be kept short and simple. List goals, starting with the least ambitious, and step them upward towards the action group's vision for the future. If we start with easily achieved goals (such as talking to the council, doing a community survey, or running a small workshop), we can then build upon our successes. When our group feels more experienced we will feel stronger to tackle the more difficult activities.

Forming *'Stepped Goals'* — easy goals leading to other, more ambitious goals — helps to break down action into manageable portions.

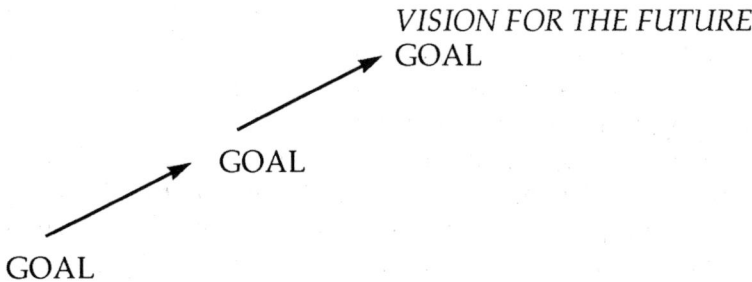

VISION FOR THE FUTURE
GOAL

GOAL

GOAL

Stepped goals also help us to focus our *plans for action*. In just a few words, write down what we hope to achieve with the particular project. For example: our ultimate goal may be to reduce street assaults (*target problem/crime*) committed by young men (*target group*) against young women (*target victims*). Our short-term goals will form part of our *Vision for a Violence-Free Community*, which can be put at the top of our *'Goal Staircase'*.

Have another look at the short-term goals which we have listed. Will they help us achieve our *Vision for the Future?* Discuss this within the workshop.

III BRAINSTORMING ACTIVITIES

'Brainstorming' is an exciting word! It indicates the *creative process* taking place by the pooling of minds and imaginations. The group becomes greater than the sum of its parts. Participants experience a sense of their own power and ability when they work together as a team.

By now there should have been some solid discussion on the selected problem. There should be a summary analysis, or a breakdown, of the problem on the board, as well as a list of the group's short-term and longer-term goals. Keep these to short simple sentences or to key words and illustrations.

During the third section of the workshop, participants increase their skills in team work, creative problem solving, action planning, resource location, and program implementation. (For an example of the brain storming process see Workbook 4 'The Abmelgorr Workshop').

12 *Action planning and implementation:*
Start to formulate the group's plan for action. Who do we want to consult with, and how will we involve the community? Our initial plan of action may be to: hold a public meeting, run a small workshop, research the extent of the problem by contacting local agencies and/or by undertaking a community opinion survey.

Discuss the setting up of community-based support groups which respond to the special needs of community members, victims, and offenders. Explore possible financial, material, and human resources which might be available. Be imaginative. Most activities will not cost very much. With the pooling of our energy, time, and talents limited funding need not be a handicap.

In exploring our community resources find out who can do what. People are a rich resource and may be pleased to be invited to help on individual projects. Outline the steps which need to be taken to achieve each goal and who could be recruited to assist. (For resource suggestions see Hazlehurst 1990: 50–73).

Example

In one South Australian Aboriginal community where offending was high among the youth and children, a 'self-discovery' bus trip was organised for those who had been in trouble with the law. The journey took the youth to some of the more traditional communities where they learnt about Aboriginal culture, arts, stories, and dance. The young people were encouraged to develop their leadership qualities on this trip by helping with the day-to-day organisation.

On their return to the town many of the young people put their energies into helping other youth and in developing youth programs. The youth offending rate in this town dropped by about 85% and remained down many months after the trip. Some of the worst offenders became positive role models for other youth.

We will need strong leaders in the future. Participation in community programs helps to develop leadership qualities in the young.

(For further guidelines on running a workshop see 'Team-Building Workshop', Workbook 5).

THE ABMELGORR WORKSHOP:
'PEOPLE COMING TOGETHER'

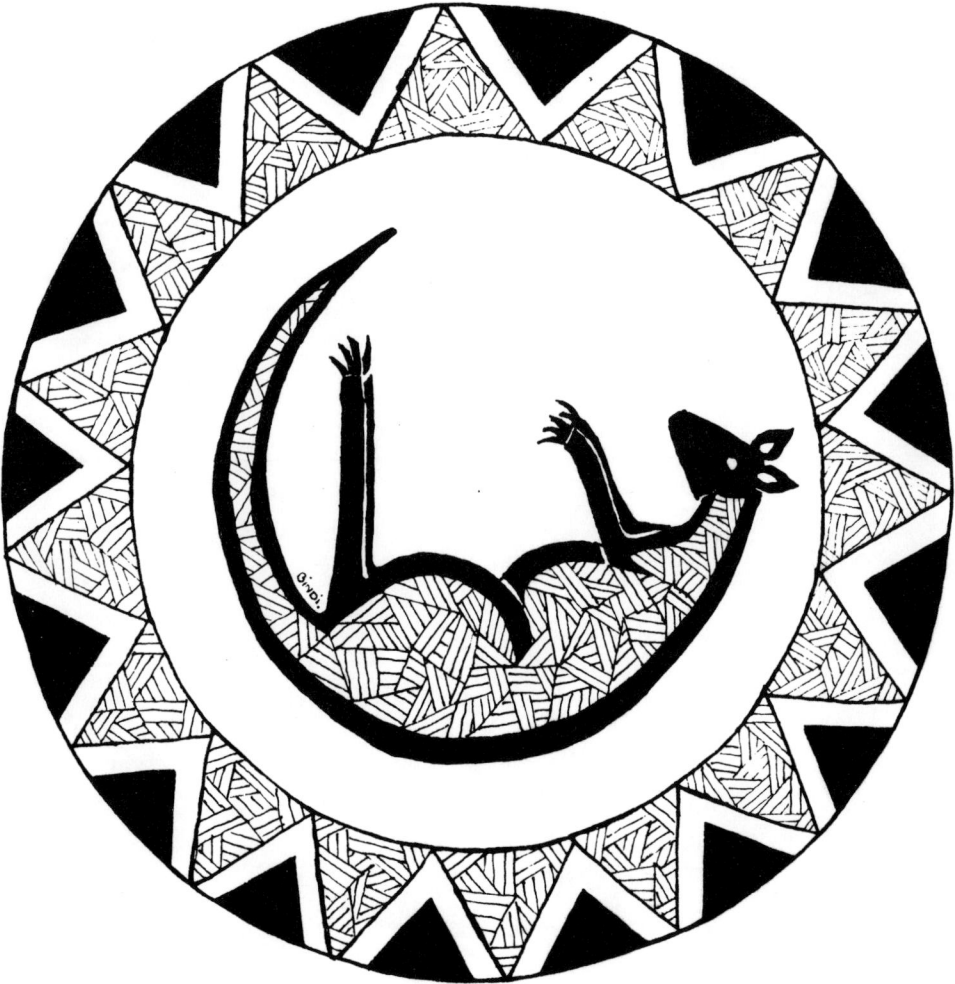

Here is an example of how one action group in far north Queensland worked through a problem and came up with an original solution. Their first task was to identify the target problem they wished to combat and the target offending group.   This is how their workshop developed:

THE TARGET PROBLEM

The Abmelgorr Action Group was concerned about the vandalism of community property, particularly the breaking of lights and windows with home-made shanghais.

THE TARGET OFFENDERS

Boys, and sometimes girls, between the ages of 12 and 16 years were seen to be the target offenders.

THE VICTIMS

The whole community was victimised by this activity.   It gave everyone a sense of insecurity on the streets due to poor or no lighting. Having their windows smashed while they were in their own homes made them feel as if they were being invaded.

ABILITY

The offenders had the ability to commit the offences.   Handmade shanghais were used to break the lights and windows.   The young people showed considerable initiative in the construction of these shanghais.   They fashioned them from local materials.   They went into the bush to obtain the right kind of wood.   They sought out old pieces of tyre–rubber for the slings.   A well–made shanghai was the source of admiration among young friends.

ENVIRONMENTAL CIRCUMSTANCES AND OPPORTUNITY

It was noted that this problem occurred mostly after school, on weekends, and during school holidays.   Apart from 'growling' at them, no adults seriously attempted to stop the problem.   Neither the police nor the council seemed able to do anything about the problem as the children ran away.

The young people had no respect for the adults of the community. Some of the offenders were not concerned whether adults were watching.   There was a general lack of interest among the young to obtain adult approval.

DESIRE

The action group spend a considerable amount of time analysing 'what was in it for the kids'.   By putting themselves in the place of the children they discovered a number of motives for the use the shanghais.

Firstly, it was fun! The competition, adventure and added sport of outwitting the adults and police brought excitement to after school hours.

The admiration of other children brought peer status and respect. Being a 'good shot' made a young person feel 'important' among his or her friends.   It gave a young person a 'position' within the juvenile hierarchy.

Accomplishment of the task of building good shanghais provided personal challenge.   Their skill as marksmen introduced a sense of pride, self worth, and the thrill of 'success'.   Younger children role modelled themselves on 'high status' older children.

CONCLUSIONS

It was concluded that bored children were committing offences for 'kicks'.   In looking at the offending group's motives the action group discovered that shanghai skills provided an opportunity to young people for personal achievement, competition, and status.   It was clearly a self-esteem building activity as well as a source of entertainment.

WHAT IS MISSING IN THE COMMUNITY?

The action group then looked to see whether the community offered their young people similar excitement and rewards.   The answer was a very loud 'No'! There were no sports facilities; social or recreational programs were sparse or nonexistent; and there were few avenues by which the young could experience or enjoy adult approval.

With little opportunity to receive encouragement from adults, the young people had little reason to prize it! In fact, the youth sub-culture of opposition had become so strong that most adults were at best irrelevant, and at worst, seen to be 'the enemy'.   Shanghai shooting had become 'fashionable' because there was nothing else much for young people to do.

ACTION PLANNING

The Abmelgorr Action Group agreed that they would need to think of other forms of recreation which were less harmful to the community and which would help bring the adults and youth back together.   Their project was to consider alternatives for the young which could divert their energies away from 'bad activities' into ' good activities'.

It was agreed that these new activities should have the same appealing components of excitement, competition, status, and personal reward.   Alcohol-free dances, football and other sports, arts and crafts, excursions, and self-learning experiences were some of the alternatives discussed.

Having analysed and understood the problem from the point of view of the offending group, the action group recognised that it was unrealistic to expect them to give up their skill of shanghai shooting —

certainly in the short term.   On the other hand, the community would continue to want them to stop vandalising town property.   Even if the action group gathered the youth together and told them how much it was upsetting everyone they were sure this would have no effect on its own.

A compromise solution was proposed.   If the skill was treated as a local sport, 'something negative could be turned into something positive'.   It was suggested that a *youth team* should be formed with the help of one or two of the more athletic men in the community.   The youth team could then be involved in making the rules for the use of shanghais in the town.

COMMUNITY RESOURCES

It was suggested that the local Aboriginal Council should be asked to prepare a shooting ground just on the outskirts of the town, and to erect a set of poles at different distances apart as marked shooting points. The young people could go there every day after school to practice their skills if they wished, with adults taking turns in supervising.   As two or three of the officers were particularly interested in youth, the police could also be approached to give their support for the project after hours.

IMPLEMENTATION

It was suggested that every Saturday, with the supervision of the adults, competitions could be held for the different age groups.   Winners could compete in a *community sponsored tournament* at the end of each month.   This would be made into a community event, with possible added fun of picnics and barbecues.   Winning shanghais from that month could be placed on display for everyone to admire.

Prizes could include a special bush outing or a piece of new sporting equipment from funds raised by the council and the youth team.   The police could be asked to attend tournaments, and help give out the prizes.   It was hoped that the police might consider providing transport for bush outing prizes.

A 'kids meeting' would be called where it would be explained to the children why people were unhappy with the situation.   The young people would be asked if they would like to set up a youth team to help run the Shanghai Competitions.   They were to be encouraged to give their view and to show off their shanghais to the adults.

The youth team would be involved in setting the rules of the 'Games'.   It was suggested that anyone who brought the sport into disrepute by vandalism during the week could be eliminated from the competitions the following Saturday — and could possibly relinquish their position at the monthly tournament.

Elders could be enthusiastic supporters.   It was suggested that a special meeting of elders be called to explain the project to them. Elders could also impart traditional knowledge to the young people and might be interested in running cultural programs through the school, if these were organised for them.

Towards the end of the discussions one elder suggested that perhaps the young people would like to learn spear throwing and other traditional skills, and that the Shanghai Competitions could later evolve into traditional sports competitions.   Everyone was very excited by this idea and it was placed on the board as a future goal.

OTHER DISCUSSION

This exercise had an empowering effect upon the Abmelgorr Action Group and increased their confidence to discuss more difficult problems in the community.   It was suggested the other sporting activities for the community might 'help overcome frustration and to build pride in our men'.

They said they wished to set up Women's Support Groups, particularly for young mothers, and suggested that 'family talks' could be held in the event of family problems, fights, and neglected children. Several local people were interested in being trained as mediators to help facilitate family and community disputes.   A shelter for battered women and children shelter was seen to be an urgent priority.

The action group was very concerned about alcoholism.   A key point was made: 'If any community-based programs were going to work at all there was a need for the community to find a way of reducing its alcohol consumption'.   The action group wanted to run alcohol-free community days — sports and other fun activities so the community could learn to enjoy itself *without alcohol*.   They decided to discuss these objectives further with the council.

It was agreed that the community needed to take charge of its own problems and to come up with its own solutions through support group activities. The action group wanted training for participants in dispute resolution, intervention skills, and family-life programs. The group wanted to find more ways of using community talents and resources — particularly the resources of the elders. There was a general consensus that the next generation needed to be diverted into healthier life-styles for the future.

COMMENTARY

It is clear from this workshop that good ideas can grow out of relevant ones! The project for the Shanghai Competitions proposed by the Abmelgorr Action Group was most likely to be successful because it had good social fit. It emerged from an understanding of the nature and context of the problem. The project also promised to empower young people in decision-making. It could be implemented at very little cost, with a modest amount of personal commitment and human labour.

As everyone agreed that they were ' tired of being shot at by shanghais', the option of 'working together' for something which promised to be fun and rewarding for the whole community, seemed a much more attractive alternative.

TEAM-BUILDING WORKSHOP: NOTES TO WORKSHOP LEADERS AND COORDINATORS

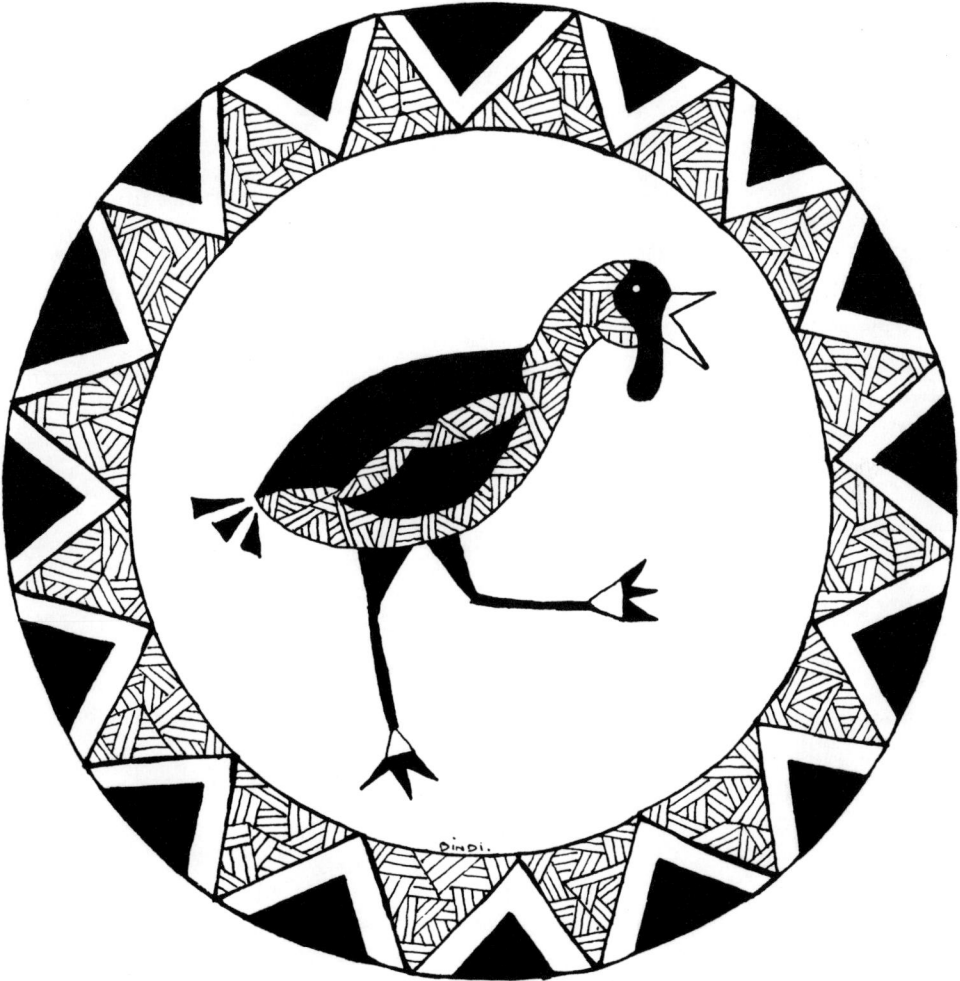

WORKSHOP LEADER'S OPENING EXPLANATION

In the workshop today I would like to invite you to participate in an experience of team-work building through the medium of role playing. It is my hope that some of you will be able to go away from this workshop with some ideas you can use for problem solving in your own areas.

The purpose of this workshop is to introduce you to techniques of ACTION GROUP FORMATION; ACTION PLANNING; AND PROBLEM SOLVING. As action planners we will be exploring techniques of PREVENTION, INTERVENTION, AND DIVERSION.

During this workshop we will act together as an action group. WE ARE THE ACTION GROUP, and the PROBLEM we have been set up to tackle in the community is [*Identify the Problem*] JUVENILE VANDALISM.

Notes to WORKSHOP LEADER

If this is at a conference say: 'Our group will role play as an ACTION GROUP set up to tackle this problem in a particular community'.

SETTING UP

In a few minutes I will ask you to break into groups of about 10 in number (*Between 8 and 15 is still comfortable depending upon space and numbers*).

But first I would like to call for one volunteer coordinator per group (*Give handouts to COORDINATORS*).

Notes to COORDINATORS

COORDINATORS lead group discussion with the help of the handout guidelines.

In the handouts there are sections which COORDINATORS read out, followed by group exercises.

COORDINATORS (or appointed 'scribes') take notes of key issues and ideas identified by the action group.

WORKSHOP LEADER

I will ask the COORDINATORS to take notes of the key issues and ideas which are developed by your team so these can be shared with other action groups (or the conference) later.

THREE-HOUR WORKSHOP

Timetable — Total 3 hours

WORKSHOP LEADER outlines the
purpose of the workshop   30 min

EXERCISES
I	Icebreaker	10 min
II	Identifying the problem	20 min
III	Setting up an action group	20 min
	TEA/SHARING	30 min
IV	Action planning	30 min
V	Support group formation	20 min
VI	SHARING	20 min
		180 min

Notes to WORKSHOP LEADER

This is about the shortest possible time in which to do these exercises. If a group has longer, give more time to each section. This workshop can be run over a 3-hour period, or up to a whole week, depending upon how long you wish to spend on each section.

HANDOUTS-INTERVENTION WORKSHOP

Notes to COORDINATORS

The job of the coordinator is to introduce each stage of the discussion, as outlined in the handouts.

COORDINATORS must also keep an eye on the time; keep to the timetable as much as possible allowing everyone to speak; and must summarise the key points to be shared with another action group, or possibly the whole conference later on.

EXERCISES — SECTION I

I ICEBREAKER   5—7 MINS

Exercise 1: Participants stand up and go over to another member to introduce themselves. Each member of the group gives their FIRST NAME AND WHERE THEY ARE FROM.

Exercise 2: Each participant tells the other member TWO THINGS THAT THEY LIKE, and ONE THING THAT THEY DON'T LIKE. Move around the group until everyone is met. *Think of something different to say to each new person.* (This should be brief, fun, light-hearted — even remember something from childhood).

Notes to COORDINATORS

COORDINATORS should start to show how this is done. For *example: 'I like: watching sunsets over the sea/climbing trees'; 'I don't like: mosquitoes; boring seminars, big dogs, noisy people'.*

II IDENTIFYING THE PROBLEM   20 MINS

We are a group of concerned parents and neighbours who live (work) in a common neighbourhood (town, community, workplace).

In our community JUVENILE VANDALISM IS RAMPANT.   We have came together to identify the circumstances in which vandalism is occurring.

Exercise 3: Identify the TARGET GROUP — who is committing the offences (be specific — age, males, females).

Exercise 4: Identify the VICTIMS — who are affected and how (be imaginative).

Exercise 5: Identify the CIRCUMSTANCES AND ENVIRONMENT in which vandalism is occurring (at night, around the pub, shops, school etc.)

There are three situational factors which need to be considered.   The where, how, and why of the offence:

OPPORTUNITY + ABILITY + DESIRE = VANDALISM

Discuss each of these:

Opportunity: When and where does the problem occur? What physical opportunities exist (dark streets, unguarded areas after hours, careless parents/community)?

Ability: How is the offence achieved (means, techniques used)?

Desire: Why does it happen? What is the offender's personal motivation in committing the offence? The ' what's in it for them' aspect of the problem (peer-group status, thrills and excitement, escape from boredom, a need to make an oppositional statement to overcome a sense of powerlessness)?

Notes to COORDINATORS

COORDINATORS should take notes on key points and issues during this session.

III   SETTING UP AN ACTION GROUP
20 MINS

An ACTION GROUP was set up following a meeting of concerned people.   WE ARE THAT ACTION GROUP.

ROLE OF THE ACTION GROUP

The ACTION GROUP will gather information about the problem to find out its social nature and seriousness.

The ACTION GROUP will INVOLVE THE COMMUNITY in information gathering and in understanding the problem.

The ACTION GROUP will help SHAPE A VISION FOR THE FUTURE for a vandalism-free neighbourhood.

Exercise 6: Discuss how our action group can gather information about the problem and can involve the community.

Exercise 7: Shape a VISION FOR THE FUTURE for a vandalism-free environment.   Write this down in a few sentences.

Notes to COORDINATORS

This is the 'problem analysis' phase. We are not looking for 'solutions' yet; only specific information about the nature of the problem, how to get information from the community (i.e. public meetings, interviews) and goals for the future. Try to keep people to these points.

TEA AND SHARING   30 MINUTES

Over tea: get together with a nearby action group to share your points so far. Each coordinator has 10 minutes to speak. KEEP AN EYE ON THE TIME.

EXERCISES — SECTION II

If you want to give others experience, a new volunteer coordinator could be sought for the next section.

IV ACTION PLANNING   30 MINUTES

Two vital qualities of an action group are:

TEAM-WORK ABILITY + ACTION PLANNING

Our action group has been through a team-building program and feels confident about its team-work ability.

ROLE OF THE ACTION GROUP

The ACTION GROUP will identify the problems and discuss possible solutions.

The ACTION GROUP will plan and organise community-based activities.

There are three main AREAS FOR ACTION in which we might work.

PREVENTION + INTERVENTION + DIVERSION.

Discuss each of these:

Prevention: When and where is prevention needed? What environmental changes are needed to reduce the *opportunities* for people to commit the offence?

Intervention: How can we limit the *ability* of people to commit the offence? What techniques or practical means of intervention will be needed?

Diversion: This is perhaps the most important, and also the most neglected aspect of any preventative exercise. If we can reduce the attractiveness of [vandalism] we can reduce its occurrence. Developing appropriate alternatives requires a good understanding of the initial motivation of the offending group. We will be replacing one motivational set for another. Whatever we offer must increase status and personal identity, it must be more rewarding and more exciting than [vandalism]. Given most circumstances surrounding offending, this is not usually that difficult to achieve.

The community is best placed at diverting the *desire* of people to commit the offence by providing alternative outlets, recreation, community support, and things which are more interesting to do. Social crime prevention, therefore, offers the greatest promise.

Remember

OPPORTUNITY + ABILITY + DESIRE =
OUR VISION FOR THE FUTURE

Exercise 8: Keeping our vision for the future in mind, discuss POSITIVE STEPS OR PROGRAMS which might be used in PREVENTION, INTERVENTION, and DIVERSION.

Notes to COORDINATORS

This is a brain-storming exercise. By its nature brain-storming is a POSITIVE exercise. Negative arguments — such as all the reasons why something cannot work — should be put aside for the moment. Keep the dialogue constructive. Avoid personality conflicts. Keep the team-work spirit active during this exercise.

V SPECIALIST SUPPORT GROUPS 20 MINS

Prevention is not just about *stopping* something from happening — such as vandalism — its about *making something happen* as well.

SPECIALIST SUPPORT GROUPS can be set up within the community. They provide safe places for sharing and mutual support. They can encourage, assist, and educate TARGET GROUPS (both victims and/or offenders). They can change ISOLATING SOCIAL ENVIRONMENTS into CARING COMMUNITIES.

Exercise 9: What kind of SUPPORT GROUPS would we like to create to reach our particular target groups?

Exercise 10: How will our support groups FUNCTION. Will they INTERVENE with, or will they merely SUPPORT target groups?

Exercise 11: What kind of DIVERSIONARY ACTIVITIES can our support groups provide (i.e. parents forums, sports/ recreation for kids, youth teams)?

SHARING   20 MINS

Share your ideas with another action group.

A 'NEW WAYS' WORKSHOP PROPOSAL

**THE GREATEST RESOURCE OF ANY COMMUNITY
IS ITS PEOPLE.**

There is a groundswell of interest in community healing and preventative approaches for community development.

'New Ways' workshops are based upon the principles of self-determination and personal re-empowerment. They emphasise *'Community control over community problems' and 'community control over community solutions'*.

'New Ways' workshops build upon existing community structures, talents, and capacities. They help workers, agencies, councils and communities to identify and to draw upon their own strengths.

'NEW WAYS' WORKSHOPS SEEK TO CREATE:

A SUPPORTIVE ENVIRONMENT — Workshops provide a positive and supportive environment for the *talents and capacities* of the participants to emerge. Where there is a need, they *encourage personal healing* in participants.

NEW SKILLS TRAINING — New skills such as teamwork building, conflict resolution, and action planning, empower individuals and groups to analyse problems, work through issues, and develop *culturally relevant and community-grounded solutions*.

COMMUNITY EMPOWERMENT — New skills, and the confidence experience generates, empower workers, families, community groups and eventually whole communities, to tackle the *hard issues* of alcohol and drug addiction, family violence, child abuse, juvenile crime and inter-family feuding.

RESOURCE IDENTIFICATION — Workshop participants are shown steps by which they can identify government, public, and professional resources in support of community development objectives. How to apply for government funding. How to attract *untapped resources of support.* How to find out about regional, state, and federal programs which could assist community objectives.

HUMAN RESOURCE DEVELOPMENT — Workshop participants are shown how to draw out and encourage the human resources and talents of their communities in support of their programs, how to train under-utilised resources, and how to create and nurture *new pools of support and talent.*

RESOURCE MATERIALS — A range of resource materials will be displayed, viewed and discussed, such as *posters, videos, manuals and leaflets.* Information about how these can be obtained and a workshop exercise on how to create our own resource materials will be undertaken.

WORKSHOP OBJECTIVES — The objective of 'New Ways' workshops is to provide the training, know-how, and positive environment for the development of paraprofessionals who can work with communities as well as with agencies and organisations for the implementation of *community-based and community empowering projects.*

EMPOWERING TOOLS

The skills or tools taught and practised at these workshops increase individual and group knowledge in the areas of:

- knowing our spiritual roots
- the meaning of self determination
- owning problems, owning solutions

- positive thought and action
- teamwork and team building

- gathering information from the community
- research and surveys
- problem identification and analysis
- solution finding and implementation

- working group formation
- action planning
- crisis intervention techniques
- mediation and dispute resolution

- rebuilding ' community'
- community involvement and organisation
- promoting leadership

- preventative programming
- program development and implementation
- locating and nurturing local support
- locating government and agency support

- funding applications and submissions
- good politics, bad politics
- negotiation and facilitation
- monitoring, evaluation and improvement

- dealing with difficult people
- keeping going when things get tough
- sharing the load, asking for help

- rewarding ourselves
- celebrating our successes.

SHARING, CARING, AND EMPOWERING OTHERS

'New Ways' participants gain individually through *personal development* and a renewed sense of their own abilities.

Teamwork action experienced during the workshops creates ties of friendship, mutual sympathy, and support. Participants will be encouraged to establish a *regional support network*, with the means for regular contact and communication between participants before they leave the workshop.

As this is a ' train the trainer' program participants will also see themselves as skilled to impart what they have learned to others in their communities. They will be encouraged to *help to empower others* through the sharing of their new skills.

NETWORKING FOR THE FUTURE

Through the *process of information sharing, community experience, and regional networking,* innovative approaches can be implemented at the community level, with community support and community involvement.

Community-based approaches begin with an understanding of the nature and structure of problems within. Solutions are shaped on the basis of this information. They should be *culturally relevant, realistic, and aware.*

Community-based approaches are carried forward through teamwork, and support group action, and are *designed to draw the strength of the community together* rather than to divide it through jealousy and opposition.

Innovations are built upon existing *community values.* They are targeted directly to community identified concerns. They are fuelled by positive attitudes and creative planning.

Developing a *Vision for the Future* liberates people from any previous sense of personal powerlessness. It empowers them to take control *collectively.*

WHO CAN BENEFIT?

Any individual who wishes to take positive action in their community can benefit. Training can help develop professionals and paraprofessionals already working in the field — youth workers, community workers, health workers, councillors, JPs, government officers, teachers or teaching aides, nurses or nursing aides, community police etc. Young people, middle-aged people, old people — those with experience and those without. *Whole communities benefit!*

WORKSHOP RESOURCES

We have a collection of leaflets, posters and videos which provide good visual illustration of issues concerning:

Youth Needs
Crime Prevention
Family Violence
Child Abuse

Drug and Alcohol Addiction
Detoxification Programs

Mediation and Dispute Resolution
Healing the Hurts

Sharing Innovations that Work
Crime Prevention.

Some of these are about Aboriginal people, others are about indigenous people of other countries. We also have a *Workshop Manual* which will be used throughout the course. Each participant will receive a copy of this manual to take home and use later themselves when sharing in their community.

WORKBOOK 7

AA Twelve Steps

WE:

Step One
Admitted we were powerless over alcohol — that our lives had become unmanageable.

Step Two
Came to believe that a Power greater than ourselves could restore us to sanity.

Step Three
Made a decision to turn our will and our lives over to the care of God [The Higher Power], *as we understood Him.*

Step Four
Made a searching and fearless moral inventory of ourselves.

Step Five
Admitted to God, to ourselves and to another human being the exact nature of our wrongs.

Step Six
Were entirely ready to have God remove all these defects of character.

Step Seven
Humbly asked God to remove our shortcomings.

Step Eight
Made a list of all persons we had harmed, and became willing to make amends to them all.

Step Nine
Made direct amends to such people wherever possible, except when to do so would injure them or others.

Step Ten
Continued to take personal inventory and when we were wrong, promptly admitted it.

Step Eleven
Sought through prayer and meditation to improve our conscious contact with God, as we understood Him, praying only for knowledge of God's will for us and the power to carry that out.

Step Twelve
Having had a spiritual awakening as the result of these steps, we tried to carry this message to alcoholics,[*] and to practise these principles in all our affairs.[†]

---

[*] A.A. uses the word 'alcoholics' here.   But different fellowships may like to use different wording, such as: 'others', ' sufferers', 'emotionally injured persons', 'survivors of violence', depending upon the nature and purpose of the group.

[†] The Twelve Steps are reprinted with permission of Alcoholics Anonymous World Services, Inc.   Permission to reprint and adapt the Twelve Steps does not mean that AA has reviewed or approved the contents of this publication nor that AA agrees with the views expressed herein.   AA is a program of recovery from alcoholism — use of the Twelve Steps in connection with programs and activities which are patterned after AA but which address other problems, does not imply otherwise.

BIBLIOGRAPHY

BOOKS, CHAPTERS, AND ARTICLES

'Abdu'l-Baha 1982. *The Promulgation of Universal Peace, Talks Delivered by 'Abdul'l-Baha During His Visit to the United States and Canada in 1912 (Compiled by Howard MacNutt)*, Wilmette: Baha'i Publishing Trust, (1st ed. 1922–1925).

Aboriginal Affairs, Department of, 1984. *Aboriginal Social Indicators*, Canberra: Australian Government Publishing Service.

Aboriginal Affairs, Department of, 1986. *Aboriginal Land Tenure and Population*, Canberra: Department of Aboriginal Affairs, January (2nd ed. 1988).

ACC, 1990. *Submission to the Royal Commission into Aboriginal Deaths in Custody*, compiled by B. Miller, Cairns: Aboriginal Co-ordinating Council, August.

Andrews, Lynn 1989. 'Mirroring the Life Force', in Richard Carlson and Benjamin Shield (eds) Healers on Healing, New York: Tarcher/Perigee Books, 42–47.

Albrecht, P.G. 1974. 'The Social and Psychological Reasons for the Alcohol Problem among Aborigines', in B.S. Hetzel, M. Dobbin, L. Lippmann and E. Eggleston (eds), *Better Health for Aborigines*? Report of a national seminar at Monash University, St Lucia: University of Queensland Press, 36–41.

Alexander, K. (ed.) 1990. *Aboriginal Alcohol Use and Related Problems: Report and Recommendations*, prepared by an Expert Working Group for the Royal Commission into Aboriginal Deaths in Custody, Canberra: Alcohol and Drug Foundation.

Altman, J.C. and Daly, A.E. 1992. *The CDEP Scheme: A census-based analysis of the Labour market status of participants in 1986*, Canberra: Centre for Aboriginal Economic Policy Research, Australian National University.

Atkinson, J. 1989. 'Violence in Aboriginal Australia', unpublished discussion paper.

Atkinson, J. 1990a. 'Violence in Aboriginal Australia: Colonisation and its Impact on Gender', unpublished discussion paper (shortened version published in *Refractory Girl*, 36, (August), 21–24.

Atkinson, J. 1990b. 'Violence against Aboriginal Women: Reconstitution of Community Law — the Way Forward' *Aboriginal Law Bulletin*, 2:46, October.

Atkinson, J. 1992. 'Indigenous Canadian Conference on Women and Wellness', *Aboriginal and Islander Health Worker Journal*, 16:1 (Jan/Feb), 12–19.

Australian Bureau of Statistics, 1987. *Census of Population and Housing*: 1981 and 1986, Canberra: Australian Bureau of Statistics.

Australia Bureau of Statistics, 1994. *Census of Population and Housing, Aboriginal Community Profile*, 1991, Canberra: Australian Bureau of Statistics.

Australian Law Journal 1982. 'Current Topics,' *Australian Law Journal*, 56:8, August, 381–383.

Australian Law Reform Commission 1986. *The Recognition of Aboriginal Customary Laws, Summary Report, No. 31*, Canberra: Australian Government Publishing Service.

Effendi, Shoghi (translated by) 1973. *Gleanings from the Writings of Baha'u'llah*, New Delhi: Baha'i Publishing Trust.

Bailey, Rebecca 1984. 'A Comparison of Appearances by Aboriginal and non-Aboriginal Children before the Children's Court and Children's Aid Panels in South Australia' in B. Swanton (ed.), *Aborigines and Criminal Justice*, Canberra: Australian Institute of Criminology, 43–78.

Bailey-Harris, Rebecca and Wundersitz, Joy 1985. 'Over-Representation of Aboriginal Children in Care Proceedings Before the Children's Court of South Australia,' *Australian Journal of Law and Society*, 2:2. ll–27.

Balendra, Jaya 1990. 'Black Violence At Home', *The Independent Monthly*, August, 23.

Barber, James. G, Punt Jeanine and Albers, Jules 1988. 'Alcohol and Power on Palm Island', *Australian Journal of Social Issues*, 23:2, May, Sydney, 87–101.

Barnett, A., Blumstein, A. and Farrington, D.P. 1987. 'Probabilistic Models of Youthful Criminal Careers', *Criminology*, 25: 1.

Bass, Ellen and Davis, Laura 1990. *The Courage to Heal: A Guide for Women Survivors of Child Sexual Abuse*, London: Cedar.

Beckett, J. 1964. 'Aborigines, Alcohol and Assimilation', in M. Reay (ed.), *Aborigines Now: New Perspectives in the Study of Aboriginal Communities*, Sydney: Angus and Robertson, 32–47.

Bell, Diane 1983. *Daughters of the Dreaming*, Melbourne: McPhee Gribble/Allen and Unwin.

Bell, Diane and Ditton, Pam 1980. *Law: The Old and the New, Aboriginal Women in Central Australia Speak Out*. Report prepared for the Central Australian Aboriginal Legal Aid Service/Department of Prehistory and Anthropology, Darwin/Canberra: Australian National University.

Bennett, Scott 1989. *Aborigines and Political Power*, Sydney: Allen and Unwin.

Benson, Allen 1993. 'Doonooch Self-Healing Aboriginal Corporation', notes provided to the author, unpublished, June 1993.

Berndt, Catherine H. 1979. 'Aboriginal Women and the Notion of the Aboriginal Man', in R.M. Berndt and C.H. Berndt (eds) *Aborigines of the West*, Nedlands: University of WA Press, 28–38.

Berndt, R.M. and Berndt, C.H. 1985. *The World of the First Australians*, Adelaide: Rigby.

Biles, David 1988. 'Research into Aboriginal Deaths in Custody'. Paper given at fourth annual conference of the Australian and New Zealand Society of Criminology, Sydney, 22–23 August.

Biles, David and McDonald, David (eds) 1992. *Deaths in Custody, Australia, 1980-1989*, 1992. Canberra: Australian Institute of Criminology.

Bird, Greta 1987. *'The Civilising Mission': Race and the Construction of Aboriginal Crime*, Monograph Series, Contemporary Legal Issues No. 4, Melbourne: Faculty of Law, Monash University.

Bogle, Deborah 1991. 'Tribal Values Key to Beating Alcoholism', *Australian*, 11 April.

Bolger, Audrey 1991. *Aboriginal Women and Violence*, Darwin: North Australia Research Unit, Australian National University.

Bonnemaison, Gilbert 1992. 'Crime Prevention: The Universal Challenge', in S. McKillop and J. Vernon, *National Overview on Crime Prevention*, Conference Proceedings, No. 15, Canberra: Australian Institute of Criminology.

Brady, M. 1985. *Children Without Ears: Petrol Sniffing in Australia*, Parkside, SA: Drug and Alcohol Services Council.

Brady, M. 1989. *Heavy Metal: the Social Meaning of Petrol Sniffing in Australia*. Report presented to the Research into Drug Abuse Advisory Committee, Canberra: Commonwealth Department of Community Services and Health.

Brady, M. 1990a. 'Alcohol Use and its Effects Upon Aboriginal Women', in J. Vernon (ed.), *Alcohol and Crime*, Conference Proceedings, 4–6 April 1989, organised by Canberra: Australian Institute of Criminology, 135–147.

Brady, M. 1990b. 'Indigenous and Government Attempts to Control Alcohol use among Australian Aborigines', *Contemporary Drug Problems*, 17, 145–200.

Brady, M. 1991. 'Making Research into Aboriginal Substance Abuse Issues more Effective', in A. Duquemin, P. d'Abbs and E. Chalmers, *Making Research into Aboriginal Substance Misuse Issues More Effective*, Working Paper No. 4. Canberra: National Drug and Alcohol Research Centre, NCADA, 55–60.

Brady, M. and Palmer, K. 1984. *Alcohol in the Outback*, Darwin: North Australia Research Unit Monograph, Australian National University.

Brady, Maggie and Palmer, Kingsley 1986. *Alcohol in the Outback: Two Studies of Drinking*, Darwin: Australian National University North Australia Research Unit.

Broadhurst R.G, Maller R.A, Maller M.G, and Duffey J. 1988. 'Aboriginal and Nonaboriginal Recidivism in Western Australia: A Failure Rate Analysis', *Journal of Research in Crime and Delinquency*, 25:1, February, 83–108.

Burger, Julian 1988. *Aborigines Today: Land and Justice*, Indigenous Peoples and Development Series, Report No. 5, London: Anti-Slavery Society.

Burman, Sandra and Harrel-Bond, Barbara E. (eds), 1979. 'The Imposition of Law', *Studies in Law and Social Control*, New York: Academic Press.

Butlin, Noel G., 1983. *Our Original Aggression, Aboriginal Populations of Southeastern Australia, 1788–1850*, Sydney: George Allen and Unwin.

Campbell, Joseph 1993. *The Hero With a Thousand Faces*, London: Fontana Press.

Carlson, Richard and Shield, Benjamin (eds.) 1989. *Healers on Healing*, New York: Tarcher/Perigee.

Carrington K. 1990. 'Aboriginal Girls and Justice; What Justice? White Justice' *Journal for Social Justice Studies*, 3.

Charny, Israel W. (ed.) 1982. *How can we Commit the Unthinkable? Genocide: The Human Cancer*, in collaboration with Chanan Rapaport, Boulder, Colorado: Westview Press.

CJC 1992. *Youth, Crime and Justice in Queensland: An Information and Issues Paper* (prepared by Dr Ian O'Connor), Brisbane: Criminal Justice Commission.

Clifford, Bill and Harding, Richard 1985. 'Australian Discussion Paper on Criminal Justice Processess and Perspectives in a Changing World', Milan: Seventh United Nations Congress on the Prevention of Crime and the Treatment of Offenders.

Clift, Jean Dalby and Clift, Wallace B. 1988. *The Hero Journey in Dreams*, New York: Crossroad.

Cobo, Jose Martinez 1986. *Study of the Problems of Discrimination against Indigenous Populations*, United Nations Economic and Social Council, (E7CN.4/Sub.2/ 1986/7/Add.1–5, Vols. I–V, 1986), New York: United Nations.

Commonwealth of Australia 1993. *Mabo: The High Court Decision on Native Title*, Discussion Paper, Canberra: Commonwealth Government Printer, June.

Community Justice Program 1991a. 'Doomadgee Dispute', internal paper, Brisbane: Community Justice Program.

Community Justice Program 1991b. 'Response to: "Towards Self-Government": A discussion paper of the Legislation Review Committee inquiring into legislation relating to the Management of Aboriginal and Torres Strait Islander Communities in Queensland', Brisbane: Department of the Attorney-General, October.

Cornish, Andrew 1985. 'Public Drunkenness in New South Wales: From Criminality to Welfare' in *Australian and New Zealand Journal of Criminology*, 18, June, 73–84.

Cristescu, Aureliu 1981. *The Right to Self-Determination: Historical and Current Development on the Basis of United Nations Instruments*, (UN E/CN.4/Sub.2/404/Rev.1.), New York: United Nations.

Crossingham, Lesley 1987. 'The Eagle has Landed', *Windspeaker* (Drug and Alcohol Special), Edmonton, 6.

Cunneen, Christopher 1986. 'Detention and Reception of Aboriginal Persons under the Intoxicated Persons Act (NSW) 1979 for the year 1986', unpublished paper.

Cunneen, Christopher 1990. 'The Detention of Aborigines in Police Cells in NSW', *Aboriginal Law Bulletin* 2, 45. August, 8–10.

Cunneen, Christopher 1992. 'Judicial Racism', paper presented to the *Aboriginal Justice Issues*, conference, 23–25 June, Cairns: organised by Canberra: Australian Institute of Criminology.

Cunneen, Christopher and Robb, Tom 1987. *Criminal Justice in North-West New South Wales*, Sydney: NSW Bureau of Crime Statistics and Research.

d'Abbs, P.H.N. 1987. *Dry Areas, Alcohol and Aboriginal Communities: A Review of the Northern Territory Restricted Areas Legislation*, report prepared for the Drug and Alcohol Bureau, Darwin: Department of Health and Community Services and the Racing, Gaming and Liquor Commission.

d'Abbs, P.H.N. 1990. 'Restricted Areas and Aboriginal Drinking', in J. Vernon (ed.), *Alcohol and Crime*, Conference Proceedings, 4–6 April 1989, Canberra: Australian Institute of Criminology, 121–132.

Daes, Erica Irene A. 1988. *Visit to Australia, 12 December 1987 – 22 January 1988*. Report by Chairman/Rapporteur of the United Nations Working Group on Indigenous Populations, Geneva: United Nations.

Darby, Andrew 1989. 'Aboriginal Health: Focus on Alcohol' *Sydney Morning Herald*, 23 March.

Devaneson, D. et al. 1986. *Health Indicators in the Northern Territory*, Darwin: Northern Territory Department of Health.

Duquemin, Anthea, d'Abbs, Peter and Chalmers, Elizabeth 1991. *Making Research into Aboriginal Substance Misuse Issues More Effective*, Working Paper No. 4, Canberra: National Drug and Alcohol Research Centre, NCADA.

Dyer, Wayne W. 1989. *You'll See It When You Believe It*, Melbourne: Schwartz Publishing (first published in USA by William Morrow and Co.).

Einfeld, Marcus (Justice) 1988. *Toomelah Report: Report on the Problems and Needs of Aborigines living on the New South Wales–Queensland Border*, Sydney: Human Rights and Equal Opportunity Commission (June).

Elsegood, Phil 1986. 'Snuff, Sniff, Snuff, Snuff, Sniff, Snuff' *Aboriginal Law Bulletin*, 21, 6–8.

Evans, Gareth (Senator) 1984. 'Human Rights and International Law,' *Australian Foreign Affairs Record*, 55:4, April, 324–328.

Fletcher, Christine 1992. *Aboriginal Politics: Intergovernmental Relations*, Melbourne: Melbourne University Press.

Friends in Recovery 1990. *The 12 Steps —A Way Out: A Working Guide for Adult Children from Addictive and Other Dysfunctional Families*, San Diego, CA: Recovery Publications, Inc.

Gale, F., Wundersitz, J and Bailey-Harris, R 1990. *Aboriginal Youth and the Criminal Justice System*, Cambridge: Cambridge University Press.

Gale, Fay and Wundersitz, Joy 1985. 'Variations in the Over-representation of Aboriginal Young Offenders in the Criminal Justice System', *Australian Journal of Social Issues*, 20:3, August, 209–214.

Gale, Fay and Wundersitz, Joy 1986. 'Rural and Urban Crime Rates amongst Aboriginal Youth: Patterns of Different Locational Opportunity', *Australian Geographical Studies*, 24:2, October.

Gale, Fay and Wundersitz, Joy 1987a. 'Aboriginal Youth and the Criminal Justice System in South Australia' in Kayleen M. Hazlehurst (ed.), *Ivory Scales: Black Australia and the Law*, Sydney: New South Wales University Press, 118–135.

Gale, Fay and Wundersitz, Joy 1987b. 'Police and Black Minorities: A Case of Aboriginal Youth in South Australia,' *Australian and New Zealand Journal of Criminology*, 20:2, June, 78–94

Gale, Fay, Bailey-Harris, Rebecca and Wundersitz, Joy 1990. *Aboriginal Youth and the Criminal Justice System: the Injustice of Justice?* Cambridge: Cambridge University Press.

Geason, Susan and Wilson, Paul R. 1988. *Crime Prevention: Theory and Practice*, Crime Prevention Series, Canberra: Australian Institute of Criminology.

Gibson, Merv 1987. 'Anthropology and Tradition: A Contemporary Aboriginal Viewpoint', paper presented to ANZAAS Conference, Townsville.

Goodale, Jane C. 1971. *Tiwi Wives*, Seattle: University of Washington Press.

Grabosky, P., Scandia, A., Hazlehurst, K., and Wilson, P., 1988. 'Aboriginal Deaths in Custody', *Trends and Issues in Crime and Criminal Justice*, No.12, Canberra: Australian Institute of Criminology.

Grabosky, Peter N. 1988. 'Aboriginal Deaths in Custody: the Case of John Pat,' *Race and Class*, 29:3, Winter, 87-94.

Grierson Centre 1988. *Grierson Community Correctional Centre Resident Handbook*, Edmonton: Native Counselling Services of Alberta.

Gumbert, M. 1984. *Neither Justice Nor Reason*, St Lucia, University of Queensland.

Gurnee, Charles G. Vigil, Doris E. Krill-Smith, Susan and Crowley, Thomas, J. 1990. 'Substance Abuse Among American Indians in an Urban Treatment Program', *American Indian and Alaska Native Mental Health Research*, 3:3, Spring, 17–26.

Haebich, A. 1988. *For Their Own Good: Aborigines and Government in the South-west of Western Australia, 1900–1940*, Perth: University of Western Australia Press.

HALT (Healthy Aboriginal Life Team) 1991. *Anangu Way*, Alice Springs, NT: Nganampa Health Council Inc.

Hamilton, Annette 1988. 'A Complex Strategical Situation: Gender Power in Aboriginal Australia', in N. Grieve and P. Grimshaw (eds), *Australian Women: Feminist Perspectives*, Melbourne: Oxford University Press, 69–85.

Hammond, Jane 1990. 'Violence Threatens Aboriginal Culture', *The Australian*, 26 June.

Hanks, Peter and Keon-Cohen, Bryan, 1984. *Aborigines and the Law*, Sydney: George Allen and Unwin.

Hazlehurst, Kayleen M. 1986. 'Alcohol, Outstations and Autonomy: an Australian Aboriginal Perspective', *Journal of Drug Issues*, 16:2, Spring, 209–220.

Hazlehurst, Kayleen M. 1988a. 'Racial Tension, Policing and Public Order: Australia in the Eighties' in I. Freckelton and H. Selby (eds), *Police in Our Society*, Sydney: Butterworths.

Hazlehurst, Kayleen M. 1988b. 'Resolving Conflict: Dispute Settlement Mechanisms for Aboriginal Communities and Neighbourhoods?', *Australian Journal of Social Issues*, 23:4, November, 309–322.

Hazlehurst, Kayleen M. 1989a. *Primary Prevention for Community Wellbeing: An interview with Jean 1989*, (video and leaflet), Canberra: Australian Institute of Criminology.

Hazlehurst, Kayleen M. 1989b. 'Violence, Disputes and their Resolution', *Violence Today* No. 7, National Committee on Violence Series, Canberra: Australian Institute of Criminology.

Hazlehurst, Kayleen M. 1990. *Crime Prevention for Aboriginal Communities*, Crime Prevention Series, Canberra: Australian Institute of Criminology.

Hazlehurst, Kayleen M. 1991. 'Australian Aboriginal Experiences of Community Justice', in R. Kuppe (ed.), *Law and Anthropology*, International Yearbook for Legal Anthropology, Law Faculty, University of Vienna, Austria 1991, 6, 45–65.

Hazlehurst, Kayleen M. 1992. '"Opportunity and Desire": Making Prevention Relevant to the Criminal and Social Environment', in S. McKillop and J. Vernon, *National Overview on Crime Prevention, Conference Proceedings, No. 15*, Canberra: Australian Institute of Criminology, 37–50.

Hazlehurst, Kayleen M. [1994a]. 'Indigenous Models for Community Reconstruction and Social Recovery' in K.M. Hazlehurst (ed.), *Popular Justice and Community Recovery*, Westport, Connecticut: Praeger Press.

Hazlehurst, Kayleen M. [1994b]. '"Prevention, Empowerment and Privatisation": Issues of the Nineties for Aboriginal Communities?', in Pat O'Malley and Adam Sutton (eds.), *Crime Prevention in Australia*, Sydney, Federation Press [forthcoming].

Hazlehurst, Kayleen M. and Dunn. Albert T. 1988. 'Aboriginal Criminal Justice,' *Trends and Issues in Crime and Criminal Justice*, No.13, Canberra: Australian Institute of Criminology.

Hazlehurst, Kayleen M. and Hazlehurst, Cameron 1989. 'Race and the Australian Conscience: Investigating Aboriginal Deaths in Custody,' *New Community: A Journal of Research and Policy on Ethnic Relations*, 16:1, October, 35–48.

Heartview Foundation, [nd] booklet, Dakota.

Heath, D. B. 1987. 'A Decade of Development in the Anthropological Study of Alcohol Use', in M. Douglas (ed.), *Constructive Drinking: Perspectives on Drink from Anthropology*, Cambridge: Cambridge University Press, 16–70.

Herd, Denise 1988. 'Drinking by Black and White Women: Results from a National Survey', *Social Problems*, 35:5, December, 493–505.

Hill, John 1989. 'Excessive Drinking Patterns in the Alice Springs Town Camps: Preventative Strategies', paper prepared for the Tangentyere Council and Central Australian Aboriginal Congress.

Hirschi, T. and Gottfredson, M. 1983. `Age and the Explanation of Crime', *American Journal of Sociology*, 89:3.

Hodgson, Maggie 1987a. 'Indian Communities Develop Futuristic Addictions Treatment and Health Approach', Edmonton: Nechi Institute, June.

Hodgson, Maggie 1987b. 'Women and Addictions: What Are the Issues?', Edmonton: Nechi Institute.

Hodgson, Maggie 1989. 'The Eagle Has Landed', paper presented at the International Conference on Alcohol Abuse, Oslo, Norway, organised by Edmonton: Nechi Institute.

Hodgson, Maggie 1991a. 'An Issue of Life or Death', Edmonton: Nechi Institute, 21 November.

Hodgson, Maggie 1991b. '"Spirituality vs Religion": and First Nation's Response to Healing of a Government's Decision to set Social Policy to Dictate Christianity as the Solution to Assimilate our People,' Edmonton: Nechi Institute.

Holman, C.D.J. Armstrong, B.K. Arias L.N. Martin, C.A. Hatton W.M. Hayward L.D. Salmon M.A. Shean R.E. and Waddell V.P. 1988. *The Quantification of Drug Caused Morbidity and Mortality in Australia*, Canberra: Department of Community Services and Health.

Hunter, Ernest M. 1988. 'On Gordian Knots and Nooses: Aboriginal Suicide in the Kimberley,' *Australian and New Zealand Journal of Psychiatry*, 22, 264–271.

Hunter, Ernest M. 1989. 'Changing Aboriginal Mortality Patterns in the Kimberley Region of Western Australia 1957-86: The Impact of Deaths from External Causes', *Aboriginal Health Information Bulletin*, 11, 27–32.

Hunter, Ernest M. 1990a. 'A Question of Power: Contemporary Self-mutilation and Other Emergent Self-harmful Behaviour among Aborigines of the Kimberley', *Australian Journal of Social Issues*, 25:4, 261–278.

Hunter, Ernest M. 1990b. 'The Inter-Cultural and Socio-historical Context of Aboriginal Personal Violence in Remote Australia', *Australian Psychology Journal*, 26:2, 89–98.

Hunter, Ernest, Hall, Wayne and Spargo, Randolph 1991a. 'Alcohol Consumption and its Correlates in a Remote Aboriginal Population', *Aboriginal Law Bulletin*, 2:51, August: 8–10.

Hunter, Ernest., Hall, Wayne and Spargo, Randolph 1991b. *The Distribution and Correlates of Alcohol Consumption in a Remote Aboriginal Population*, Working Paper No. 12. Canberra: National Drug and Alcohol Research Centre, National Campaign Against Drug Abuse, NCADA.

IWGIA, 1987. *IWGIA Yearbook 1986: Indigenous Peoples and Human Rights*, compiled by Andrew Gray, Copenhagen: International Working Group for Indigenous Affairs.

Johnston, Elliott (Commissioner) 1991. *Royal Commission into Aboriginal Deaths in Custody, National Report: Vol.5,* Canberra: Australian Government Publishing Service.

Justice and Consumer Affairs Committee, 1987. *South Australian Aboriginal Fine Default Intervention Study 1986–987,* Adelaide: Aboriginal Task Force, South Australian Cabinet.

Justice J.H. Muirhead, 1988. *Interim Report: Royal Commission into Aboriginal Deaths in Custody,* Canberra: Australian Government Publishing Service.

Kamine, M. 1975. 'Aborigines and Alcohol: Intake, Effects and Social Implications in a Rural Community in New South Wales', *Medical Journal of Australia,* 1: 291–298.

Keon-Cohen, B.A. 1981a. 'Native justice in Australia, Canada, and USA: A comparative analysis' *Monash University Law Review,* 7, 250–325.

Keon-Cohen, Bryan 1981b. 'The Makarrata: A Treaty within Australia between Australians, Some Legal Issues,' *Current Affairs Bulletin,* 57:9, February, 4–19.

King, Michael 1988. *How to Make Social Crime Prevention Work: The French Experience,* NACRO Occasional Paper, London: National Association for the Care and Resettlement of Offenders.

Kirby, Michael, Justice 1988. 'Domestic application of International Human Rights Standards,' *Australian Foreign Affairs Record,* 59:5, May, 186–188.

Kuper, Leo 1981. *Genocide: Its Political Use in the Twentieth Century,* London: Penguin Books (also New Haven: Yale University Press 1982).

Kuper, Leo 1985. *The Prevention of Genocide,* New Haven/London: Yale University Press.

Langton, Marcia 1989. 'Seeing the Grog for What it is', *Land Rights News,* March, 29.

Langton, Marcia 1991. 'Grog: Too Much Sorry Business', *Yarranma,* 4:1, 8–9.

Langton, Marcia and Ah Matt, Leslie et al 1991. '"Too Much Sorry Business": The Report of the Aboriginal Issues Unit of the Northern Territory', *Royal Commission into Aboriginal Deaths in Custody, National Report: Vol.5,* Canberra: Australian Government Publishing Service, Appendix D (1), 275–512.

LaPrairie, Carol 1992. 'Who Owns the Problem? Crime and disorder in James Bay Cree communities', *Canadian Journal of Criminology*, 34:3/4, 417–434.

LaPrairie, Carol and Craig, Barbara 1985. *Native Criminal Justice Research and Programs: Inventory Update*, Ottawa: Solicitor General.

Law Reform Commission of Australia, 1986. *The Recognition of Aboriginal Customary Laws: Summary Report*, No. 31, Canberra: Australian Government Publishing Service.

Life Education Centre 1990–1991. *Synopses of Programs* (handbooks and flyers), Sydney: Life Education Centre.

Lyon, P. 1990. *What Everybody Knows about Alice: A Report on the Impact of Alcohol Abuse on the Town of Alice Springs*, Alice Springs: Tangentyere Council.

Lyons, Gregory 1983. 'Aboriginal Perceptions of Courts and Police: A Victorian Study', *Australian Aboriginal Studies*, 2, 45–61.

Mail, Patricia D. 1989. 'American Indians, Stress and Alcohol', *American Indian and Alaska Native Mental Health Research*, 3:2, Fall, 7–26.

Mam, Steve 1991. 'The Torres Strait Islander Viewpoint into Men Against Violence', *Healing Our People: Aboriginal Community Justice and Crime Prevention Forum*, conference, Alice Springs 2–5 April, organised by Canberra: Australian Institute of Criminology.

Marshall, M. 1983. '"Four Hundred Rabbits": An Anthropological View of Ethanol as a Disinhibitor', in R. Room, and G. Collins (eds.), *Disinhibition: Nature and Meaning of the Link*, NIAA Research Monograph, No. 12, U.S. Berkeley: Department of Health and Human Services, 186–204.

Mattingley, Christobel and Hampton, Ken (eds.), 1988. *Survival in Our Own Land: 'Aboriginal' Experiences in 'South Australia' Since 1836*, Adelaide: Wakefield Press.

McCaskill, D 1985. *Patterns of Criminality and Correction Among Native Offenders in Manitoba: A Longitudinal Analysis*, Saskatoon: Correctional Service of Canada, Department of the Solicitor General, Prairie Region, March.

McCorquodale, J.C. 1985. 'Aborigines: A History of Law and Injustice, 1829–1985'. Ph.D thesis, Armidale: University of New England.

McCorquodale, John 1984. 'Alcohol and Anomie: The Nature of Aboriginal Crime', in B. Swanton (ed.), *Aborigines and Criminal Justice*, Canberra: Australian Institute of Criminology, 17–42.

McCorquodale, John 1987. *Aborigines and the Law: A Digest*, Canberra: Aboriginal Studies Press.

McLeod, Robert 1992. 'Doonooch Self Healing Centre: Executive Summary', paper presented to the *Aboriginal Justice Issues* conference, 23–25 June, Cairns: organised by the Australian Institute of Criminology.

McNeil, E. 1987. *Inner City Kids*, report to the Department for Community Welfare, Adelaide, September.

Medicine Eagle, Brooke 1989. 'The Circle of Healing', in Richard Carlson, and Benjamin Shield (eds) *Healers on Healing*, New York: Tarcher/Perigee, 58–62.

Metis and Non-Status Indian Crime and Justice Commission 1977. *Crime and Justice Commission Study*, Ottawa: Justice Department and the Solicitor General.

Milera, Doug 1980. 'Walkabout to Nowhere', Canberra: Australian Foundation for Alcoholism and Drug Dependency.

Miller, B. 1990. 'Report on the Social Control Project'. Cairns: Aboriginal Co-ordinating Council, unpublished.

Miller, Calvin 1982. 'A Haven for Alcoholics Ditching their Addiction', *The Medical Journal of Australia*, 2:12, 602–605.

Miller, James 1986. *Koori: A Will to Win: The Heroic Resistance, Survival and Triumph of Black Australia*, Sydney: Angus and Robertson.

Morgan, Sally 1987. *My Place*, Fremantle: Fremantle Arts Centre Press.

Moss, Irene (Commissioner) 1991. Report of the National Inquiry into Racist Violence in Australia, Canberra: Australian Government Publishing Service.

Mountain View Rehabilitation Centre, Inc. [nd] handout on intervention.

Muirhead, J.H. (Justice) 1988. *Royal Commission into Aboriginal Deaths in Custody: Interim Report*, Canberra: Australian Government Publishing Service.

Muirhead, J.H. (Justice) 1989. *Report of the Inquiry into the Death of Edward James Murray; Kingsley Richard Dixon; John Clarence Highfold; Charles Sydney Michael*, (four reports), Royal Commission into Aboriginal Deaths in Custody, Canberra: Australian Government Publishing Service, January.

Muirhead, Justice J.H. 1988. *Royal Commission into Aboriginal Deaths in Custody: Interim Report*, Canberra: Australian Government Publishing Service (December).

Mukherjee, S. and Scandia, A. 1988. 'Aboriginal Imprisonment,' *Crime Digest*, 88:1, January.

National Aboriginal Health Strategy Working Party 1989. *A National Aboriginal Health Strategy*, Canberra: Department of Aboriginal Affairs.

National Committee on Violence 1990. *Violence: Directions for Australia*, Canberra: Australian Institute of Criminology.

Native Courtworker Services of Saskatchewan 1983. *Community Residential Centres for Native Offenders, A Feasibility Study*, Saskatchewan: Correctional Service of Canada.

NCSA 1985a. *Family Life Improvement Program: Final Report*, Edmonton, Alberta: Native Counselling Services of Alberta, July.

NCSA 1985b. *Native Counselling Services of Alberta: Annual Report 1984–85*, Edmonton, Alberta: Native Counselling Services of Alberta.

NCSA 1987. *Native Counselling Services of Alberta: Annual Report 1986–87*, Edmonton, Alberta: Native Counselling Services of Alberta.

NCSA 1991. *Native Counselling Services of Alberta: Annual Report 1990–91*, Edmonton, Alberta: Native Counselling Services of Alberta.

NCSA 1993. *A Family Affair* (produced by Esther Supernault) Edmonton, Alberta: Native Counselling Services of Alberta.

NCSA [1994]. *The Native Counselling Story*, unpublished manuscript of book by the Edmonton, Alberta: Native Counselling Services of Alberta, unpublished.

NCVAW 1991. 'National Committee on Violence Against Women Position Paper', Office of the Status of Women, Department of the Prime Minister and Cabinet, Canberra: AGPS.

Nechi Institute 1992. *Data Base Study of Nechi Participants: 1974–1991: Final Report*, Edmonton: Nechi Institute on Alcohol and Drug Education and Research Centre.

Nettheim, Garth 1981. *Victims of the Law: Black Queenslanders Today*, Sydney: George Allen and Unwin.

Nettheim, Garth 1983. 'Justice and Indigenous Minorities: A New Province for International and National Law' in A.R. Blackshield (ed.), *Legal Change: Essays in Honour of Julius Stone*, Sydney: Butterworths.

Nettheim, Garth 1984. 'The relevance of international law', in P. Hanks and B. Keon-Cohen (eds.) *Aborigines and the Law*, Sydney: George Allen and Unwin, 50–73.

Nettheim, Garth 1987a. 'Indigenous Rights, Human Rights and Australia', *The Australian Law Journal*, 61, June, 291–300.

Nettheim, Garth 1987b. 'Justice or Handouts? Aboriginals, law and policy' in Kayleen M. Hazlehurst (ed.), *Ivory Scales: Black Australia and the Law*, Sydney: New South Wales University Press, 8–29.

New South Wales Community Justice Centres 1988. *Community Justice Centres 1987–88 Annual Report*, Sydney: Attorney General's Department of NSW.

NSW Bureau of Crime Statistics and Research 1973. *City Drunks — a Possible New Direction*, Statistical Report No.7, Sydney: NSW Bureau of Crime Statistics and Research.

NSW. Ministry of Aboriginal Affairs, 1987. *The Final Report of the Working Party on the Bourke Disturbances of August 1986* Sydney: New South Wales Ministry of Aboriginal Affairs, May.

O'Connor, Alan 1990. *'Dry Areas': Preliminary Views on their Impact on Communities in South Australia. A report prepared for the Justice and Consumer Affairs Committee of the South Australian Cabinet*, Research Section, Adelaide: SA Aboriginal Affairs.

O'Connor, I., 1990. *The Impact of Queensland's Family and Child Welfare Law and Juvenile Justice Legislation, Policy and Practice on Aboriginal and Torres Strait Islander Families and Children*, Brisbane: Royal Commission into Aboriginal Deaths in Custody.

BIBLIOGRAPHY

O'Donnell, Marg 1992. 'Mediation within Aboriginal Communities: Issues and Challenges' paper presented to the *Aboriginal Justice Issues* conference, 23–25 June, Cairns, organised by the Australian Institute of Criminology.

Ober, Coralie 1991. *A Community Work Book* 1991, Brisbane: Queensland Corrective Commission.

Payne, Sharon 1990. 'Aboriginal Women and the Criminal Justice System', *Aboriginal Law Bulletin*, 2:46, October, 9–11.

Payne, Sharon 1991. 'Aboriginal and Torres Strait Islander Women and the Law', *Women and the Law* conference, 24–26 September, Sydney, organised by the Australian Institute of Criminology, .

Pearson, Carol S. 1989. *The Hero Within: Six archetypes we live by*, San Francisco: Harper and Row.

Pearson, Carol S. 1991. *Awakening the Heroes Within: Twelve archetypes to help us find ourselves and transform our world*, San Francisco: Harper.

Potas, Ivan, Vining, Aidan, and Wilson, Paul 1990. *Young People and Crime: Costs and Prevention*, Canberra: Australian Institute of Criminology.

Poundmaker's Lodge 1988. Leaflet, 'Alcoholism and Drug Abuse Treatment Centre', Edmonton: Poundmaker's Lodge.

Poundmaker/Nechi Centre [ca. 1988]. 'Poundmaker's Lodge, Alcohol and Drug Abuse Treatment Centre', leaflet, Edmonton: Poundmaker's Lodge and Nechi Institute.

Prather, Hugh 1989. 'What is Healing?', in Richard Carlson, and Benjamin Shield (eds.) *Healers on Healing*, New York: Tarcher/Perigee, 12–30.

Queensland Domestic Violence Task Force, 1988. *Beyond These Walls*, Report and Summary to Hon. Peter McKechnie, Brisbane: Minister for Family Services and Welfare Housing Department.

Reid, Janice and Trompf, Peggy (eds) 1991. *The Health of Aboriginal Australia*, Sydney: Harcourt Brace Jovanovich.

Reynolds, Audrie 1977. *A Mighty River: Selections from the Baha'i Writings*, Wilmette: Baha'i Publishing Trust.

Reynolds, Henry 1981. *The Other Side of the Frontier: An interpretation of the Aboriginal response to the invasion and settlement of Australia*, Townsville: James Cook University.

Reynolds, Henry 1987. *Frontier: Aborigines, Settlers and Land*, Sydney: Allen and Unwin.

Reynolds, Henry 1992. 'Mabo and Pastoral Leases' *Aboriginal Law Bulletin*, 2:59, December.

Roberts, Greg 1990. 'Damned Children on the Islands of Despair', *Sydney Morning Herald*, August 11.

Roberts, L., Chadbourne, R and Rose, M. 1986. *Aboriginal/Police Relations in the Pilbara: A Study of Perceptions*, Perth: Special Cabinet Committee on Aboriginal/ Police and Community Relations.

Room, R. 1984. 'Alcohol and Ethnography: A Case of Problem Deflation?', *Current Anthropology*, 25, 169–191.

Ross, Russell 1990. *A Probit Analysis of the Factors Influencing Labour Market Success of Aborigines in New South Wales*, Social Policy Research Centre, Discussion Paper, No. 27, Kensington: University of New South Wales.

Royal Commission into Aboriginal Deaths in Custody 1991. *Final Report*, Canberra: Australian Government Publishing Services.

Sackett, L. 1988. 'Resisting Arrests: Drinking, Development and Discipline in a Desert Context', *Social Analysis*, 24, 66–84.

Sansom, B. 1980. *The Camp at Wallaby Cross: Aboriginal Fringe Dwellers in Darwin*, Canberra: Australian Institute of Aboriginal Studies.

Scutt, Jocelynne. 1983. *Even in the Best of Homes*, Ringwood: Penguin.

Scutt, Jocelynne. 1990. 'Invisible Women? Projecting White Cultural Invisibility on Black Australian Women', *Aboriginal Law Bulletin*, 2:46, October, 4–5.

Shaw, Geoff 1991. 'Working Together', speech notes *'Healing Our People': Aboriginal Community Justice and Crime Prevention Forum*, 2–5 April, Alice Springs, organised by the Australian Institute of Criminology.

Stafford, Christine C. 1988. *Between the Rock and Another Hard Place: Aborigines and the Criminal Justice System in the East Kimberley Region of Western Australia*, Canberra: Criminology Research Council, Australian Institute of Criminology.

Supernault, Esther 1993. *A Family Affair* ... see NCSA 1993.

Sutton, Adam 1991.`The Bonnemaison Model: Theory and Application', in B. Halstead (ed.) *Youth Crime Prevention*, Proceedings of a Policy Forum, 28 and 29 August 1990, Canberra: Australian Institute of Criminology.

Tatz, C. 1980. 'Aboriginality as Civilisation', *The Australian Quarterly*, 52, 352–362.

Thompson, Ruth (ed.) 1986. *The Rights of Indigenous Peoples in International Law*: Workshop Report, Regina: University of Saskatchewan Native Law Centre.

Thomson, Don 1985. 'Drunk in a Public Place: Dinosaur or Trojan Horse?', *Legal Service Bulletin*, 10:2, April, 79–82.

Thomson, N. and Smith, L. 1985. 'An Analysis of Aboriginal Mortality in NSW Country Regions, 1980–1981', *Medical Journal of Australia*: Special Supplement for Aboriginal Health, 143:9, 49–54.

Thomson, Neil 1984. 'Aboriginal Health: Current Status', *Australian and New Zealand Journal of Medicine*, 14, 705–18.

Thomson, Neil 1985. 'Review of available Aboriginal Mortality Data, 1980–1982. *Medical Journal of Australia*: Special Supplement for Aboriginal Health, 143:9, 46–49.

Thomson, Neil and English, Bruce 1991. *Drug Use and Related Problems among Australian Aborigines and Torres Strait Islanders: Current and Potential Data Sources*, Aboriginal and Torres Strait Islander Health Series, No. 6, Australian Institute of Health, Canberra: AGPS.

Torzillo, Paul and Kerr, Charles 1991. 'Contemporary Issues in Aboriginal Public Health', in J. Reid and P. Trompf (eds), *The Health of Aboriginal Australia*, Sydney: Harcourt Brace Jovanovich.

UAICC, Uniting Aboriginal and Islander Christian Congress (Bathurst Island) 1989. *Family Fighting/Killing: Wrong Way!* (handbook, manual and video), Darwin: Northern Territory Department of Aboriginal Affairs.

United Nations, 1948a. *Convention on the Prevention and Punishment of the Crime of Genocide* (adopted by General Assembly resolution 260 A (III), 9 December).

United Nations, 1948b. *Universal Declaration of Human Rights* (adopted by General Assembly resolution 217 A (III), 10 December).

United Nations, 1955. *Standard Minimum Rules for the Treatment of Prisoners* (adopted by the First United Nations Congress on the Prevention of Crime and the Treatment of Offenders, also approved by the Economic and Social Council by its resolutions 663 C (XXIV) 1957 and 2076 (LXII) 1977).

United Nations, 1965. *International Convention on the Elimination of All Forms of Racial Discrimination* (adopted by General Assembly resolution 2106 A (XX), 21 December).

United Nations, 1966. *International Covenant on Civil and Political Rights* (adopted by General Assembly resolution 2200 A (XXI), 16 December).

United Nations, 1975. *Declaration on the Protection of All Persons from Being Subjected to Torture and Other Cruel, Inhuman or Degrading Treatment or Punishment* (adopted by General Assembly resolution 3452 (XXX), 9 December).

United Nations, 1979. *Code of Conduct for Law Enforcement Officials*, (adopted by General Assembly resolution 34/169, 17 December).

Walker, J. and Biles, D. 1982–1986. *Australian Prisoners: Results of the National Prison Census 30 June*, Canberra: Australian Institute of Criminology.

Walker, Jamie 1993. 'Mean Season, Mean Times', *The Weekend Australian*, January 9–10: 15.

Walker, John and Henderson, Monika 1991. `Understanding Crime Trends in Australia', *Trends and Issues Series*, No. 28. Canberra: Australian Institute of Criminology.

Walker, John., Hallinan, Jennifer and Dagger, Dianne 1992. *Australian Prisoners 1991: Results of the National Prison Census 30 June 1991*, Canberra: Australian Institute of Criminology.

Warrior, Chris 1992. 'Change the Environment and You Change the People' in S. McKillop and J. Vernon, *National Overview on Crime Prevention, Conference Proceedings No. 15*, 4–6 Canberra: Australian Institute of Criminology, 219–226.

Watson, C. Fleming, J. and Alexander, K. 1988. *A Survey of Drug use Patterns in Northern Territory Aboriginal Communities: 1986–1987*, Darwin: Northern Territory Department of Health and Community Services, Drug and Alcohol Bureau.

WCC 1981. *Justice for Aboriginal Australians, Sydney:* Report of the World Council of Churches.

Williams, Nancy M. 1985. 'On Aboriginal Decision-making' in D.E. Barwick (ed.), *Metaphor of Interpretation: Essays in Honour of W. E. H. Stanner*, Canberra: Australian National University Press.

Williams, Nancy M. 1987a. 'Local Autonomy and the Viability of Community Justice Mechanisms' in Kayleen M. Hazlehurst (ed.), *Ivory Scales: Black Australia and the Law*, Sydney: New South Wales University Press, 227–240.

Williams, Nancy M. 1987b. *Two Laws: Managing Disputes in a Contemporary Aboriginal Community*, Canberra: Australian Institute of Aboriginal Studies.

Wilson, Paul 1988. *Black Death White Hands*, Sydney: Allen and Unwin/ Winchester; Mass: Unwin Hyman Inc. (first ed. 1981).

Windspeaker 1987. 'Editor's Note', '"Everybody's Problem": Successes Inspiring Communities to Rediscover their Roots', (Drug and Alcohol Special), Edmonton, 3.

Windspeaker 1987. 'Drug and Alcohol Special', Native Newspaper, Edmonton, 6.

Windspeaker, 1990 Native Newspaper, Edmonton, 8:12, 31 August.

Woititz, Janet G. 1986. *Guidelines for Support Groups: Adult Children of Alcoholics and Others who Identify*, Florida: Health Communications, Inc.

Woititz, Janet G. 1988. *Adult Children of Alcoholics: Common Characteristics*, Florida: Health Communications, Inc.

Woititz, Janet G. 1989. *Healing Your Sexual Self*, Deerfield Beach, Forida: Health Communications Inc.

Wong, Bennet and McKeen, Jock 1992. *A Manual for Life*, Gabriola Island, British Columbia: PD Seminars, 'Haven by the Sea'.

Working Group for Follow-up of Aboriginal Women's Conference, 1991. *Record of Proceedings of Remote Area Aboriginal Women's Conference*, 1–4 July, Laura, Cape York Peninsula, organised by the Working Group for Follow-up.

Wundersitz, Joy and Gale, Fay 1988. 'Disadvantage and Discretion: The Results of Aboriginal Youth in Relation to the Adjournment Decision', *Adelaide Law Review*, 11:3, June, 348–358.

Wynter, Jo 1991. 'Central Australian Aboriginal Alcohol Planning Unit: A Challenge for Change', *Aboriginal Law Bulletin*, 2:51, August, 7–8.

YALP 1992. *Youth and the Law Project —Youth Action*, Newsletter, Sydney: Law Foundation of New South Wales, December.

VIDEOS, MANUALS, AND OTHER RESOURCES

A Community Work Book 1991. Compiled by Coralie Ober, Queensland Corrective Commission, Brisbane.

A Damned Good Job 1991. A video documentary, from the Pioneer Women's Series, Produced by Pamela Meeking-Jones, Channel 1, NZTV (45 mins).

A Family Affair 1993. Manual on family violence, (produced by Esther Supernault) Edmonton: Native Counselling Services of Alberta.

A Love Stronger Than Poison 1987. A video documentary on a community seeking sobriety produced by the O'Chiese reserve, Alberta with NNADAP, 1189 Jeanne Mance Building, Ontario K1A 0L3.

Aboriginal and Islander Community Police Training Manual, with *Aboriginal Community Policing*, 30 min. video, 1988. Sponsored by the Aboriginal Co-ordinating Council, Cairns; Police/ Aboriginal and Islander Liaison Unit, Queensland Police Dept, compiled by Kayleen M. Hazlehurst, Australian Institute of Criminology, Canberra.

Alcohol Education for Aboriginal Offenders Package 1988. The Institute of Applied Aboriginal Studies, Western Australian College of Advanced Education. Four videos:

BIBLIOGRAPHY

What Alcohol Does to Us (10 mins); *Drinking, Driving, Surviving* (15 mins); *Driving Blind* (30 mins); *All Time Loser* (30 mins); also posters displays. A program on alcohol and how it affects us.

Alcoholics Anonymous 1976. *The Story of How Many Thousands of Men and Women Have Recovered from Alcoholism'*, New York: Alcoholics Anonymous World Services, Inc. (3rd ed.).

Andersen, Bob 1992. *Justice Committees and Traditional Native Justice*. A discussion paper on committees of Elders and Criminal Justice personnel mandated to recommend appropriate sentences for young offenders found guilty by the court. Edmonton: Native Counselling Services of Alberta.

Bass, Ellen and Davis, Laura 1990. *The Courage to Heal: A guide for women survivors of Child sexual abuse*, London: Cedar.

Beyond Violence: Finding the Dream, 1990. Video and manual on the handling of domestic violence in Aboriginal families and communities, produced by Judy Atkinson, Canberra/Brisbane: Office of Status of Women, Dept of Prime Minister and Cabinet/ Office of Aboriginal Women, Aboriginal and Torres Strait Islander Commission (50 mins).

CADAP 1988.*Community Worker's Manual: A Community Action Approach to Preventing Drug Misuse*, produced by George van der Heide, Canberra: Alcohol and Drug Foundation.

Children See, Children Do 1987. A video on family violence in Native communities, how it affects young people, and how the cycle of violence is perpetuated from one generation to another. Edmonton: Native Counselling Services of Alberta (11 mins).

Cianci, Donato 'Pathmaker' and Nadon, Suzanne 'Sunshine' 1989. *Walking the Medicine Wheel Path in Daylight: An exploration of The Medicine Wheel Teachings on Human Relations*, Ontario: Maplestone Press.

Crime Prevention for Aboriginal Communities 1990. A workshop leader's manual on community-based crime prevention techniques and action group strategies, produced by Kayleen M. Hazlehurst, Canberra: Australian Institute of Criminology.

Crime Prevention for Native Communities Part I: Crime Prevention Works 1988. Video, Canadian Indian programs for crime prevention, Edmonton: Native Counselling Services of Alberta (9 mins).

Crime Prevention for Native Communities Part II: How to get it working 1988. Video, Canadian Indian programs for crime prevention, Edmonton: Native Counselling Services of Alberta (12 mins).

Crossingham, Lesley 1987. '"The Eagle has Landed"', *Windspeaker* (Drug and Alcohol Special), Edmonton, 6.

Family Fighting Wrong Way 1989/1990. Video, poster and manual package. Northern Territory Aboriginal Program showing that family violence and alcohol dependence is a personal and community responsibility, Darwin: The Remote Areas Domestic Violence Project, United Aboriginal and Islander Christian Congress/ Department of Aboriginal Affairs (25 min).

First Time Last Time 1988. Video on the Canadian First Offenders Alternative Program - particularly for youth, Edmonton: Native Counselling Services of Alberta (15 mins).

Friends in Recovery 1990. *The 12 Steps for Adult Children from Addictive and other Dysfunctional Families*, San Diego: Recovery Publications.

Grateful Members 1975. *The Twelve Steps for Everyone Who Really Wants Them*, Minneapolis: CompCare Publishers.

Grateful Members, 1977. *The Twelve Steps for Everyone*, Minnesota: CompCare Publishers.

H. Arthur with McPeek, George 1988. *The Grieving Indian: An Ojibwe Elder Shares his Discovery of Help and Hope*, Winnipeg: Indian Life Books.

Healing the Hurts 1989. Video, Produced by the 'New Directions' Training Program, Alkali Lake Band Council, Alkali Lake BC with the Four Worlds Development Project, Lethbridge, Alberta: Faculty of Education, University of Lethbridge, (60 mins).

Healthy Aboriginal Life Team (HALT) 1991. *Anangu Way*, Alice Springs, NT: Nganampa Health Council Inc.

Heartview Foundation, [nd] booklet, Dakota.

Henley, Thom 1989. *Rediscovery: Ancient Pathways — New Directions. A Guidebook to Outdoor Education*, Vancouver: Western Canada Wilderness Committee.

Hodgson, Maggie 1987a. 'Indian Communities Develop Futuristic Addictions Treatment and Health Approach', Edmonton: Nechi Institute, June.

Hodgson, Maggie 1987b. Women and Addictions: What Are the Issues?', Edmonton: Nechi Institute.

Hodgson, Maggie 1989. 'The Eagle Has Landed', paper presented at the International Conference on Alcohol Abuse, Oslo, Norway, organised by Edmonton: Nechi Institute.

Hodgson, Maggie 1990a. 'Impact of Residential Schools and other Root Causes of Poor Mental Health', paper presented to the Health and Welfare Branch, Indian Health National Assistant Regional Directors/Zone Directors Meeting, 6–8 November, Edmonton: Nechi Institute.

Hodgson, Maggie 1990b., 'Restructuring the Legal System', Edmonton: Nechi Institute.

Hodgson, Maggie 1990c. 'Shattering the Silence: Working with Violence in Native Communities', Edmonton: Nechi Institute.

Hodgson, Maggie 1991a. 'An Issue of Life or Death', Edmonton, Nechi Institute, 21 November.

Hodgson, Maggie 1991b. '"Spirituality vs Religion": and First Nation's Response to Healing of a Government's Decision to set Social Policy to Dictate Christianity as the Solution to Assimilate our People,' Edmonton: Nechi Institute.

Honouring Our Voices 1993. Video on dealing with family violence, (Executive Producer, Eileen Knott) Edmonton: Native Counselling Services of Alberta.

Lerner, Rokelle 1988. 'Boundaries for Codependants', leaflet, USA: Hazelden Foundation.

Let only Good Spirits Guide you 1987. Video on the joint Canadian Indian/Royal Canadian Mounted Police crime prevention campaign throughout Alberta, Edmonton: Native Counselling Services of Alberta (23 mins).

MacLeod, Linda 1987 *Battered but not Beaten: Preventing Wife Battering in Canada*, Ottawa: Canadian Advisory Council on the Status of Women.

MacLeod, Linda 1989 *Wife Battering and the Web of Hope: Progress, Dilemmas and Visions of Prevention*, Ottawa: Health and Welfare Canada.

Martens, Tony 1988. *Characteristics and Dynamics of Incest and Child Sexual Abuse* (with A Native Perspective by Brenda Daily and Maggie Hodgson), Edmonton: Nechi Institute.

Mediation can Change the World 1988. Video on mediation and alternative dispute resolution, Sydney: New South Wales Justice Centres Mediation Service (15 mins).

Moore, Robert and Gillette, Douglas 1992. *The Warrior Within: Accessing the Knight in the Male Psyche*, New York: William Morrow and Company Inc.

Mountain View Rehabilitation Centre, Inc. [nd] handout on intervention.

Mousseau, Marlin *Working with Indian Men who Batter* (video), Duluth: Minnesota Program Development Inc.

Nadeau, Denise 1991. *A Resource Kit based on the Evaluation of the Native Family Violence Training Program*, Vancouver: Native Education Centre.

NCADA, Posters covering subjects of alcohol addiction, smoking, community care approaches, sports and self-development, Canberra: National Campaign Against Drug Abuse.

Nechi Institute on Alcohol and Drug Education, 1987. *O'Chiese Information Package: Guidelines for Community Sobriety*. Edmonton: Nechi Institute.

Nechi Institute on Alcohol and Drug Education, 1989. *An Educational Process for Children in the Prevention of Solvent Abuse: Teacher's Guide*, produced by Moir Management Systems Inc, Edmonton: Nechi Institute on Alcohol and Drug Education.

Nechi Institute on Alcohol and Drug Education, 1991. 'Keep the Circle Strong', Edmonton: Nechi Institute.

Nechi Institute on Alcohol and Drug Education 1992. *The Eagle Has Landed: Data Base Study of Nechi Participants*, produced by Trish Merrithew-Mercredi, Nuniyah Consulting Servicing Ltd, Edmonton: Nechi Institute on Alcohol and Drug Education.

BIBLIOGRAPHY

New Directions Program, 1990. Leaflet, Alkali Lake, BC: Alkali Lake Band.

Ponce-Montoya, Juanita 1978. *Grief Work*, Hicksville, New York: Exposition Press.

Poundmaker's Lodge 1988-90. Leaflets and resource materials, 'A Healing Place: Helping each other on the Pathway to Recovery'; 'Alcoholism and Drug Abuse Treatment Centre'; 'Poundmaker/Nechi Centre' Edmonton: Poundmaker's Lodge.

Poundmaker's Lodge: A Healing Place 1987. A video sharing experiences of Indian participants in the Poundmaker's Lodge detoxification program, produced by the Poundmaker's Lodge, Edmonton with the National Film Board of Canada (30 mins).

Primary Prevention for Community Wellbeing: An interview with Jean 1989. Video and leaflet, on the use of primary prevention for the community healing and positive growth, produced by Kayleen M. Hazlehurst, Australian Institute of Criminology, Canberra (25 mins).

Rage: Men and Violence Video, which explores the causes of violence as seen through the eyes of a group of male inmates who are now dealing with the consequences (David Cunningham, Director) Edmonton: Native Counselling Services of Alberta.

Richard, S. 1985. 'Releasing Anger', leaflet, USA: Hazelden Foundation.

Sharing Innovations that Work 1985. A video on the Alkali Lake Sobriety Program, Alkali Lake, BC (26 mins).

Solvent Abuse Prevention Program: An Educational Process for Children in the Prevention of Solvent Abuse 1989. Teacher's Guide, produced by Moir Management Systems Inc., Edmonton: Nechi Institute.

State of Shock, 1989 Video, an intimate look at a broken culture following the stabbing of a young woman by her boyfriend in a drunken rage (David Bradbury, Director), Ronin Films, PO Box 1005, Civic Square, Canberra, ACT 2608.

Super Shamou, (Native comic book), Dept of Social Services, Government of the NWT, PO Box 1320, Yellowknife, NWT X1A 2H9

Talk About It: Mediation for Aboriginal and Torres Strait Islander Communities, 1992. Video, Community Justice Program, Alternative Dispute Resolution Division, Department of the Attorney-General, GPO Box 149, Brisbane, Qld 4001 (30 mins).

The Honour of All, Parts 1 and II, 1986. Videos, the Canadian Indian, Alkali Lake Story of How a Community Detoxified its People, produced by the Alkali Lake Band Council, British Columbia (58 mins).

Through Black Eyes: A Handbook of Family Violence in Aboriginal and Torres Strait Islander Communities, 1991. Compiled by Maryanne Sam, Sydney: Secretariat of the National Aboriginal and Islander Child Care.

Walk Tall, 1987. A video giving Aboriginal youth a futuristic vision for a better life, Sydney: New South Wales Alcohol and Drug Foundation (15 mins).

Weber, Rick 1976. 'Help for Ourselves: Twelve Steps to Recovery for Native Americans' (with Native illustrations, art work by Sam Wilson).

Windspeaker — A bi-weekly Native newspaper which promotes an alcohol and drug free future for Native people and their children.

Windspeaker,
Bert Crowfoot, Chief Executive Officer,
15001–112 Avenue,
Edmonton, Alberta, T5M 2V6, Canada
Tel. (403) 455 2700; Fax: (403) 455 7939.
(Subscription:$26.00 Canadian addresses,
$40.00 Overseas addresses)

Woititz, Janet G. 1986. *Guidelines for Support Groups: Adult Children of Alcoholics and Others who Identify*, Florida: Health Communications, Inc.

Woititz, Janet G. 1988. *Adult Children of Alcoholics: Common Characteristics*, Florida: Health Communications, Inc.

Woititz, Janet G. 1989. *Healing Your Sexual Self*, Deerfield Beach, Forida: Health Communications Inc.

CONTACTS

Australia

Marg O'Donnell, Director,
Community Justice Program,
GPO Box 149, Brisbane, Queensland 4001.
Tel. 227 4933; 008 017288 (country districts).

Bobby McLeod, Director,
Darren McLeod, Assistant Executive Director,
Doonooch Self Healing Centre,
PO Box 489, Nowra,
New South Wales 2541.
Tel. (044) 230 048; Fax. (044) 214 526.

Judy Atkinson and Coralie Ober,
'We Al-li', Program for Personal, Family
and Community Healing,
PO Box 269, Yeppoon,
Queensland 4703.

Douglas Walker, Director,
Douglas Abbott, Chairperson;
Lana Abbott, Program Co-ordinator,
Eric Shirt, Consultant,
Central Australian Aboriginal Alcohol Planning Unit,
(CAAAPU Treatment Program),
PO Box 8695, Alice Springs,
Northern Territory 0871.
Tel. (089) 555 336; 555 375;
Fax. (089) 555 385.

Eric Shirt and Associates,
8 Kekwick Ave, Alice Springs NT 0870.
ph/fax. (089) 522 747 (messages via CAAAPU).

'Living with Alcohol' Program,
Department of Health and Community Services,
Health House, Mitchell St,
PO Box 40596, Casuarina,
Northern Territory 0811.
Tel. (089) 892 553; 892 691.

Basil Sumner, Director,
South Australian Aboriginal Sobriety Group for
Drug and Alcohol Rehabilitation,
128 Wakefield St., Adelaide,
South Australia 5000.
Tel. (08) 223 4204.

Jean Jans,
PO Box 248, Weipa,
Queensland 4874.

Aboriginal Co-ordinating Council,
PO Box 6512,
Cairns Mail Centre,
Cairns, Queensland 4870.
Tel. (070) 312 623; Fax: (070) 312 534.

Val Carroll and Jim Carroll,
Administrators,
Benelong's Haven,
South West Rocks Road,
Kinchela Creek,
New South Wales 2440.
Tel. (065) 654 880; Fax. (065) 654 932.

Selena Seymour,
Administrator,
Namatjira House Aboriginal Rehabilitation Centre,
PO Box 14, Alstonville.
NSW 2477. Tel/Fax. (066) 281 098.

Salvation Army Man Care Community for
Drug and Alcohol Dependency,
PO Box 4181, Kingston,
Canberra, ACT 2604.
Tel. (06) 295 1256; Fax. (06) 295 3766.

Sister Pat Quinn,
'The Portiuncula' Centre for Spiritual Development,
189 Herries Street, Toowoomba,
Queensland 4350. Tel. (076) 331 383.

Author: Dr Kayleen Hazlehurst,
Program in Cross-Cultural Studies of Community Regeneration,
Faculty of Arts,
Queensland University of Technology,
PO Box 284, Zillmere,
Queensland 4034. Australia.
Tel. (07) 864 4771;
Fax. (07) 864 4711.

Canada

Executive Director,
Poundmaker's Lodge/Nechi Institute Centre
Box 3884, Station 'D', Edmonton,
Alberta T5L 4K1.
Tel. (403) 458 1884; Fax: (403) 458 1883.

Dr Maggie Hodgson, Executive Director,
Nechi Institute on Alcohol and Drug Education,
Box 34007, Kingway Post Office,
Edmonton, Alberta T5G 3G4.
Tel. (403) 458 1884; Fax: (403) 458 1883.

Andy and Phyllis Chelsea,
Alkali Lake Band Council,
P.O. Box 4279, Williams Lake,
British Columbia V2G 2V3.

Lorraine Brave, Executive Director,
Hey-Way'-Noqu', Healing Circle for Addictions Society,
206–33 East Broadway,
Vancouver, British Columbia V5T 1V4.
Tel. (604) 874 1831; Fax: (604) 874 5235.

Dr Chester R. Cunningham, Executive Director,
Alan Benson, Assistant Executive Director,
Native Counselling Services of Alberta,
#800 Highfield Place,
10010–106 Street, Edmonton, Alberta T5J 3L8.
Tel. (403) 423–2141; Fax: (403) 424 1173

Professor Phil Lane,
'Four Worlds' Development Project,
University of Lethbridge,
4401 University Drive, Lethbridge,
Alberta T1K 3M4.
Tel. (403) 329 2065; Fax: (403) 329 3081

Ben Wong, and Jock McKeen,
'Haven by the Sea',
PD Seminars, (Personal Development),
Gabriola Island, Vancouver,
British Columbia VOR 1XO.
Tel. (604) 247 9211.

Executive Director,
Hey-Way'-Nogu,
Healing Circle for Addictions Society,
206-33 East Broadway, Vancouver,
British Columbia V5T 1V4.
Tel. (604) 874 1831; Fax: (604) 874 5235.

Mercy E. Thomas, Executive Director,
Helping Spirit Lodge,
205–96 East Broadway, Vancouver,
British Columbia V5T 4N9.
Tel. (604) 872 6649.

CONTACTS

Brian Madarash,
Native Education Centre,
Urban Native Indian Education Society,
285 East Fifth Avenue, Vancouver,
British Columbia V5T 1H2.
Tel. (604) 873 3761.

Walter Knott,
Family Focus Co-ordinator,
Squamish Nation,
Social Development Department,
345 West 5th Street, North Vancouver,
British Columbia, V7M 1K2.
Tel. (604) 985 4111.

GLOSSARY

'New Directions Training' — a reserve-based intensive personal development program run by the Alkali Lake Band Council, British Columbia.

'The Honour of All' Parts I and II — the Alkali Lake Story is a video docudrama about the Alkali Lake experience. It imparts first hand knowledge of the stages of community alcoholism and eventual recovery. Community members re-enact their parts in the Alkali Lake story. A community which was once almost totally alcoholic slowly wins almost complete sobriety

'Life-Springs Program' is a program for personal growth. Individuals are helped to rebuild ourselves — emotionally, socially, culturally, spiritually. This program has 'New Age' roots and is non-culturally specific.

'The Healing Circle' (or sometimes called 'The Sharing Circle') — originally for children of alcoholic parents. Group exercises and activities are used to introduce positive experiences of caring and mutual support.

Sweetgrass Ceremony — an Indian ceremony which involves the burning of sweet grass (a sweet smelling incense) and appropriate chanting and spiritual incantation.

The Sweat Lodge ('The Sweat') — the Indian Sweat Lodge functions very much like a sauna. Heated stones are placed in the centre of a low circular enclosure. Participants are seated around the stones. Purification rituals symbolise the cleansing of the human body, spirit, and mind.